THE GOLDEN YEAR

THE POETRY SOCIETY OF AMERICA
ANTHOLOGY (1910-1960)

The
Golden Year

edited by **MELVILLE CANE, JOHN FARRAR,**
and **LOUISE TOWNSEND NICHOLL**

foreword by **CLARENCE R. DECKER**

Granger Index Reprint Series

BOOKS FOR LIBRARIES PRESS
FREEPORT, NEW YORK

Copyright 1960 by The Fine Editions Press
Reprinted 1969 by arrangement with
The Poetry Society of America

STANDARD BOOK NUMBER:
8369-6004-1

LIBRARY OF CONGRESS CATALOG CARD NUMBER:
73-76941

MANUFACTURED
BY
HALLMARK LITHOGRAPHERS, INC.
IN THE U.S.A.

Original Publishers Note

ALL PRESENT MEMBERS of the Poetry Society of America were invited to submit a maximum of three poems for consideration by the editors of this Anthology. Those who failed to respond, or submitted work past the deadline, or who did not observe the conditions, or imposed conditions which were found unacceptable are, regrettably, not represented.

The editors faced a difficult task in keeping the book within bounds; much additional material (second and third poems) originally selected for inclusion had to be omitted, and most poets were necessarily restricted to representation with a single entry.

The decision to include a poem was based on a unanimous or two-thirds vote in favor. In case of a doubt, the poem was voted in. The editors sought to include at least one poem by every member submitting. Authors are not always the best judge of their own work, and this fact may have caused a number of poets to be shut out who, otherwise, had they made a better selection, might have been included.

Assembling an Anthology such as this is always a shared labor, representing not only the work of the editors, but the participation of many others who gave of their time and counsel without stint or thought of reward. These others will be nameless, since they wish it to be so. However, it would be unchivalrous not to mention several whose contribution was so considerable that, without it, publication of the Anthology could not have been realized. The publisher therefore takes this occasion to acknowledge, with thanks, the assistance of Florence Putnam, who reduced a mountainous mass of biographical data to usable form; to Myra Reddin, for systematizing records and preparing copy for the printer; and to Michelina Buoncore, who did much of the final proofreading.

The publisher also wishes to thank other publishers, editors, authors' agents, copyright owners, as well as the contributing members themselves, for the free use of copyright material. Above all, the publisher wishes to express his gratitude and indebtedness (and he speaks here in behalf of the whole Society) to the three editors, Melville Cane, John Farrar, and Louise Townsend Nicholl, for the expeditious and highly creditable manner in which they handled a very exacting and always thankless task.

Foreword

ON THE EVENING of January 21, 1960 the Poetry
Society of America celebrated its 50th Anniversary, a
semi-centennial that is being observed in appropriate
ways throughout the year, preeminently by the publication of this Anthology.

Anniversaries are occasions for retrospect and pros-
pect. On both fronts, the PSA has reason to be proud.
The notable record of its past presages its future. For
poets and lovers of poetry, the Society's Golden Year is
a year of rejoicing.

The notion that a society of poets is a contradiction
in terms is a mischievous half-truth. From time im-
memorial, poets as priests, prophets and philosophers
have, like other professionals, pooled their interests to
promote fellowship and to protect their wares (Burns
called his "rhyming wares"). Even the late Oliver
Gogarty, who took a dim view of "societies"—he
thought the ideal setup was a table of six in the back
of a pub — became and remained to the end an active
member. But whether in a pub or a parlor a benevolent
and protective order of poets has its uses.

The founders themselves pondered the wisdom of
forming a "collective" of rugged individuals, but in
1910 more than two score of the country's leading poets
and men of letters enrolled as charter members. And
once the Society was a *fait accompli*, other literary
figures, equally distinguished, joined. Today, after
half a century of continuous service, with a membership drawn from every section of the country as well

as from many other parts of the world, and deferentially including (as associate members) editors, teachers, critics, scholars, and patrons — in fact, all who render yeoman service to poetry—the Poetry Society of America is the largest and oldest and most influential organization of its kind. Numerous regional groups that have sprung up since 1910 look to it as a model and guide. And now, as in the beginning, its membership embraces novitiates as well as masters.

The purpose of the Society, as set forth in its constitution, is "to secure fuller recognition for poetry . . . to kindle a more intelligent appreciation of the art . . . and to perform such other acts as may be deemed necessary to assist poets." Through its meetings, open discussions, readings, lectures, monthly bulletins, publications and awards, the Society has advanced the cause it set out to serve, so much so that today it enjoys the enviable position of being regarded, by friends and foes alike, as the foremost organization in the field.

In the war between the old and the new, the traditional and the experimental, the PSA has been hospitable to both: it is committed to the proposition that all sides of an issue must be known and heard if the cause itself is to flourish. At the monthly gatherings and at the annual banquets, the Society has been host, over the years, to such varied voices as Yeats, AE, Masefield, James Stephens, Siegfried Sassoon, Housman, Amy Lowell, Pound, Sandburg, Frost, Colum, Millay, Mac-Neice, Auden, Spender, Graves, and Marianne Moore.

The Society has pioneered: it initiated the Pulitzer Prize for poetry; established the book and holograph collections at the New York Public Library; started public readings and discussions of poetry; created permanent funds and scholarships for needy and deserving poets; honored — by way of citations, medals, cash awards — exceptional service to, and distinguished achievement in, poetry. It has fought censorship, authoritarianism, the stranglehold of cliques, and has sought to preserve the fruits of the past. The Society welcomes any protagonist with an honorable grievance or a debatable issue, and provides him with a ready platform from which he can declare his conviction, and an audience that asks nothing better than to be stirred into dissent or admiration.

In a word, the Society has helped people to remember poetry and poets to remember people, as this Anthology so eloquently testifies.

CLARENCE R. DECKER
President

Contents

Contents

Contents   xxiii

George Abbe

HORIZON THONG

Go back now; pause to mark
that hill town cut in two:
one half, green summer's charm,
the other, chasmed in snow.
Horizon, a thong of red
knotted by smoldering sun;
wind, the wind in the drifts,
and crystal blossoms flung
downward — so near, so warm —
to where orchards bend and lift.

And father — father who kneels
to pull snowshoes from his back,
looks down to the shining field
where his son runs, easy and fast;

he must follow, follow to save,
but the snowshoes will not free;
they are rooted to shoulder blade,
they are flesh of paternity.

Only a quick run down,
but helpless he kneels in cold,
watches his young boy run
over meadows lyric and full
towards woods, a woods of his own.

Wrenching, and wet with pain,
the father downward bows;
the village of homes and men
grows faint in the blizzard's glow.

The boy flashes under trees
and fades. The horizon mark
binds throat of man on his knees;
the sun-knot tightens to dark.

NEW YORK CITY

Flying in plane's rib,
cribbed and yearning for earth-touch birth,
watching, down-reaching, I saw worlds below
that intransigent city adrift by night,
bright-pulsed, flung-upward, flamed with silver,
white-fountained, love-finned, embossed by tumult.

The plane leaned, the city grew, rose to ensnare
brain's eye, blood's finger-tip, all desert hope.

Yet lovely far, yet hung like rose,
yet known to thirsty and the proud,
suspended out of time, ungeared
from mesh of soil and flesh and metal,

released, as was the angel from stone,
flown, out-flung as virtue's rocket
locked in God's dream, wistful as man.

Ellen M. V. Acton

EXODUS FROM A RENAISSANCE GALLERY

Every towered city, every street
Was thronged with knights and horses, hounds and hawks
And leashless doves that flew along above.
Every forest was the flower-starred retreat
Of gracious ladies, elegantly gowned,

Who fondled lamb or child in arms of love,
While small itinerant animals paused, mute,
Enchanted in the populated grove.
There acquiescent slender hands were bred
To hold the staff that blossomed, or the lute,
Which curious birds descended to approve,
Encircling the music-leaning head.

Up which steep background path has trod
The race of sturdy mystics, lately vanished,
Who from the lion's paw withdrew the thorn,
Who tamed the griffin and the unicorn,
Attained to the endearing ways of God,
And left us, modern, futile, banished?

Marjorie L. Agnew

On GOING HOME

When I return I search for myself
Among the dark streets, and question the night
For some trace of the child that I was.
I stand on the top of the hill and
Stare up and down, seeking my face, or a print,
Or a thread from my coat on a vine.
The names of the streets are the same,
And even the trees and the stars and the birds
Seem the same, and my name is still mine,
But I never find out where I went,
What I thought, what I knew,—
And the village still holds me somewhere,
And I can't find the child that I was
Or even be sure in what town
The person I have become now
Can be found.

Samuel L. Albert

AFTER A GAME OF SQUASH

And I thought of how impossibly alone we were,
Up in the room where the lockers are and the showers.
He with wiping the sweat from his face and head;
And I bending over, loosening the laces from my sneakers.

We had just finished this long game of squash.
Then, we were much closer; smashing the same ball;
Lurching forward, out-maneuvering each other
Hard down the sidelines, death to the opponent.

It was a battle, the killer's eye in the middle
Of the round black ball. Two men struggling
To find each other out. What made each one's mind work
And with what heart each fell to the long odds.

And when the game was over we thanked each other generously;
Complimented one the other on his skill, his finesse.
And I thought of how impossibly alone we were,
Up in the room where the lockers are and the showers.

HONEYMOON
Remember, Phyllis,

When we walked from the hotel across the street
        at three in the morning
O'clock and smiling
And all undressed (though fully dressed really)
We held each other's hand?

Remember, how positively exploratory we felt;
How positively, as a new adventure even this business

Of buying toasted-English under the bright light at Waldorf's;
Especially remembering where we came from and
    why we were there?

And here how self-conscious we were
Looking at this driver, late and tired;
(And the bellboy in, I am sure, for his third coffee)
Wondering if they knew what had happened to us
And more than physically and forever.

Now that I think of it, Phyllis,
This business of scrambled eggs at three in the morning
Comes more to my mind than almost anything else, almost.
The amazing difference of all that love
In the hush and dark of that hotel room;

And the still-life of this place across the street
Its search and its glare, almost too much to bear.
The blazing difference of all that love
In the hush and dark of that hotel room.

Remember, Phyllis?

Frances Alexander

THE CONTENTMENT OF WILLOUGHBY

Willoughby liked being Willoughby
Because he was used to it.
There had been times when
He had envied other men
Their fishing leisure
Or some gadget-treasure;
But Willoughby's house-shoes were soft
After the day's hard chores

And his evening loft
Was angled toward the stars.

Willoughby's wife let him be Willoughby
Because she was used to it.
There had been times when
She had noticed other men
Brought their wives more dresses
And more railroad passes;
But Willoughby brought himself home,
And it was wealth enough
To know he would come
With a new theory or a laugh.

Grace Elisabeth Allen

PINKLETINKS

To Vineyarders in cold Korea,
Louisiana or Berea,
Spring means the hidden mayflower pink;
Spring also means the pinkletink —
A word no one will come upon
In the most learned lexicon.
Who loves the Vineyard snail or winkle
May never yet have seen a pinkle —
Tink inside his hideout, sprinkling
The woods and swamps with tiny tinkling.
If one day, searching, we should tree him,
How would we know which speck could be him?
Spring would be a springier, I think,
If we could meet a pinkletink.

Sara Van Alstyne Allen

THE ZOO IN THE CITY

Enclosed the lacquered, coiling snake
Within a web of glass.
Offer for his devious need
A subsidy of grass.

Hollow out the bitter stone.
Provide the bowl for a neat sea.
The sleek and polished city seal
Detects in this no irony.

Crowd into a music-box
A hundred birds to sing,
And measure out the humming air
For every slanting wing.

Circumscribe the panther's grace
Within a cell of steel and wire.
Dim to a dull processional
The stealthy pace, the hunter's fire.

Here between stone and rearing stone
Man adds a fillip to his feast,
Keeping to round his holiday
The netted bird, the futile beast.

MARBLE STATUETTE HARPIST
(Metropolitan Museum)

Seated, the harpist waits,
His shaven head erect.
Marble his arms, marble his quiet face.

The gates of sound will open soon
In this forgotten place,
In this forgotten noon.

The strings are carved of air,
And should the music wake,
The silken curtain shake,
The sober chair
Hold more than waiting now,
A hundred notes will come,
Fresh-fallen from the tree
Whose fruit is love,
Where music is the bough.

Julia Cooley Altrocchi

THE PIGEON-FEEDERS IN BATTERY PARK

It is not the young whom we find feeding the pigeons,
The young whom the world abundantly feeds
With the seeds of life, the hope of the harvest-deeds.
It is the finished, the frustrate, where no hope breeds.

It is age that gives largess of crumbs to the pigeons,
The wintered people, whom life, with an ultimate shove,
Thrusts to the park bench. Too late for deeds, or for love,
It is the old who must give what they have, — to a dove.

Dorothy Alyea

KEEPSAKE FROM QUINAULT

I have brought berries on a grape-leaf.
It is a slight gift, but my hands were scratched for it.
Under the hemlocks the path was cool
But the clearing smelled of blackberries
And spruce-chips where the loggers had been.
There were bees with orange bags and the sound
  of a woodpecker,
And a goldfinch on a clump of thistle.
Vines over dead trees led me by trails of moss
Upward until I could watch the sea.
I have brought you a gift. Come away from these people.
The ripest fruit you must eat from the spray.

Evelyn Ames

TWO SOLITUDES

When I see carved so clearly on your face
The life in you which I shall never share —
The shocks endured alone, the wars which trace
The grandeur of the spirit's struggle there —
I long to take into my hands and heal
Whatever is still wounded in your soul,
Give you that self-forgiveness which might seal
The open vein, make past and present whole.

Yet love for you demands the opposite:
Proves that the deepest love consists of freeing

Even from the touch of guardian wings which it
Would fold around you; so I stand apart,
Beyond the outmost circle of your being
And let you be, and let this break my heart.

BECAUSE I LIVE

Because I live — and you, not —
Waves that traveled the ocean of our years
On their long way to the edges of the world,
Shatter, broken, against that rock.

However much I had become
Terraced to vineyards and grown up to wheat,
A net of towns and roads across my heart —
I am compressed to one hard fact.

Stone does not stay bare stone for long:
The armored pine cone's seed discovers cracks,
Growth and forgetting generate new loam:
I meet an unexpected look or word
And all but break under orchard bloom.

Charles Angoff

A LITTLE GIRL

Spring is in her eyes
And soft ecstasy
Is in all her ways.

The warm echoes
Of every yesterday
Are on her lips,

And the quiet memories
Of every year
Are on her cheeks.

The gentle laughter
Of Heaven
Surrounds her.

She is
The constellation
Of all creation.

Howard Ant

BUCKET OF SEA-SERPENTS

On the skim of the wharf where the planks split,
and old car-tires stuck to be tug-catchers
tarred the brine down with their rank rubber smell,
I spied a boy with a bucket of eels.
They writhed and pretzeled in a ropy mush
up the dank seams, and he'd a grin
so big it smeared his tonsils with horizon.
Everyone else had crabs in their steep buckets,
or finny fish. His eels set him apart,
much as a ditch would. I never knew
eels spawned where cities scummed and sewers emptied,
or that a boy could pluck them up like posies,
his slick line dipping like a bobbin
in the sea's boil, hooking their squirmy rumps
the way tall Lancelot might've speared an ogre.
On, on he grinned as eels piled in the bucket,
proud of his differentness as any eagle.

"What's those you've hooked?" I said. He said "Sea-serpents.
They swallow ships up when they get bigger.
Every one here's one ship'll never sink."
So there it was! it wasn't supper he saw
all cooped and wriggling under the rope handle,
or what they'd bring by the pound in fish-stores.
He saw that bucket awash with saved ships,
woody, white-canvased, the kind he'd seen in bottles
I'd guess, not any steamy steelers;
and none to know the proud deed but I now.
Some crab-hunters up the pier turned their crabs loose,
and they scuttled over the rotting wood
snicking their tough claws like nutcrackers.
Ah, those were jointy devils! lunging sideways,
bow-legged and deadly, it was Hop, Mister!
all mid-day, and Nip Your Nose Off, Charlie?
I thought, as monsters go they'd the eels beat
from here to Canada — but smoke's all they seemed
to my wee ship-saver! no fist-size crab
could wipe that chuckle off or scotch *his* vision.
Not sea-serpents — there was the pith of it!

Shoving my fancy loose I saw a rope,
a cable of eels stretching to mid-ocean,
funneling in from the far hatcheries
to where a boy's hook called sea-serpents shoreward
for his imagination to make myths of.
I stayed aloof from the grizzled fishers,
fearing they'd tell me eels thick as guppies
slithered their dark loops under the mud-knuckles
in the sink of the silt,
spoiling my dream as I'd not spoiled the boys'.
I left with sunset slopping the planking,
speckling his mild face to a fire-splash,
piling the heaped eels in a blood-bucket.
I waved; he grinned, but his hands on the stubby rod
might've been screwed there. I knew the reason.
Ship-savers can't indulge such courtesies,

not where it means a clipper sucked under,
thirty years on, off the Canaries.
"Haul 'em in good!" I hollered, "those sea-snakes."
"Not snakes," he called. "Serpents. And they eat ships."

Kate Rennie Archer

THE LAIRDLESS PLACE
(Comox, Vancouver Island)

Grey, low ceiling, sough of sea wind along forest,
Hawk-wings low, questing the warrened shore;
Gaunt, toothed wreckage of barn and forgotten fencing
And home no more!

Rutted road, its sea-beach gravelling scattered,
Half-ploughed field, its unsown furrows grassed;
No glass to window or door, and the weathers enter
Where once he passed.

But birds talk yet in the places he loved to hear them.
Bees still harvest the heart of his best-loved rose.
Sometimes there seems a word in the wind, I listen
For perhaps . . . who knows?

Maybe the hawk sees something that still loves woodlands.
Maybe the birds, the hives in the rose-sweet glade,
Black Angus, wagging his tail by the white laburnums,
Greet their Laird's shade!

Richard F. Armknecht

CROW'S NEST

The lookout watch must climb and climb
An iron ladder into time
Unlike earth time — the swaying sum
Of sea's eternal pendulum.

Unquiet the horizons lie,
Now low and slant, now skewed and high,
While from the mast-roots he may feel
The ocean tugging at the keel.

The wind is salt and sinewy
And sings one song, *the sea! the sea!*
And as the seabirds wheel and cry
They write *the sea!* against the sky.

The waves, the winds, the birds combine
Into an intricate design
That is the sea itself, known only
To lookouts watching high and lonely.

Flora J. Arnstein

TIMERS

The early have a miser's insinuating rub
Of thumb and forefinger,
Are virtuous cocks —
Stealing the morning

From between locked lids,
An inch or so higher than any walker.

The punctual ride the clock lightly
With the snaffle hand,
Allowing for stumble or for saddle-cinch,
But stepping neatly to the tryst
Without righteousness or bouquet.

The later-comer stutters the pebbles in his mouth,
Wears a one-shoulder cape,
Or carries a vacant cane
With an eye to shapeliness.

All timers dial their own faces,
Confession escaping from the tiny gears,
Candor in the slow circumference
But unknown to the slim hands' betrayal.

Sarah Leeds Ash

CHANGELESS SHORE

Nothing will ever change beside this river:
There will be reeds bending, the water whisper,
forgotten oars tossed

where tides brush alluvial grasses,
a dinghy, ancient in sunlight,
fast to a broken wharf.

Loneliness, heavy as smoke,
will fall from wings of a heron;
a fish will shatter copper solitude

in a swift, reliable arc.
Nothing will ever be different here, no never.
Except freight of dead leaves on a dark tide:

the solemn removal of withered September
nothing progresses, not even time.
We shall return to this place where silence whittles

shavings of time, drops them over the shore.
We shall return when blunt shadows fall.
We shall come back in the mind's long evening.

Sylvia Auxier

BREAKING POINT

She might have borne them had they come
By two's and three's as ravens do,
Saving a space for sun and sky
To filter through.

She might have borne them had their caws
Been intermittent as the crows',
Crying a sorrow that the mind
Already knows.

She might have borne them had there been,
Among her spreading tree of mind,
Branches not burdened by the clutch
Of their raven-kind.

But coming as they did, — at once,
All black, all clamor, all dread freight, —
Small wonder that the tree had cracked
Under their weight.

Robert Avrett

RENAISSANCE

Sly merchants plotted newer, greater gains;
Ambitious clerics fattened in their stalls;
Proud nobles trod resplendent Gothic halls;
And slaves' resentment strained against their chains.

Stout sailors scanned the charts of unknown seas;
Astrologers observed the planets' course;
Kings warred for realms beyond their utmost force;
And Art knew Titian and the tapestries.

Ethan Ayer

LIKE A WHISPER

The day that ends the world will be the one
Where all the mystery will be explained,
And everything that's dark shone down upon,
And everything that's deep explored and drained.

The day that ends the world will not be loud,
For sound can only swell where there is room.
It will be like a whisper in a crowd;
No one has ever heard the crack of doom.

The day that ends the world will be drab and still,
Neither gay nor sad nor natural nor strange.
Brightness is next to darkness; death to kill
Must make an end of something — even change.

Karle Wilson Baker

BEAUTY'S HANDS ARE COOL

Beauty's hands are cool:
They fall on fevered clay
And mute the sob half-uttered
Into a listening breath;
Beauty's hands are cool
As a crab-apple spray,
And Beauty cares no more for tears
Than Death.

Come thou before her
Shriven of thy sighs,
Lay aside thy tumults
Like a tattered dress;
Beauty's hands are cool
As her quiet eyes —
She will not dim her lucid peace
With bitterness.

Mary Newton Baldwin

LONELY ARE THE FIELDS OF SLEEP

When night plows the meadows of darkness,
Striking stars from unseen stone,
We follow through furrows of midnight
Silent and alone;
Not knowing where they lead us
In fields knee-deep in sleep,
Where each one must go lonely
Through dream-worlds wide and deep;

Through mysteries unfathomed
Whose solitary way
Forbids us ever choosing
Companions from the day.
And from the eyelids' closing
To rising of the sun,
We wander unremembered ways
With consciousness undone.

Frances Barber

PLAY-ACTING

She spent her time recalling
What other folk forgot, —
Small doings unrelated
With neither plan nor plot.

They could not serve for patchwork
To piece in or complete
The pattern of a story
Her lips would not repeat.

Until her mind, supported
By an attitude naive,
Kept real experience hidden
In a lasting make-believe.

So gossip never garnered
What rumor never sowed
And scandal left her presence
For person more endowed!

Melanie Gordon Barber

SONNET FOR MY SON

You know the answer to the last surmise —
The truth you loved — the truth your life expressed,
For He who answers all things has addressed
That awful knowledge to those clear brown eyes.
Was it for this that you were born so wise?
For this, was it, with courage you were blessed?
Beneath what weight of waters your young breast
Released the element of Paradise.

The transmutation sure, serene your mind;
Before all you had spent your life to find,
You were the scientist who kept the faith;
Thus was your ruling purpose firm in death,
Ready with level gaze and quickened ears
To face Eternity at eighteen years.

Edna L. S. Baker

CHILD OF THE WORLD

I am the child by the Yangtse running
In the wind and the cold,
To find a crack in the rocky shelter;
For my few years I am old.

I have no bench, no quilt, no pillow
On which my head is laid.
I am the child of the earth, hungry,
The one afraid.

You heard me cry in the dark,
You knew me and tossed in your sleep,
But the night is huge, and the river
Is wide and deep.

You knew of the waves, the wind rising,
Snow on the rocks —
I have a coat like paper, my feet
Have mud for socks.

I am the child of the world, hungry,
Savage and wild,
Inarticulate, forgotten —
I am your child.

Isabel Harriss Barr

MADAKET BEACH
(Nantucket)

They speak of time, as if the hour were split
Into atomic parts, each grooved to each,
And barbed with sixty seconds; the knife-whet
Enmeshed, to chill with its steel touch

Both you and me. It is not true. There on the broad,
Cleft beach at Madaket, pillowed on sand
You asked, "Where has the morning gone?" The tide,
A net of shells, moved closer to my hand.

And then the sea came in and flooding, swept
In one momentous wave, toward the green dune.
The spindly sandpiper stopped short and leapt
To air, while time rose, circled and was gone.

Elizabeth Bartlett

AFTER THE STORM

That morning, after the storm,
Everyone gathered about the tree
And marveled at its fall,
The body leaning gently on one arm,
Its mighty head now cushioned by deep
Branches, seemingly asleep.

"You wouldn't think a storm," one said,
Then broke off, staring at the fruit
That never would be eaten red
And sweetened by the sun, or set
In jars and slowly left to cool,
The ripening years ahead gone, too.

"It was the wind." "The rain." Each spoke
A part of truth out of his own mouth
With words that could not make it whole,
Because the naked roots showed
How much there was to doubt,
The secret in the darkness crying loud.

Even a tree, she thought, biting her tongue
And bringing her childish thoughts down,
Remembering the climbs, the stout swing hung
On rafters soaring to the sun,
A tree built like a tower
So you could visit God and talk for hours.

The men sawed logs and timber all that day,
Until there was nothing left, not
Even a shadow where you could wait

And hide to see if it would wake;
Then they buried the hole and forgot
What else they might have covered with the sod.

Dead trees tell no tales, she thought,
Nor empty nests, nor little girls who see
How helpless all things are when caught
By storm, no matter how big or
Strong or secure, and she walked quietly
Into the house to help with the next meal.

Victor E. Beck

SIFTING

My life is cast
upon the sieve of Time;
The winnowing years
will prove it chaff or wheat.

Alice Behrend

SNOWFLAKES

On crystal rims, they wheel in space —
Six spokes against six tangents pinned —
And though a myriad million fall,
No two are twinned.
Most fragile of created things, they curl;
Earth holds her breath to hear
White silence on white silence, whirl.

Laura Benét

THE ROWERS

Have you not fallen asleep to strong men's rowing,
    Hearing their oars touch water found deepest peace?
What matters it where the boat is going, going,
    Like grass before a sickle in mowing, mowing,
Wave and rowers are blended calmly at ease.

In dream I saw a mysterious boat go drifting,
    Her men were stalwart though aging and weatherworn
As the wet blades in unison lifting, lifting,
    Under the ghostly moonlight ever shifting,
No sound of voice on the creeping wind was borne.

Before my waking I heard those long oars dipping
    Into colder seas on a widening, wilder shore,
Stroking and sculling, lifting, dripping, dripping,
    Thunderous was the sea water's distant roar.

What manner of burden was it they proudly bore?

MOUNTAIN CONVENT

A sinister presence changed life in a twelvemonth,
    An alien something, rare
As the ghostly peaks, the canyon where great eagles
    Measured the air.

Amazed nuns gazed in wonder from the doorway,
    Drawn from sacred things
By the exotic scent of flaming blossoms,
    The swooping wings.

Kneeling to tell their beads, paused in their praying,
 As in the painted dawn,
Ominous shadows drifted past the windows,
 Darkened the lawn.

The corridors held whispers and the candles
 Lighted within the chapel, flared, blew out.
And tongue-tied native children gave no answer,
 Themselves in doubt.

So if they fled the convent, who could censure?
 But passive shapes that stood
At every turning beckoned veiled intruders
 Into a midnight wood.

Anna Elizabeth Bennett

CANDLE SONG

Out of my longing, dusk-aware,
I take this candle, white and new,
white as an April bough of pear
(white as my love, my love for you).
The match inquires, the wick's reply
blooms on the window like a sigh.

A pattern spreads like a web of dew,
clear as dawn on a shaken wing,
(clear as my love, my love for you);
the flame is a finger beckoning.
Will you come by this way tonight —
be drawn, be snared into my light?

I lean into the shadows, yearning;
beyond the window, stars unclose

deep as my love. The candle's burning
breaks in the darkness like a rose.
It will be spent when night is through,
(but never my love, my love for you).

Gertrude Ryder Bennett

DIARY OF A RACCOON

Here on this open, ancient book
Of sand beside a fern-bound brook,
Inscribed by paws all silver-tipped
Upon a moonlit manuscript
In writing cuneiform and bold
The raccoon's diary is told.
Here in a silent pool of night
The polliwogs were stirred to fright —
A score of comets, fat and black,
Scooting away and wriggling back.
And here the grottoes of the trout
Were searched and morsels raided out.
Tracks, retraced and blurred, express
His ritual of cleanliness;
With etiquette of innate laws
He gripped each bit in eager paws
And washed it, feasting all alone.
Then here beside a moss-grown stone
He paused, content with his repast.
He left his signature at last
In ink of night, and he was gone,
His page concluded with the dawn.

Murray Bennett

FUNERAL

You shall not vanish into dust today,
And never in this world will I confound
A stricken mind with ghosts of yesterday,
Nor celebrate a grief above this mound.
There was no past, no future, while you breathed:
You were the dearer breath become my own,
The full estate of living once bequeathed, —
The miracle that now must change to stone.

I will return an alien to our land,
I will be patient in my thin disguise,
No one shall guess the substance of my hand,
I will be cautious to deceive the wise.
You were my love. There are no tears to start.
There is no pain for me. I am your heart.

Patricia Benton

DESERT RIVER

Follow the long snake
Find salt
Where the coyote meets daybreak:
No sea-journey here.
Only stone-hand
Searching thirst-end,
Salt without tears.

Henry Birnbaum

WHEN SILENCE DIVESTS ME

When silence divests me of ornament,
let me stand outside with the mourners
in the great terror of knowledge.

Let me remain like a white family
of ducks that glides on innocence
with all their energy submerged.

And where I have fallen like a tree,
may I lie in the soft decay
while I blend early into stone.

Or sometimes like a cut carrot
to be useful in some gifted way
beyond desire. Let me be

the unobserved leaf in the vast
unburden of love, more like clouds
than those which farmers see.

A ROOM I ONCE KNEW

Outside the world crackles like a daily. A lion
Prowls the edges of my dream and stalks the back
And forth of my senses. I sleep in coils
While the moon streaks across the padded tympany
Of my restiveness. Within the pulse of dark,
I stretch my soul over the drum and reach deep
Into the hollow of crepuscular anxieties.
    Let us open another door:

Here is the lamp beside the table. Here is
The kitten on the couch. Patterns of innocence
Diapasoned among my childhoods. And once I sat
Beneath the kitchen table, cross-legged in my own
Evolution, and my love was kneaded like
A morning pastry.

               Here is the same door to open:
Two sticky flies jettisoned into reality buzz their stain
About Victorian corners. The dust, like the hoarse
Sound of an oboe, lies in the weariness of cardboard
Boxes, hidden in thick closets and behind the virtue
Of worn bedspreads. I am adult
And reflected in the eczema of tarnished mirrors.

There are simple spaces between knowledge which lie
Fallow in our growth. And in that house I knew,
The animals purred their intact memories
And were received as we receive our domestic
Bowls of milk. But in that room, the dust
In souvenirs grows hoarse like the roar of a lion.

               Close the front door. This is
The front porch. Goodnight, house.

Earle Birney

A WALK IN KYOTO

All week, the maid tells me, bowing
her doll's body at my mat, is Boys' Day.
Also please Man's Day, and gravely
bends deeper. The magnolia sprig in my alcove,
is it male? The ancient discretions of Zen were not shaped
for my phallic western eye. There is so much discretion
in this small bowed body of an empire —
the wild hair of waterfalls combed straight

in the ricefields, the inn-maid retreating
with the face of a shut flower — I stand hunched
and clueless like a castaway in the shoals of my room.

When I slide my parchment door to stalk awkward
through Lilliput gardens framed and untouchable
as watercolors, the streets seem much the same;
the Men are being pulled past on the strings of their engines,
the legs of the Boys are revolved by a thousand pedals,
and all the faces as taut and unfestive as Moscow's
or Chicago's or mine.

Lord Buddha help us all there is vigor enough
in these islands and in all islands reefed and resounding
with cities. But the pitch is high as the ping
of cicadas, those small strained motors concealed
in the propped pines by the dying river, and only
male as the stretched falsetto of actors mincing
the women's roles in *kabuki*, or female only
as the lost heroes womanized in the Ladies' Opera.
Where in these alleys jammed with competing waves
of signs in two tongues and three scripts
can the signature of man be heard?

By the shogun palace, the Important Cultural Property
stripped for tiptoeing schoolgirls, I stare at the staring
penned carp that flail on each other's backs
to the shrunk pool's edge for the crumbs this non-fish
tosses. Is this the Day's one parable?
Or under that peeling pagoda the five hundred tons
of hermaphrodite Word?

At the inn I prepare to surrender again my defeated
shoes to the bending maid. But suddenly the closed
lotus opens to a smile and she points
over my shoulder, above the sagging tiles, to where
tall in the bare sky and huge as Gulliver
a carp is rising golden and fighting

thrusting its paper body up from the fist
of a small boy on an empty roof higher
and higher into the endless winds of the world.

Walter Blackstock

OLD VOYAGER

His landlocked dreams were rainbow-tides that ran:
Of clippers cutting ebony and spume
Through silver shatterings, a caravan
Of fractured waves. Always he saw the bloom
Of hyacinth-weather turning ships to sea.
He saw Orion and Arcturus burn
For mariners who steered toward Napoli;
He watched their transports leave, and then return.

He lived for one last voyaging — but one —
When he would sail beyond the Pleiades —
Past Sirius — to find eternities
Of hope bright-garlanded around the sun.
He dreamed of calm, of everlasting blue:
The port was known — the reckoning was true.

Harriet Gray Blackwell

FOREST

This is no wood for me to walk,
Not as the great oaks breathe the word,
For hither flies the golden hawk
To prey upon the scarlet bird.

Here in bright pools the sun has made
Leaves slither in soft avalanches,
Yet mystery mingles with the shade
When sable patches fall through branches.

And in this jungle that I planted
The painted tree-snail feeds on bark
Until its covert place is haunted
By hands not waiting for the dark.

I, neither song-bird, snail nor hawk
Watch time when fairest or when black,
This is no wood for me to walk,
Yet always I keep coming back.

Frederika Blankner

REMAINDER

Eyes do not lie,
And so,
Robbed of the after-glow,
Caught in this laughter-woe,
I must remember:

Once without anodyne
How your eyes looked in mine
And through an opened door
I saw as then before
Friend beyond time
And love more than lover.

    Is it because you fear
    Music that comes too near?

Is it because you kill
What might offend your will?

Is is because you die
Rather than falsify?

Be it or not, I have
Something in this to keep:
Once you looked deep, yes deep,
And what I saw no sleep
    Can undiscover—
And what I saw, I keep
    Forever.

Etta Blum

WHEN YOU REACH TIIE HILLTOP THE SKY IS ON TOP OF YOU

The sky was on the hill
the sky leaned over
white and blue and inbetween
feather-cushioning
the scythed hay.

I had all I could do
    between sky and dry
    brown clover, between
    blue tattered white
    and the inedible cherries
    (which I reached for just the same)
I had all I could do
    twirling time and
    again to see
    downward slope

hill on summer hill
green-breasted
in tempest of
eye-clasping
all I could do
to keep my feet
walking
a certain way,
contain my heart's
merry-making.

Arthur S. Bourinot

SNOW ANTHOLOGY

Snow
is an anthology
full of variety
in form and rhythm.
Here is a Hokku
by the partridge
whose sparse words
go single file
up and down the page
with meticulous care;
with fabulous nothings,
fairy lyrics
by the imagist mice,
free verse by the squirrels
scattered helter-skelter
on page after page,
and slow Miltonic blank verse
by the craftsman fox
following the scansion of the rabbit
whose onomatopoeia and alliteration
become, at times, a trifle monotonous.

To cap them all,
an occasional work
by that great artist, the deer,
written with delicacy and grace,
stamped with the deep feeling
and consummate artistry
of the master prosodist.

The edition is limited
and will soon be out of print.

Charles A. Brady

DIMIDIUM ANIMAE MEAE

We used to shadow-box on the shining grass
Against the dark dripping green of barberry and bridal-wreath
In the rainbow-mist of the sprinklers that spread their peacock
    fans slowly, stately in the westering summer sun.
And I was fleeter, but you were stronger.
And first I was the giant Willard, because I was the taller,
And then I was Carpentier, the fair Frenchman, because I
    liked him better,
But you were ever the swart Dempsey,
And ever the champion.
And we were happy, O my brother.

There was the time at the carnival when you spent your
    money quickly
(While I hoarded mine, for I had ever the double soul,
    and you were always a single heart)
On the swirl-wound long distaffs of taffy, flax-threaded,
    honeyhued,
And the popcorn hydrangeas on their wooden stalks,

So that there were no pennies left for tickets at the
    weathered kiosks,
To ride the shaggy ponies in the weedy paddock;
And I bought you screed after screed of green-stamped
    talismans;
And you rode round and round, easily, and confident
    as I need us
And we were happy, O my brother.

And once, swimming to the raft, by the bright bobbing floats,
While the loud-speaker trumpets husked out the
    Pagan Love Song over the choppy wavelets,
With the sand warm and white on the beaches, I tired,
And you helped me.
And once we fought after the hard-played tennis
On the raised court by the whistling Cape grass
    and the opal Bay,
Over who should take a girl to the *Blue Moon*
    that enchanted night.
And I won, and victory harshed brass on the tongue,
    and the magic drained pale from the evening;
And the girl had cow eyes and thick ankles.
          *   *   *

Tonight it tastes cold and clear. The fire burns sweet
    by the burnished andirons.
But there is snow in the Vosges passes; the moon glints
    sharp on your gun barrel.
And I am lonely, O my brother.

Joseph Payne Brennan

RACCOON ON THE ROAD

The asphalt morning found him; he was dead.
He lay as if asleep; his eyes were closed
Within his robber's mask, his glossy coat

Was wet with dew, his satin paws lay still.
I saw in retrospect the swath of blinding light,
The burning wheels that found him where he froze.
I mourned him in my mind—the quiet one
Who came at dusk, stealing the succulent grubs,
Seizing the saffron fish that swam too high.
I saw him, stippled in shadow, prowling the swamp,
Probing the maple stump, exploring the pool.
The hot sun came up; the asphalt smoked.
Soon enough the racing wheels arrived.
I carried him off the road into the woods.
Under a cool catalpa tree where the wild grape
Was growing, I turned the fragrant earth
And laid him in.

Olga Hampel Briggs

BRIEF HISTORY

Poetry, Emily:
Curiously, in two-times-three
Syllables—biography.
Quietly, Emily
Walked her ways with poetry:
Not unharried, not carefree
Who lives her days with poetry!
Carefully, Emily
Worked her thoughts in poetry:
Dower-chest embroidery,
Sampler for posterity.
Secretly, Emily
Folded-by her poetry:
Not for careless eyes to see
Such delight and ecstasy.

Happily, Emily
Cherished rainbow, blossom, bee,
Blended bird and star and tree,—
Shaping immortality.

Zoe Kincaid Brockman

THE GRAPEVINE

Someone has lived here where twin chimneys,
Shorn of warm timbers, stand up alone;
Someone who left a vibrant message
Graven deep on the vital stone.

Carved on a block of deathless granite
Set in the ravished chimney-piece,
Here in the autumn sun I read it;
"Thunder of pulse shall never cease."

Here in the thin, bright sun I ponder
On one who cherished that burning line,
While, from his sunken grave in the garden,
Nourished, a grapevine sings of wine.

In this still place my soul must ponder
On the oldest truth his soul had won:
Here where his voiceless dust reposes,
Singing, a grapevine climbs the sun!

Florence Kerr Brownell

COIN IN THE FIST

Level with duty, days ride a city-express across the
    calendar page,
Lights primed an hour ahead for the tunnel-night,
Tomorrow's news already platform-stacked.
Trial begun, trial over—
Wait, was he hanged before the crime?

Time was once measured by anticipation's pulse:
It could be now or later—whistled to as Gyp came running—
A short or long way to the window-front.
It is years since we have traced rainbow veins in a
    glass-alley
Or bounced a simulated orange over the jacks.

Where has Saturday gone, a coin clenched tight in the fist,
The wings of a moment pinned down—
A bright butterfly for our slow perusal?

Elizabeth Mabel Bryan

FATHER OF THE MAN

No fence will keep a growing boy outside
Even if it be spiked and tall to boot.
Can wanton whirlwind stem the morning tide?
Can rock defy the reach of living root?
In dreams of storming bastions he will see,
For toe-hold, widened crevices that slant,

And he will ferret hide-outs with a knee,
One hand cupped stoutly on a dagger point.
Your boy can come to terms with any fence:
A postern gate or fretted barricade.
He means to climb such tall impediments
Rather than scuff thick blue-stone newly laid.
And having set his lance and made his vow,
Your embryo knight has never questioned how.

Frances Westgate Butterfield

TIME OUT

Lay out the minutes, row on ordered row,
Vast acres of dismembered days and weeks,
Departed months and years, in bloody streaks,
Across the field of separation show;
And none return, in measure swift or slow,
Nor gather in commemorative cliques.
Each next-of-kin, a harassed victim, speaks,
Eye-hungry, spirit dragging low,
"Where are the medals for this loss of time?
I hear no volleys for its brave release.
Surely some monument with ponderous rhyme
For parted love should epitaph surcease."

What balance sheet can tot the hideous score
Of this, the least considered crime of war?

Witter Bynner

AN AUTUM WALK

Here at this sudden age of mine
I listen to leaves along my walk:

My foot becomes the moving vine,
    My step the talk.

I lift a foot and the other foot,
But still I hear along the way
Less of what I am about
   Than a leaf can say.

Leaves lie down so lightly dead
That they are neither there nor here,
And I remain alive instead
    Along the year.

AGED FISHERMAN

You fish for people
And not even their names
Come up for you
But the sun is still there
And you sit in it
Fishing for people
And hooking the sun.

Melville Cane

EACH TO EACH

We were closed, each to each, yet dear.
We were taut with a covert pride;
We were tied
With a throttling fear;
We were undefined
And blind.

We were caught when we sought to reach;
We were mute when we strove for speech.
We were closed, each to each, yet dear.
We were vapid, polite, obscure
Through a merciless flood of pain;
We were trivial through strain;
We were desperate to endure.

Then a locked word slipped from your heart,
Like warm rain dropped on mine,
And the fog that had held us apart
Thinned, —we could dimly divine
The one we had groped for in vain.

And my hand touched yours, and the pain
That clutched and withered had fled,
And the fear and the pride lay dead,
And at last we were free, we were plain.

We were closed, each to each, yet dear.
We are close; we are clear.

PRESENCE OF SNOW

So rare, so mere,
You cannot hear
It brush against the stillness or impair
With faintest stir
The poised, suspended air.

So rare, so mere,
And yet imponderably clear;
You cannot see, yet see
The secret flow
Of immanent snow,
Although

The softest breath has yet to free,
The gentlest current yet to take
The first bewildered flake.

Eleanor Hollister Cantus

FAME

Wear it as a bangle on your arm,
It may shield you from all harm.

Use it as an anklet, when you run
It will glitter in the sun.

Thread it like a ribbon through your hair—
Do not wear it everywhere.

Weave not a robe nor put it on,
Winds are cold when it is gone.

Mary E. Caragher

TREE TAG

Three children dash in the dim dooryard.
Ready! Get set! Go!

Run, Ellen, Lena, Elizabeth!
Touch the Russet, the Baldwin, the Sheepnose!
The Red Astrachan tree is goal.

Wind is rising among the leaves;
An apple thumps to the darkening planet,
Rushing through space toward the winter solstice.

Lena, Elizabeth, Ellen,
Don't you hear the calling?
It is late and cold.
The short day turns toward a harsher season.

Sara King Carleton

LATE OCTOBER

The scent of rotted apples,
    day-steeped in sun,
Leads us on and on up the
    rutted road, where
Maple leaves fall languidly,
    one by one,
Shifting and drifting in the
    quiet air.
The dog sniffs along the faded
    asters, the sedge,
Along the stiffened goldenrod
    at the wood's edge.

It will be good to remember
    leaves and orchard musk
On the shining hard pavement
    of the city street in the
    winter dusk.

It will be good to remember
    the moist barnyard,

And the cowbells' haunting
    sound,
And the dancing light of the
    lantern, homeward bound.

Margaret Haley Carpenter

SEPTEMBER AFTERNOON

Around us summer wrote its last farewell
In legends we were swift to comprehend;
And reading leaf and shadow we could tell
That something more than summer was to end.

Tincture of autumn stained the darkening air
With color of loneliness, and we could see
Chromatic tones of richness changing there,
Resolving even then to memory.

An elegy of wind began to blow
Over and over its insistent theme:
"This is the way all lovely things must go,
Leaving behind the substance of a dream."

The lingering light began to perish under
A spell of stars that ushered evening in,
And we were left an image burned in wonder,
More beautiful than summer once had been.

Constance Carrier

FUGUE

Behind the granite church
the sky has taken on
the quality of stone,
its weight, its triple tone
from gray to purple hue:
the pigeons dip and wheel,
purple, slate-gray, and blue.

Purple, slate-blue, and gray,
the shadows blend and shift,
the shadows load and darken
the late December day—
darken and fade and lift,
resume and fade—a chord
that swells and dies away,

that dies away and swells,
against whose dominant
the birds in spiral flight
go up across the stone,
up like the sound of bells,
then, like the overtones,
drift downward past the stone.

Pigeons and cloud and church
resolve their medley toward
both counterpoint and chord—
the sullen troubled slow
clouds, moved against their will,
the church, a silent *No*
to motion, and the birds'
nervous arpeggio.

Perceive, O innocent,
here in this triad plain
(dead calm, and flying storm,
and motion grave and slow)
the ancient argument
of bone and blood and brain,
whose tones, tho they remain
antiphonal, afford
both counterpoint and chord.

TRANSFORMATION SCENE

Returned, a wraith from her defrauded tomb,
she haunts an empty house,
stares thro the window at a scrawl of boughs,
wanders from room to legendary room.

Weightless she roams: with printless fingertips
touches the polished table tops, and looks
at the long rows of books:
turns then and slips

thro an unopened door and past the stair.
Nothing must be neglected: she will check
lest there be change, lest there be flaw or fleck
to dim the house whose keeping is her care ...

till, in a sunlight grown lackluster, she
who cast no shadow even in full sun,
comes on a mirror where there should be none,
sees her reflection who had none to see—

watches it sharpen, grow opaque and clear,
while silence gathers and like summer thunder
splits the high cupola, swells downward under
a gray light, and explodes upon her ear

here in a house that will not fall but fade
as her own body takes on life once more.
Not she is unsubstantial, but the door
she passes thro, its locks again betrayed.

She walks on ground grown firm: the house, receding,
dissolves behind her: from a bough she breaks
a branch of blossom, and the branch-end rakes
her arm, her flesh, warm in the sun, and bleeding.

Mabel MacDonald Carver

CODICIL

Let certain holdings of stocks and bonds
be distributed in legal process
        to legal heirs;
accrued interest on savings,
        plus capital,
        be assigned.
That, too, my heirs may squander on fol-de-rol:
        I shall not mind.

Give the *blanc de chine* Kwan Yin
to someone blind, that he may
touch white loveliness with seeing fingers.
Give the museum piece of purple cloisonné
to one whose four walls have been too gray.

But keep the shabby, world-traveled Chinese shawl
        close by.
Wrap it for extra warmth around your shoulders
        in spring or autumn chill.
        Keep it close by,
knowing a part of me is with you still.

Jean Valentine Chace

VISIT TO A HOSPITAL

I have come to where the world drops off
Into an emptiness which cannot bear
(Or lacks the center to compel)
The weight of one sparrow's feather falling.
Perhaps the sparrow's furthest calling
Is, after all, to fall
Numbered by some most tender care;
But here, the air
Has grown too thin: the world drops off
That could imagine Heaven, or so much care.

I fall, still in the earth's monstrous pull,
To kiss your quiet hands, your planeless face.
Oh, our dearest, you are right
Not to know your deathbed's place,
To wander in your mind from Framingham
To Salters Point's blond beaches where
As a girl you skipped stones and swam.
The iron bedstead there was much like this;
And in this grave, unspeakable night,
Beyond the pull of gravity or care,
You, oh our dearest, have no place.

Katherine Garrison Chapin

PORTRAIT IN WINTER

There is much to be said for the portrait painted in winter,
Winter of age, and winter of season.
Light from snow clouds is no sharper

Than sun of Spring. It is clearer.
Colors hold their right, shapes define their reason,
Values are neither increased nor changed.

Time's winter has marked brow and hair,
Iced a thin nose, cupped the eyes,
Chiseled a final story on the mouth,
No longer curved in wonder or surprise.
Winter is too late to alter what is there.

Within the room warmth from the hearth glows
Against fuchsia dress. Under a chair
The black dog sighs contentedly.
Against a northern window barbed sleet blows.

And the painter, moving in a sinuate pattern,
Mixes thought and color, line and perception.
His brush a sharp dissecting instrument
Bears down against bone, or delicately
Finds a secret pulse. From chromatic palette
He builds flesh and weight; movement
Poised, at rest; form dominated
By the mind's perspective.
Ambience of the past discarded—
Soft air of summer, or the appled autumns—
In disembodied light of winter
He paints a portrait for a candid future.

Jeannette Chappell

NEWTON TO EINSTEIN

Welcome, friend.
Two hundred years I've waited for this day,
two hundred years and more.
But I'm a patient man; stubborn, too, some say.

The Christmas I was born
the midwife prophesied I would not last the night:
fourscore-and-five full years went past
before they bore me through the Abbey door.

Twice welcome, friend.
What of the planet Neptune, what of that?
I left precise directions
where 'twould be,
and yet it took a century for anyone to see!

But what is time when you're outside of time?
Let's talk of Relativity.

Mary Grant Charles

FLOOD

It is impossible to find anything good
about water during a flood:
to relate it to dew on the feet
in refreshing grasses;
or to playful whitecaps
on a sudden, inland sea.

It is unrealistic,
when water assaults our cities,
to say, "This is the wand of rain
that waved Edens into a Kansas
dust bowl;
this is the long drink of water
to them lost in Saharas of thirst."

While the enemy is at our door
it is irrelevant to tell,

"He is the kin of dew, of mist, of summer
rain."
Yet . . . too much or too little,
one drink or a flood:
All, all is water!
Without which there is no living thing.

Joseph Cherwinski

MANHATTAN MENAGERIE

Off Broadway, where they sell those photographs
Of glossy nudes beneath the glassy eye
Of a jaundiced man who perches priestly high,
The buyers reach for dreams like dry giraffes.

In front of Tiffany's, a mewing cat
Is caught and fondled in Italian arms.
On Madison, a model's frozen charms
Halt traffic with a red mink coat and hat.

And down in cellars mercifully dim,
Musicians weave like cobras in a spell,
Exuding, with their hiss, a jungle smell
Of the hunted one and the hunter after him.

And off in Central Park, behind their bars,
The prisoners who sulk on cold cement.
Are waiting to burst their iron tenement
And stalk these trees of glass, these caves of stars.

Thomas Caldecot Chubb

PRAISE OF NEW ENGLAND

Let me now set down a picture of New England that will
    show it to you and explain it,
And soften the edges of its outline, and make kindlier its
    raw rain.
Let me fill in its Spring wonder, Fall glory—its fragile greens,
    flambent crimsons.
It is not always frost-nipped. It smells of new earth after
    Winter.

It smells of lilacs in May when the furrows are straight in
    the sun.
It smells deeply of roses when the lawns are shadowed with
    Summer.
It is colored with mallows, creamy white, delicate pink in the
    marshes.
You can always sense the salt air. The sea is not ever far.

Let me now make a saying about New England, running
    north to Vermont,
Running east to the cleft rocks of Maine, being shielded by
    Cape Cod,
The bent right arm of a fighter that wards off heavy blows:
It is a firm land, a solid land, a land worth the knowing.

Its men are true men, terse, frugal. Their hearts are kept
    locked.
They are careful of speech. Their coin is secured in safe box.
Their thoughts are spare thoughts. Their minds are tough
    and austere,
Yet smart as a whip. Where they do not see far, they see
    clearly.

And they know beauty. They can neither deny nor gainsay it,
Whose fine white houses still stand like some breathless
    Greek vase,
Whose spiralled stairways arise as a fluted shell does,
Who made exquisite ships and silver as true as a bell.

Let me now praise New England. Though it forge for itself
Chains to bind its own soul, it is good past the telling.
It is not alloy, not base. It is made of pure metal.
Oh, my New England where true worth is valued yet!

Gertrude Claytor

GRANT AT APPOMATTOX

Now it was Spring,
Buds were thick on the shattered bough,
Now you could hear the high bird-trill,
The rustle of wind, the rain—
For guns were still.
Fields that were choked with blood
Thawed in the rain, drew breath,
Conquering spears of green rose from the load of death.

Though a hundred years go by
Rhythm is still the same,
Shadow and shock of steel,
Smoke and the fruit of flame,
Blue of the sky, the Gray—
Caught and forever bound,
The old that is folded away,
The new that peoples the ground.
The fallow dust must yield,
The soldier turn from the field.

Grant looked on the sodden land
With the plume of life just showing,
On the tree with the shattered bough,
On the bough where the buds were growing;
He looked on the field of death,
On wheat that prodded the loam
And he said to the vanquished men,
"Take the horses and mules, go home,
Go home for the Springtime plowing."
The weary men went home,
And remembered the words of Grant,
The seed of the word was sown
In the fields they were soon to plant.

As a tide will rise from the sea,
The heart will rise in flood
Breaking its barriers—free—
Cool with the cooling blood—
This was his day, his theme,
His flood in the sea of time,
Warrior, dreamer and dream.
Here at the end was Lee,
Strong in a vast defeat,
So had the cycle turned—
So was the dream complete.
Lee and the proffered sword—
After the Wilderness—Peace,
Out of the wilderness, Lord.

E. R. Cole

OH, YOU WHOLLY RECTANGULAR

Oh, you wholly rectangular, totally sinuous
immeasurably abstract
proud-of-your-crystalline-viens-and-arteries
Cezanne!

Were you to blame (or your metallic leg)
for engendering impossible diameters
instead of flowers
for us?

Or was it a blame on your granitic hand
to have gone spilling the jugulars
of our futurity:
your horal testament of cubes and spheres?

Hours
hours
proceeding steadily,
vertically downward, ubiquitously around, osmotically in.

Hours
mocked by an invisible laughter
that tears to the horizons
unravelling deserts behind.

Lucile Coleman

WITH LILACS IN MY EYE

Now I shall reach over
This dividing line
And touch the lilac tapers
Lighting purple toward the sky.
If you want to know why....
Say they are my neighbor's
(Indifferent as a goldfish
Or a sunblind mole;
Or a chrysalis that never
Turned into a butterfly).

I should be the owner,
They should be mine ...
So I'm a next-door beggar
With lilacs in my eye.

Horatio Colony

GHOST PET

My ghost pets are like shadows on the wall,
Moving there back and forth. A cat I had
That lay upon my chest to rise and fall
With my own breath like spirit dark and bad.

But he repulsed me even from the first,
Complaining ever of his delicacy,
Himself so brittle, and my hands accursed
That worked around him smooth and lovingly.

One day he backed himself into the fire.
His eyebrows mixed with stealth fell downward slowly.
I saw him in a flame of blue expire.
I saw him become cinders small and lowly.

The fire did that around his furry throat
Which I could never do; and his abdomen
Heaved in the fire; his spirit seemed to float
Along my room: I took it for an omen.

Padraic Colum

GARLAND SUNDAY

On Garland Sunday, the weaver told me,
Things grown gloomy with years' disuse,

Their marching orders we straight will give them,
And send them hopping out of the house.
And this includes the spoutless kettle,
The backless chair with the missing rung,
The short-legged bench and the snoutless bellows—
No wake we'll give them—let them begone!
Man alive! Let them begone!

No luck nor grace can be about them,
The balked, the broken, the mouldy lot;
We'd grow like them and our thoughts go shabby,
And even our prayers might catch dry-rot.
The long-tailed coat that is as rusty,
As nail that hangs it in cob-webs thick,
The clouts and the combs, the duds and the druggets—
Their march to the dock is the double-quick—
Man alive! Make it double-quick!

The porch and the wall we'll whitewash finely,
And posies set on the window-ledge,
And daub the door with a lively color
To match the haws in the garden-hedge.
And Garland Sunday will see the curtains
As fresh as daisies on window lids,
And whin and fern and yellow iris
Lighten the house as old custom bids—
Man alive! As old custom bids!

And things of choice, the weaver told me,
Will raise our hearts like the winning goal,
The crock on the table that shows deep lustre,
The figured dish and the well-shaped bowl.
Tatterdemalions all gone to the gallows,
The rest of the ballad is right as rain:
We'll favor the well-shaped, the clean and comely
Till Garland Sunday comes round again—
Man alive! It comes round again!

AFTER SPEAKING OF ONE DEAD A LONG TIME

"She should have had . . .," I said, and there I stopped:
Knowing her loss, how could I speak of it,
I who have only words of men befriended?
I should have had the language used by men
Who stood outside their tents, the waste before them,
And looking towards some great star made a poem
Of tenderness and grief—all manliness—
The words as lonely as their desert marches:
I should have had possession of that speech
To make the poem that rises to my mind
Of one who grew into a life forsaken.

And there were men in Ireland, annalists,
Unfailing men for whom all things had failed,
Whose chronicle was pillage would destroy
The vellum that they wrote on, and make blank
A thousand years a people could take pride in,
And on the page that was the volume's end
Wrote of a personal loss, a wife or child
Dead, in words that have eventfulness
Being taken off the loom of history:
I should have had reversion of those words
To tell of all she lost in one short life time!

"She should have had . . .," you said, reached by
        what held me,
"The simple things that we will always have."

Hasye Cooperman

THE MISTS ARE RISING NOW
(based on "Great Expectations" by Charles Dickens)

Child,
You are my brother.
You that were
And I that am.
Across the broad expanse
Of tranquil light,
Across this distant solitude
I see you as you trod.

The iron band of solemn years,
The nettles,
Oh the dark, flat wilderness
That held the tombstones where my mother and my
    father lay,
The crying heart the earth spun round,
For these
We are.
We need not be ashamed.

Our tears
"are rain
upon the blinding dust."
We left the forge.
We roamed. We sorrowed.
And we sought.
Close together
In this darkness,
Crying evil, go.

Empty sky, and
Empty exile,

And the tread was azure dawn.
Once, just once, you turned your eyes
And said:
The hand of God
Has touched my shoulders
And my head is light.
I feel the earth after a flood.
And underfoot I stamp the sod.
I know the folds of living earth
And of the trampled land.
Your voice was clear. You spoke into the dawn.

I, wastrel, idling in the moorlands,
Playing there among the tombstones,
Looking out to sea.
The scattered cattle gazing quietly
And feeding,
As the earth spun round the childish heart
That knew a cold fatigue.

Beyond were dikes and mounds of green
And enigmatic gates.
There was a leaden river line
And then the savage lair, the sea, the distant sea.

There stand the dreams
In frozen awe.
The morning mists, they rose so long ago.
The evening mists are rising now.

Annette Patton Cornell

SAILOR'S WOMAN

An opal ring and a holly tree:
the gifts my true love brought to me.

The tarnished sea and the pewter sky
met with a crash and the waves leaped high
to a crest of pearl, pitting the sand
with talisman shells where they rushed and fanned.

The dark came close . . . and the stars burned low . . .
and I knew all I had hoped to know.
The depths of the opal were as desire—
reflecting the flames of the driftwood fire . . .
The night and the stars whirled out in space
and there was nothing but my love's face.
The fire and the sky and the moon-drawn sea
swirled in the kiss my love gave me.

I twist the jewel upon my hand . . .
The tree grows tall at the edge of the sand.
I wait again . . . as I waited then . . .
as sailors' women wait for their men.

Mildred Cousens

AMERICAN VINEYARD

This is an ancient pattern on these hills—
The lines of silvery stakes
Climb up the contoured rows of terraces;
The unseen shuttle of the sun
Has woven them all about with myriad leaves
Guarding the ripening clusters with their green.

Some patterns are erased by time and place;
Others are dimmed, remaining echoes only—
The pomegranate, bird of paradise,
The lotus blossom and the Persian pear
Survive on clay or wood, parchment and tapestry.

This one withstands
The stormy rigors of a harsher land;
This is a living theme enacted here.
It once knew Canaan and Assyria,
And then the isles of Cyprus and of Crete,
Provence and Andalusia, Tuscany—
Remember? You have even heard it named
Within the rhythms of the Odyssey—
The gardens of Alcinöus, the sea as dark as wine—
Think how the strand weaves through the web of years,
A many tendrilled vine.

Elizabeth Cox

MASK

Image in the bulb-ringed mirror
incomparable I, this decent face.
    Now line and shade define
        familiar planes.
    (Buskin, cap and bells)

Unnatural length along the jaw;
accent the brow; hint heightened mouth
    wider than truth to speak
        no fact but life.
    (Spirit gum and grease)

It startles with a star-fringed terror.
Cry love or hate upon it now,
    mask in the mirror framed,
        this naked face.

    The call boy rudely raps.

Christine Turner Curtis

VILLA SCIARRA: ROME

Everything shall be erased,
all scars from the acids of life
shall be smoothed away
in the alleys of the pleached laurels;
and where cedars of Lebanon
hang their Persian-blue shawls over the fountains,
and satyrs in scarves of rose-tendrils
frolic with the long-haired goat,
bending to see their shirred reflections
in the bottle-glass of the scarcely perturbed pool.

And the sound is only
the wind rising up from Rome
to slant the strings of water,
diffusing the drops into subtler sequences.
Is it not true that the Roman marbles
are in danger of dust? and yet this garden,
lifting its cypresses, its palms,
the hollies, the little firs shaped into peacocks,
would comfort, I think, even one survivor,
walking, shaken, in its sighs and shadows.

Betty Page Dabney

EARTH'S BONDMAN

When man has conquered space
What will be his gain?
The moon's pocked face
Unmollified by rain,

The far cold reaches
Between star and star,
The blast-carved beaches
Where no seas are

Nor any wind sings
Nor any gull cries;
Where no herb springs
Nor germinates nor dies?

Though the universe be his,
The last void spanned,
Not all the galaxies
Can break his ancient bond

With cloud and leaf and sod.
The earth is in his flesh,
The tide is in his blood;
So intricate the mesh

That moors him to his star.
Adventurer by will,
By nature insular,
He wears Earth's livery still.

Rae Dalven

MY FATHER

My father tore out his native roots
when middle-aged, unskilled, proud.
He sailed for this golden land
when it was quota-free, hope-endowed.

He found a job in a factory
owned by a man from his own home town;

his compatriot workers all spoke Greek,
he enjoyed a clannish-renown.

And he sweated for a dollar a day
recalling a mother's lament,
"Are these all the drachmas you earned today?"
A limited life, void of event.

And at night he'd amble across
to the coffee-house on Rivington Street,
where the old and the new
would never, never meet.

And his oriental "amanedes"
soared in revel-release,
soaring him back in flight,
serenading his wife in Greece.

And he sent for his loved ones,
their passage he took on a loan,
found a flat in a slum tenement,
started to work on his own.

Why did he fail?
Why was his presence fatherly weak?
He couldn't learn the language they spoke,
"They speak in English, I speak in Greek!"

Inhospitable, suspicious
of the friends his children made,
"A shoe from our own home town, let it be patched!"
Out of his orbit afraid.

This was my father,
this was our sin,
he couldn't come out,
we wouldn't give in.

Olive Tilford Dargan

RESCUE

Ruthless unrest has urged slow feet
Out and down to the siren river
That murmurs of sleep no sun disturbs.
Suddenly on night's shore
The vigil gold of a flower
Shines in the first quick shaft
Of dawnlight parting the night's gray mist,
And in the heart stirs an infant joy.

A lily on the water
Quiets the waves with beauty,
Beauty that trembles up and climbs
Through rescued veins of welcome.
From morn-lit flower
And wave-kissed lily
Rises an essence more preciously woven
Than roots unaided can yield.

Pervasive charm uniting
Disjointed self with calm of strength
That veils its source
In far dividing distance,
But near as breath to human need,
With unfelt touch of power cleanses
The shambles of maddening fate,
And a heart that begged to die
Is keen again to face
A beckoning life.

Mariana B. Davenport

SUSPENDED MOMENT

A welcome freshness over the garden lay
As the sprinkler turned, making a circle of rain
An archway of mist, a plume of silver spray
Repeating the curve, falling and falling again.

Into the mist where a perfect rainbow grew
As water rose and fell on the parched brown lawn
Suddenly into the arc a hummingbird flew
Miniature bird and bow—and the moment gone.

Gustav Davidson

AMBUSHED BY ANGELS

Ambushed by angels and by demons bound
    I wrestle with that hierarchic host,
    Knowing them to be only phantom, ghost,
    Legend or fable, incantation, myth,
    Spirits of air fit but to conjure with.

By day, by night, thronging on every hand,
    They stalk and leaguer me, a myriad band.
    Vainly I rout them out of sight and mind—
    Upon the instant, horned or aureole-crowned,
    They shape themselves anew and hem me round.

Thus tricked by fancy or the wintry wood
    Wherein I loiter, baffled and beguiled,

I sense, in the vast hush and failing light,
Tall presences, like a believing child.
Nor can I tell the evil from the good,

Demons from daevas, satans from seraphim;
    Aeons from thrones, archons from kerubim;
    Nor if that world I cannot hope to prove,
    Flaming with heavenly beasts, holy and grim,
    Is any less real than that in which I move.

NEVERTHELESS

Wisdom is better than bread,
Charity sweeter than wine;
What is not loved is dead—
Yet love may be bitter as brine.

Hope is a lovely wraith;
Freedom, life's very breath;
Truth is more precious than faith—
Yet truth may be bitter as death.

For all that, it were best
To seek and love and burn—
Though dust return to dust
And all our striving vain.

Irene Dayton

EAR IS NOT DEAF

After long journey in sun
light penetrating marrow bone.
One comes to terms with summer

as summer ends, arm shading
upturned face in the knowing all
of light; understanding ear

listening, the same way one comes
upon paradoxes of living, wrestling
with meaning through longer season.

The experienced ear is not deaf—
listening—it is hard, however,
to hear among hordes of locusts

singing, bushed in dry burnt air;
the nuances of speech encountered
in fever of noon-day pitch. Sound

moving out from dry, cluttered season
extends the year's invisible reach.
There are rustlings in dove-tailed light,

enfolded throughout summer's heat,
hours of inverted speech. In this
interval it is hard to hear broken

vowels of the longer season; continually
they turn in blue magic light. The ear
hears time's cadence, her ontoward flight.

Elma Dean

OLD MEN'S WARD

Now we are civilized, the old men die
in white and formal anonymity;
bed after bed, defeated all, they lie

and no familiar thing to touch or see;
wakened too early, tucked to sleep too soon,
and fed the smooth and tasteless infant diet;
their last days dribbled out by glass and spoon
in timed and dull and antiseptic quiet.

Weep for them—not for the old one found
dead with his clothes on in his dirty shack;
companioned only by the blue-tick hound
whose deep-bell baying could not call him back.
Spare him the pity——he departed whole,
spitting the dear brown weed, owning his soul.

Miriam Allen deFord

WE SHALL SAY

Now with earth riven and a bloodied sun
Comes the hour of affirmation.
Love, we shall say, is not rutting only—
The coupled beasts wear wings:
Death, we shall say, is not decay alone—
The dying beast can gaze beyond horizons.
Still runs the ancient quicksilver,
Still under the seemly coat
The hidden and personal creature
Burns with the lawless wish,
Is tranced in the snow-cold dream.

This hurricane-age, we shall say, will have its riders
        and tamers,
Will be possessed of heroes, rebels, saints,
Children of fathers destroyed,
But children of their fathers.

Blood on the sun, and the earth riven, we shall say,
But a new earth healed, and a new sun rising.

Harriet L. Delafield

NO ESCAPE

If I were a chipmunk
And you a star
I could not scramble
Half so far:
If I were a squirrel
And you a bee
You'd always buzz
Ahead one tree:
But as we've heads
To rule our feet
It must occur—
You'll see—we'll meet.

Joanne de Longchamps

BLIND, I SPEAK TO THE CIGARETTE

No longer casual hand to lip
but habit remains. Finding you,
I lift to my ready mouth a round familiar
that teeth can test and tongue tamp down.
The match another matter—like a friend
no longer trusted, having brittle ways—
a firework threat remembered red,
the scent of sulphur known salute.
Not as sister to another act,
I seek you singly, turning it to play
as you ride in my right hand up and down

to meet the left hand midway with its tray.
I wonder am I daft—or sly
to flail at ashes on my coat,
to fear the cinder in your cyclop's eye?
Possessing you, your bitter warmth,
I know the better part goes forth on air
in dissipating coils—a serpent track
unimaginable, the frolic of form I lack.

August Derleth

THE PLANETARY ARC-LIGHT

A neighbor thought that they
had put an extra streetlight at the far end
of the street.
"I never saw it there before,"
he said, chancing to meet
me out at his side door.

It looked like surplus amperage to spend,
before it changed from white to red.
There were any number of things I could have said,
but telling him the truth was hard to do.

"That light a star?" He laughed and went inside.

He might have seen it on another night; on only
     one or two
would Venus hang there in the line of lights beside
the corner pole. It *might* have been a light
put up by men—
it was unwinking and as bright.
But it shone too whitely and then
too amber and too red at last
before it went out of line and down

under past the street's end, past
the last house at the edge of town.

Snug and secure inside his house, a leaf curled
winter-wise, he could never know
he had looked briefly on another world,
because he saw it in an arc-lights' row.

If it mattered, I could not say—
it *had* looked like a streetlight in the evening air,
an alien light indeed that did not stay.
The important thing was that he noticed it out there.
What he called it did not count. Perhaps somewhere
far outside, somebody pointed Earth to say,
"I see they've put a new streetlight out there."

Samuel A. DeWitt

TWO SONNETS FOR A LOST LOVE

I

"There is no permanence," you sagely said;
    "Why mummy every kiss and fervored vow
With the balmed tape of faith? This love once dead
    Will shrink into a grisly shape, while now
"It pulses quickly, radiates, and springs
    Like a young beast prime passioned for the stud.
This is the way of all terrestrial things;
    This is the ordained manner of the blood.

"And why make votive nonsense over flesh,
    When it be meant for open gluttony . . .
Then gorge and revel while the game is fresh . . ."
    All this and more you sagely said to me.
But when love died, I fled the proffered feast,
To find a permanence in pain, at least.

II

If I were less the man, I might have kept
    A show of worship at your trammelled shrine,
Or in a swinish incarnation crept
    To snout your crumbs and lap the dripping wine.
But being more the man, and more the fool,
    I fashion outrage for your simple sins,
And mouth it frothing with fanatic drool.
    Now all your smiles are like gargoylian grins,

And lurking madness frames a silhouette
    Against my wall of thought. Your fragrant form
Contorts into a monstrous thing, and yet,
    My reason rides its anchor through the storm.
However passion fume, and fog and blur,
I still can see the light I dreamed you were.

Alice Fay di Castagnola

MORTAL COMBAT

When I come groping back through mists of sleep
To where the floodgates now stand open wide,
Where sentinel-thoughts, by day, were trained to keep
Stern watch, with lock secure and you outside,
I wonder if I can again retire
To sober worlds, renounce th' enchanted land
All iridescent with celestial fire,
And where you lead me always by the hand;

If I succeed at last, and bar the door,
A horde of hungry memories will beat
Upon it, as they did, and try once more
To break the lock, invade my last retreat,—
This is a mortal combat we are in,
And no one can foretell which side will win.

George Dillon

A KIND INN

I dreamt I came to a kind inn.
I left my boat with fallen sail
At the curb, filling the dark street.
It was a winding strait. Within,
I stood uncertain at the door.
Half glare, half darkness, half-discerned
Faces. I thought it might be hell.
Yet all was kindness: every eye
Could tell me (though I could not tell)
Why I had come, where I had been.
But I could only stand and pour
Coins into a telephone,
While in remembered rooms that burned
At various levels in the night
The pleading of the distant bell
Drilled, in a city I had known.
A voice would answer and go dead,
But I could only stand and cry
Repeatedly, as though for days,
"How shall I have the boat returned
When I have come to the last mile?"
But someone near me in the gloom
In a jersey, with a child's clear gaze
But all the rest in shadow, said,
"Let me go with you for a while
And pilot you to the sea-foam.
Trust me: I know these waterways."

Celia Dimmette

APOLOGY OF THE YOUNG SCIENTISTS

Near the river with white waves, we probed,
In the floor of grass and groves jeweling
Inland waters, through country with the moon in palms.
To the border holding the final miracle,
We came for the first of light, the hidden seed.

In alien cold and deep in the mind's harbor
We searched, through icy cover, welled and walled,
For the secret cell. The eye of vortex burning
Or severed bead of sun, we could not know.

In the watery dark, we held, breast-wrapped and fanned
Alive the seeds of growth to plume the earth—
Hosanna green the hour, no cornucopia
Spilling the lurid fruit. We proffered terror
And hope, the good and evil that we found.

Alfred Dorn

CHALLENGERS

Tapering stars glint cool;
No wind intrudes.
Phalanxed miles of feathery wheat
Glisten in dawn's red gloom.
Slowly the wide bare hills are maned in lion-colored light.
All lies vast and silent.

Like a Chinese character on the horizon,
One hut clears through the glimmer.

Small as a blade of grass against the sky,
A farmer plows his star-far field.
I leap on a rock and wave the air to splinters.—
At last he waves reply.

Crisscrossing space with laughter,
We stand undwarfed,
Fused by a wordless gesture
That foils the sun,
And know the earth is smaller than a man.

Leah Bodine Drake

PRECARIOUS GROUND

On the volcanic hill
The small brave village clings
And the rich grapevine swings.

In wheat foredoomed to fall
Beneath the reaper's blade,
Meekly and undismayed
The field-mouse makes her nest,
And down to the sea's false arms
The harbour alleys run,
And farmhouse windows burn
Each with its tiny sun
Against the tremendous night
Arching this tilting dust
That is a world in flight.

On such precarious ground
Life rears its endless house
For meadow-lark and mouse
And fiery-rotted flowers,
And love itself must shape
Its vulnerable towers
On the uncertain sands
Of the wild human heart,
Raising its reckless port
Beside an unknown sea,
Building with desperate trust,
Building because it must
Only upon the slope
Of old catastrophe.

Carleton Drewry

EVENSONG
(for David)

Sit quiet in my lap while solemnly
The evening gathers all the daylight hours.
Now watch the moon climb past that crooked tree
Where the star-seeded sky, a thicket, flowers.

Your time runs down, but only for a day;
Tomorrow's tense will take it up in you.
And when you sleep your world will wink away,
But when the earth wakes you will waken, too.

Would it were so with love that holds you here,
The circle that I close about you now,
So soon to slacken, too soon disappear
In sleep I know not why, you know not how.

Mary Ballard Duryee

HOMESTEAD—WINTER MORNING

Clocked with the sun and by his journey paced,
A shadow moves across my winter lawn
Immense and black—a frosty polygon
Where wall and gable are exactly placed;
But in the solid cube no door is traced
To open on the evening or the dawn;
Only the outlined replica is drawn
And cast in dark reflections, silver faced.

Here there is no concern with filigree;
No latticed light; no leafy foil of boughs
Or flattery of ornament afforded;
But in its bold austerity I see
How beautiful the years have made the house—
Trifles deleted and the strength recorded.

Virginia Earle

A DREAM AS REPORTED

. . . you were with me and it wasn't flying, exactly,
but landing on a mountaintop on one foot
with the knee bent, tensed, just so,
and the pushoff—
the leap through air, it wasn't
floating, exactly, it was the muscles
doing just what they were told.

You said, *Look down.* The valley
opened below us
and all the trees were small and very clear,
filigree miniatures, too tiny for toys,
green dust-catchers in the gold air.
And a bee, or a buzz-saw, droned in the day's green calyx,
and looking down I thought
At last we have learned how to do this, now
we can do it any time we want to.
And reaching with one foot through the resilient air
for the next landing
I waked, and there I lay,
startled and stupid in the usual
limp muscles. My eyes
were sore with sun
from the aggressive window, where you stood
less tall than I remembered you.

Heavily I rose and began to climb the morning.

... you were with me and it wasn't morning, exactly,
it was more like a mountain.
Marking place, marking time,
my tired thighs pistoned up and down, the rocks
rolled under our feet like a treadmill.
And once a wind blew warm with pine and sun
and twice we heard the trickle of ground-water
in rocks behind the ferns
but mostly there was only dust and climbing. The lost peak
thrust on and up into the hard bright sky
far as forever;
and morning was a mountain, and the rocks
rolled under our feet like years.

And all at once you said, *Look down,*
and I turned, and looked. The valley

opened before us
and all the trees were small and very clear,
filigree miniatures, too tiny for toys,
green dust-catchers in the gold air.
And a bee, or a buzz-saw, droned in the day's green calyx,
and I took your hand, and we smiled.

Burnham Eaton

TECHNIQUE

Fra Pandolf, have you tried to reproduce
the faint half-flush that lies along the snow
when sun is slanting westward? It's no use.
Color along the lady's throat has no
comparison to this. You have observed,
and subtly, satisfactorily unnerved
milady to your purpose. That's the glow,
the soon-made-glad, responsive, gently sensual,
your brush has done so well to the eventual
approval, somewhat cold, of Duke Ferrara,
who mostly keeps your picture under cover,
as dated and as temporal as Mascara,
as incidental as an orchard lover.

How could you deal with honesty of snow,
Fra Pandolf, with your art, however much
you sensed the cooler values, and although
some surfaces responded to your touch?

Charles Edward Eaton

A PEONY FOR APOLLO

O peony, O pink inverted bell,
Sun-glutted, with your clapper hidden,
I, who listen with an ancient ear
Yet speak my modern speech, foretell
A time, if such an image were forbidden,
When death would have dominion here.

O riot of images in my own brief span,
Hardly to be rifled by one who would not spend
Anything he loves unto exhaustion's end,
Nor would I be that dissolute, divided man:

Such a one as wastes the world
By thinking it too closed or too unfurled—
This music of the upside down
Is like a campanile cast,
Subverted, yet tolling to the town
Or to some idler strolling past.

A motive, a manner, a way to feel—
If sorrow must refine our pleasure,
Give us the courage of our leisure
To make the unimagined world more real.

Evelyn Eaton

THE GARDENER

He used me today,
I felt His hand on my life,
grip, turn, lift,

high,
low,
flail,
hoe,
one with Him,
tool in His light.

He left me
propped by the trunk of this old apple tree.
I think He intended to mow the weeds round it,
but I was too dull to be used.
Ant and spider jeer,
travelling my rust,
"Where is now Thy Gardener?"
I believe . . . I believe He has gone for the whetstone.
Lord, return,
take me up,
sharpen me,
cut!

I will be His,
held or discarded,
used or useless,
shining or covered with rust.

Night with its dark corrosion comes,
day with its heat;
not yet my Lord's feet.

Richard Eberhart

SPRING MOUNTAIN CLIMB

Till thinking had worn out my enterprise,
I felt, and felt the flesh
Salt-swart, blood-sweet,

To which bird-song stung mysterious
And the white trillium mysterious in the wood;

I saw the mountain and the lake,
I followed where the source sounded,
Over boulders, crossed logs,
Up rugged reaches, where
The gates of mystery increased;

Sacred justice moved me, I entered
The ancient halls of visionary grace,
Bird-call sounded, sky
Appeared miraculous along,
And evil thickets held red histories;

Here divine justice made me sweat;
While an eye nebulous and profound
Partook of a huge nature, endless
Sufferings redeemed in rushwater,
Song falling, searching the world.

Such were the signatures I saw
Written by the hand of God
In knotted density, mysteries
Of incontestable day, while I
Passed the singing brook, so

Controlled by its eternal sound
As to be a living witness
To spirit, and to spirit reaching,
And to the sound falling back,
And man fallen to his endless burden.

Jeannette Slocomb Edwards

HESTER MACDONAGH

Hester MacDonagh of Murderkill Creek
hazards the marsh when the winds are bleak.
With the changeful glass a-dropping a blow,
the captain's daft girl will up and go
out over the marsh with anxious eye,
searching the muck, the bay, the sky,
down to the flat and desolate sand
to Bower's Wharf on the oozy land.

Gulls wheel and mew over Murderkill Creek
the leaden sky lowers to a livid streak,
threatens the bay past Ship John Light,
again foreboding a howling night
when sharp winds whine. Seas roar in thunder
that sucked the little schooner under
with the crew and catch off Martinique
and Captain MacDonagh of Murderkill Creek.

Hester MacDonagh of Murderkill Creek
with bitter bay-wind lashing her cheek
will sit ... and wait ... and watch the water.
Old folk take warn from the captain's daughter,
and fisher boats turn to wharf and quay,
for peril rides in from the open sea,
when Hester MacDonagh of Murderkill Creek
haunts the marsh, when the winds are bleak.

Richard Burdick Eldridge

THE SOUL REMEMBERS

Let the eye remember the loved face,
Let the heart beat, let the blood dance
Remembering the cheek's curve, the soft grace
Of the eye's shadow. Let thought trace
The dream born in a swift glance.

Here in the brain a face dwells
Like a constant song, like an old prayer
Spoken at dusk. The pulse tells
How the throat aches, how the breast swells
As the mind mirrors the soft hair.

When the winds fail, when the stars die
And the soul walks in a strange place,
Though the stilled heart and the closed eye
Are one with earth where the leaves lie,
The soul remembers the one face.

Jean Elliot

EXERCISE IN A MEADOW

Retrievers run through the meadow
and the grasses are parted before them
like seas by the strokes of a swimmer,
are rolled up and parted before them
in a surge of sweet smelling freshness
that submerges all but their shining

black heads and shining black shoulders.
By the farther edge of the pasture
the racers break out into sunlight
and the waves they stirred up behind them
recede in the wake of their going
till the field lies flat and unruffled
as a cove where no swimmer is swimming.

Frances D. Emery

LONG-BILLED GANNETS

We came to the high cliffs of Bonaventure
Shining flamingo red in the departing sun.
A thousand or more long-billed gannets,
Black-tipped wings and chalk-white bodies,
took off from the narrow ledges
darted like arrows into the St. Lawrence.
We watched these birds upon the red-gold water
these feathered fishermen who rear their young
In saucer-like nests of seaweed.
At length the broad and steady beam
Of the lighthouse fell across our path,
We turned home, night at our shoulders,
And the flutter of wings in our minds.

Rhina P. Espaillat

FROM THE RAIN DOWN

This is the way a tree: from the rain down,
Black pencil-drawn thin multitudes inrunning
Down all the myriad forkings, gathering earthward,
As in gay womb a filigree of veins.

Past all the drenched snows and the dreary now
To the ghost of trees silk-leaved and golden-fruited,
Imperishable, rooted in the heart's ground,
In the still child, where every wonder grows.

Summertime is late to trace
In the pale core the hollow star.
God's signature is in its place
Before the bud, before the scar,
For stars were new when blossom's face
Was fashioned for all Springs that are.

Through death uncasual, season's range,
From rain to flower to fruit we go,
No more miraculous or strange
Than stars above or stones below
Or seed before, or past all change,
The starry blossoming of snow.

Lillian Everts

PLAYMATES

I looked into a lake and saw a forest
standing on its head—as though in jest—
beckoning to me to dare to join it,
chiding me to try it in a test.

I dived into the very spot to prove that
humans can perform the feat as well,
only to discover when I touched it,
it disappeared without a sound to tell
where or why it left as suddenly
as if it had to lose identity.

Yet strange enough, when I returned to shore
and looked again, the same reflection wore
the evidence inviting me to trace
it where it was before it left its place.

John Fandel

THE BEE

A zig-zag bee, *zzz* and *zzz*-ing, came
Out of the flowers in my room; his claim
For being there was he had been carried there
While he worked in a flower, unaware.

He swayed, buzzed toward a window where a screen
Stopped him, sieved the universe between
A green beyond and his desire for
A green beyond: he was neither/nor.

From flowers to screen, he hummed a sort of thunder—
Nothing, yet olympic to my wonder;
His song stopped when the network stopped the bee.
He inspected man's ingenuity.

The screen was there to keep him out, not in.
I wanted to let his ecstasy begin
Again—to let it continue as it was.
Let a bee have his summer: what he does

With his brief season is a song for hours;
Let a bee have his privilege of flowers,
I thought. Therefore, I took an envelope
(He did not know this was his one white hope)

And tried to maneuver him to crawl inside.
Something, maybe fear or maybe pride,
Prompted him to be difficult:
He had his bee-wise reason to consult

Whether this should be or should not be.
I learned some independence from the bee.
Yet, because I could not watch him strive
Futilely, and wanted him alive—

I could not let him die, with honeysuckle
Just in view—I nudged him with my knuckle,
Then carried him outside like a note for mailing;
I opened the envelope, and the bee went sailing

Into his freedom as his thunder began
Again. I felt aliveness as a man
Should. I felt the summer rise in me.
I saw a million flowers for the bee.

Norma Farber

BEYOND THE TAPESTRIES

Someone has opened and undone
the work of seven tapestries:
the chase; the baying; the cruel escape
surrounded; the creature fierce in turn;
the taming by girl; the taken beast;
the closure round that steepled nape.

Someone has opened up the paddock.
The stableboy? the huntsman's daughter?
The beast is free to graze the fern,

and we to guess the tangy burdock
and planted kinds—no blossom whiter
than his pure flank of unicorn.

An edict? or an accident?
or negligence, while deep indoors
they celebrate the priceless win?
For no one guards the game. No hand
strains to recover him by that terse
uprising, and re-imprison him.

O not indifference? after such hard
pursuit, past lion and lioness,
and laying on of poignant spear,
and straining dogs, and one hound gored?
Do men so lightsomely release
the life they sought? Is life to spare?

Or is there mystery beyond
the capture at a maiden touch:
an eighth, an ultimate, never perhaps
accomplished cloth?—its cord unbound,
its freedom loosened from the swatch,
in flight such as no weaver stops?

In flight no wefting threads arrest . . .
But flight itself may choose to pause
by glad imagined carpet-grove,
abide domestic, and adjust
toward pasture-wold and garden laws,
though wildness wait beyond the weave.

And as we watch, our textile fills:
a company completes the field,
where folk and unicorn immerge
upon a sward so placable
the very fountains are unsealed,
and pheasants preen on the moist verge.

Jessie Farnham

GARLAND FOR A STORYTELLER

My father thought that fact was dull,
And so he wandered wide
Down far, enchanting labyrinths,
Where fancy might abide.

My father gathered ribbon lengths
Of stories that beguiled
And tied them into lovely bows
To please a wide-eyed child.

I used to keep my fingers crossed,
For even then I knew
And held my breath, the while I feared
He might revert to true.

Oh, fact may be a worthy thing,
And truth a star of gold;
But I would gladly forfeit both
For tales my father told.

Janice Farrar

A THOUGHT OF MARIGOLDS

When I opened your letter,
The day looked green enough,
And I was thinking of marigolds,
Until beneath the warmth of morning sun

Your letter gleamed in laconic black,
While back in memory the cancer clawed,
And I cursed te ignorance that thought him cured.
He is alive, you said.
But in a week, please God, he will be dead.

I had believed in antiseptic hands
Chipping away the chill disease,
And I cursed the ignorance that thought him cured.
But now, in California's warm December,
Your letter heaved with unadmitted pain,
And all at once I knew that in New York,
Ice skates were glinting on frozen lakes,
And snowballs caked in childish gloves
Splattered on ill-fated hats,
While you caressed his hollow face
And watched the flakes interring the sill,
The icicles fingering towards the grave.

But I stand in a different sun,
I see a palm tree leaping in the breeze,
There are flowers in the garden,
There is noon-warmth on my hands,
A single leaf turns gold, a single petal folds.
How can I face you, death in the East?
I send a thought—of marigolds.

John Farrar

THE TIME IS TODAY
(For Jonathan Haydn)

I have been figuring that in a way
Tomorrow is two halves of yesterday;
That yesterday and all the days before

Fill me for days ahead with a rich store
Of bright and dark, of close things and of far,
From the hall candle, from the evening star.
Tall grandfather, the clock, talks of this matter.
His voice is wise, not like the tiny chatter
Of the desk clock. She's silly but he's serious
And Time, he says, is not at all mysterious
But that it covers you and you can crawl
Inside it, too, as though it were a ball
Hollowed and huge and hung upon the hill
Like the dawn sun, rising but seeming still.
The sundial, too, explains that every light
Whether of sun by day or moon by night
That marks a shadow on his mossy face
Is not destroyed but held within a space
Rich with the things before and things to come—
Storehouse of Time—the universal sun
Filled for tomorrow and the days ahead
With everything that's thought or done or said.

VICTORIAN SONG
(For Sara Kit Cousins)

I and my sisters three
Will grow one day to be
A ladylike quartette.
But oh! Not yet!

We'll win our elders with our charm,
Walking slowly, arm in arm,
Clad in sweeping black with pearls,
Demure—when we're no longer girls.

Father'll be delirious
When we become serious,
Dainty, sweet and prim,
We'll curtsey just for him.

But now we'll jump and laugh and play,
We'll make each day a circus day,
We'll be the imp, we'll play the clown,
We'll scandalize the quiet town.
We'll climb the trees and twist the swing,
We'll dance round father in a ring
Until in frantic desperation
He plunges for the railroad station.

But when he's back at night,
When mother's clicked the light,
We'll all be kind and meek—
Four kisses on his cheek!

Thomas Hornsby Ferril

THE TRAIN BUTCHER

I sit on the back platform of the train
Dragging my patent-leather buttoned shoes
Through embers of fireweed growing along the ties.
How slowly I go by! How long I use
The wonder of the mountains in my eyes
As if I were that very boy again.

There is a beautiful train butcher who comes
Still as a cat to the platform where I sit,
He props his basket on the hand-brake wheel,
He gives me grapes, he gives me chocolate,
He does not make me buy, he does not sell,
He gives me cornucopias of plums.

He's older than the hills and I am young,
He gives me colored eye-glasses through which
To see the whole wide world and all that's in it,

But I am rich with train whistles, I'm rich
With cinders falling half a dream a minute
On the sag of the rails the weight of the train has sprung.

The train butcher whispers under his cavernous coat:
Stop staring at the hills, no one will know!
Here are pictures of men and girls with no clothes on!
All yours! All yours! See what they're doing now!
All yours! These childish mountains now be gone!
All yours! No foolish woodlands in your throat!

All mine! And every cross-tie nudging *yes!*
All secret interlockings, all my own!
I finger the tongue of steel that snubs the brake
In the ratchet-wheel . . . but a strange new train moves on,
Slides into satin valleys that awake
To naked music wilder than wilderness.

Far as tomorrow, this, and far ago,
The platform of the car, the hills, the smoke,
The smell of windrowed hay, the terrible shadow
Of the great train butcher's blue serge cowl and cloak,
Good and evil, Eden's ageless meadow,
A boy's new shoes the weeds go snatching through.

Gone is your train, my ancient, whistle and bell,
Gone are the rails, and I am come and gone
And gone and come through centuries I gauge
By crags the wings of butterflies grind down
A flick a season, so I say how sage
You were! How sage for teaching me so well!

Fine fellow, did you die in church or bed?
I miss you as I walk these rotted ties
Among the canyons of lost valley floors,
No tempter but the sunrise in my eyes;
Such grapes were yours, such sweets, such pretty whores,
And all love's wisdom that you left unsaid.

Jeanne Robert Foster

JOHN BUTLER YEATS

We shall remember him
As a man who had a little in him of the men of all time.
We shall remember him—
This tall lean-shouldered, witty Irishman,
Master of the art of conversation,
Jesting with us in his high-pitched Irish voice,
That lilted to a delicate string
Beyond our hearing.

"Shakespeare was a kindly man," he often said.
John Yeats was a kindly man
Who gave lavishly of himself
As if life had no end.
Around him gathered
The tangible aroma of life
Full-flavored with intense living.

"Ireland is kind," he said.
"She has many faults but I feel about her
As I do about Heaven.
If Heaven were a perfect place it would bore me.
I like to think of Heaven as a place with discords;
As a beautiful orchestration with Love as master of the music."

"Montaigne said"—that phrase was often on his lips,
Stories of wits and poets and artists,
Memories of Samuel Butler, John O'Leary, and Dowden,
Brilliant debris of irrecoverable personality.

"The artist is the only happy man," he told us
"Art springs from a mood of divine unreason.

Unreason is when a man cannot be at peace with
    external conditions."

We shall remember him intimately
As we knew him—his room, his pipes, his drawings.
We shall remember him sitting at his easel,
Keen-eyed, young, eager to live a thousand years,
Unwearied by life,
Sheltered beneath the green tree of his own thoughts.
We shall remember him
Ripening like an apple in quiet sunshine,
Responsive to human affection,
And—patient of our human limitations—
Writing under his own portrait
(Painted from his reflection in a mirror),
"Myself seen through a glass darkly."

Marilyn Francis

NEIGHBORS

Our backyards touched somewhere upon the hill
Along a mass of litter and neglect,
A barricade of brambles grown so high
That everything was hid but chimney smoke.
A few had seen them when they came to town:
His eyes were only guides to place his feet,
She followed at a distance in his path
And never spoke, except once at the store
In such a babel no one understood.
The townsfolk told us, "Better stay away,
Whatever he is hiding, he means to keep it hid.
You cannot clear the brambles of his fears."

We worked to move the barrier time had made
Observed by hostile, calculating eyes.
He buttoned up his ragged coat and stood
As if to measure us. His lined brown hands
Hung limp, then beckoned suddenly, against his will;
We found ourselves upon his land as guests,
Accepting round blue grapes he plucked for us.
She came to see and stood and looked so long
We had to turn away to miss the tears.
They followed us to where our work had stopped
And waved farewell until we reached the house.
It took the next day's sun for us to know
The chimney smoke we saw was bramble fire.

Florence Kiper Frank

NOW IN THE BLOOM

Now in the bloom
And ache of the earth
The dead are stirred
To unseemly birth.

The dead tug hard
At root and stone
And gnaw at ashes
And worry bone.

And he who walks
In the April wind
Walks with the dead
Not far behind.

And he who breaks
The alder branch

Feels blood drip
That he cannot stanch.

The sun that troubles
The living heart
Pulls the thoughts
Of the dead apart.

And no soul goes happy
Through rains of spring
But hears the proud dead
Whimpering.

John Frederick Frank

ONE NO. 7

Eggs from a chain store grocery
Candled by No. 7:
Any complaints, egg not an egg,
See "Candler No. 7."
Not Joe Miles, nor Miss Grande;
Not Mae Lee with a heartfelt hand.

No one any one whole thing now:
Just lifter, tightener, holder,
Opener, closer, commodity loader.
Just one No. 7 somehow
Who, if not at bench 11,
At TV in Apt. 15b, East 187.

Robert Frost

A TUFT OF FLOWERS

I went to turn the grass once after one
Who mowed it in the dew before the sun.

The dew was gone that made his blade so keen
Before I came to view the leveled scene.

I looked for him behind an isle of trees;
I listened for his whetstone on the breeze.

But he had gone his way, the grass all mown,
And I must be, as he had been, —alone,

'As all must be.' I said within my heart,
'Whether they work together or apart.'

But as I said it, swift there passed me by
On noiseless wing a bewildered butterfly,

Seeking with memories grown dim o'ernight
Some resting flower of yesterday's delight.

And once I marked his flight go round and round,
As where some flower lay withering on the ground.

And then he flew as far as eye could see,
And then on tremulous wing came back to me.

I thought of questions that have no reply,
And would have turned to toss the grass to dry;

But he turned first, and led my eye to look
At a tall tuft of flowers beside a brook,

A leaping tongue of bloom the scythe had spared
Beside a reedy brook the scythe had bared.

The mower in the dew had loved them thus,
By leaving them to flourish, not for us,

Nor yet to draw one thought of ours to him,
But from sheer morning gladness at the brim.

The butterfly and I had lit upon,
Nevertheless, a message from the dawn,

That made me hear the wakening birds around,
And hear his long scythe whispering to the ground,

And feel a spirit kindred to my own;
So that henceforth I worked no more alone;

But glad with him, I worked as with his aid,
And weary, sought at noon with him the shade;

And dreaming, as it were, held brotherly speech
With one whose thought I had not hoped to reach.

'Men work together,' I told him from the heart,
'Whether they work together or apart.'

A DRUMLIN WOODCHUCK

One thing has a shelving bank,
Another a rotting plank,
To give it cozier skies
And make up for its lack of size.

My own strategic retreat
Is where two rocks almost meet,
And still more secure and snug,
A two-door burrow I dug.

With those in mind at my back
I can sit forth exposed to attack
As one who shrewdly pretends
That he and the world are friends.

All we who prefer to live
Have a little whistle we give,
And flash, at the least alarm
We dive down under the farm.

We allow some time for guile
And don't come out for a while
Either to eat or drink.
We take occasion to think.

And if after the hunt goes past
And the double-barreled blast
(Like war and pestilence
And the loss of common sense),

If I can with confidence say
That still for another day,
Or even another year,
I will be there for you, my dear,

It will be because, though small
As measured against the All,
I have been so instinctively thorough
About my crevice and burrow.

DEPARTMENTAL
or, The End of My Ant Jerry

An ant on the tablecloth
Ran into a dormant moth
Of many times his size.
He showed not the least surprise.

His business wasn't with such.
He gave it scarcely a touch,
And was off on his duty run.
Yet if he encountered one
Of the hive's enquiry squad
Whose work is to find out God
And the nature of time and space,
He would put him onto the case.
Ants are a curious race;
One crossing with hurried tread
The body of one of their dead
Isn't given a moment's arrest—
Seems not even impressed.
But he no doubt reports to any
With whom he crosses antennae,
And they no doubt report
To the higher up at court.
Then word goes forth in Formic:
'Death's come to Jerry McCormic,
Our selfless forager Jerry.
Will the special Janizary
Whose office it is to bury
The dead of the commissary
Go bring him home to his people.
Lay him in state on a sepal.
Wrap him for shroud in a petal.
Embalm him with ichor of nettle.
This is the word of your Queen.'
And presently on the scene
Appears a solemn mortician;
And taking formal position
With feelers calmly atwiddle,
Seizes the dead by the middle,
And heaving him high in air,
Carries him out of there.
No one stands round to stare.
It is nobody else's affair.

It couldn't be called ungentle.
But how thoroughly departmental.

Vi Gale

SHORE BIRDS

In that rapacious littoral now slaked by sea,
Now parched by sun, the shore bird is his own
Bird, in a sense gregarious, but movably.

High, low, between the tide lines of this zone,
The willet, peep and plover know instinctively
That gifts are brief and must be gulped or counted gone;

Yet quizzical in flocks they stand their range
On sand, peer surfward at the striate roar
With equanimity. When luck brings change,

Brings headlong flight to crack a clam on shore,
Pursued by neighbors, whirled in a raucous interchange,
Forcibly out over dune and rock they soar

In that rapacious littoral now slaked by sea,
Now parched by sun. The shore bird is his own
And makes his briefest ground a solid flange
To serve him in the thing he does so well—endure.

Marguerite George

PRISONER

Aeons of history float
in the blood,
tug at the deep nerve center,
hold memory taut
with instinctive fear
inexpressible, obdurate ...

I turn with instant misgiving
as an unbratile form creeps by,
perhaps only a small bird shadow
or a bit of the past moving on.

A noise immediate, strange
crashes the brain's locked door
and a sound of feet goes padding
through the core of forgotten things.

I startle as a word is whispered
in a savage unknown tongue
as though I had known the language
millenniums ago ...

So tied to the past
I can never escape,
a prisoner without number
or guard.

Louis Ginsberg

MORNING IN SPRING

One morning when I went downtown,
I felt such sunlight capsize down
That streets were glutted with more gold
Than all my heart could ever hold.
I thought a glory much like this
Must have been poured from Genesis.
I had not noticed until now
Such glittering of leaf and bough.
Not for a moment could I doubt
Telephone-poles might start to sprout.
Brilliant gas-stations, like bazaars,
Were jubilating with the cars.
Traffic in some triumph went
In pageant of astonishment.
And all the things in all the stores
Were like abundant metaphors.
More than the sun illumined sight;
More than the sun and more than light
Seeped on the avenue a wonder
That everything grew porous under.
Houses and people, trees and I
Replied to each, as earth to sky.
I felt all objects linked and set
As in a vast, transparent net;
I felt that everything was part
Of rapture answering my heart;
Until I knew, until I knew
I was the world I wandered through.

Emilie Glen

CAT BALLERINA ASSOLUTA

The white cat
    Light paws about the studio,
Dances cloudsome among Madam's pupils
    Aching, stretching at the *barre*,
Mocks them with her *pas de chats*,
Teases with her *en l'air*,
Down stares them with her lemon drop eyes

Is Madam a spit-spite,
    A catty teacher?
Showing up her groundlings,
Sly dealing them a puss
    Who leaps with a *ballon* beyond them
For ribbons they try to bind round taffy ankles,
She neat points a pop pearl,
Jetés a lost earring,
    Such batterie, *battement*,
The *pas de bourrées*, the *entrechats*,
Prima without pulled ligaments,
Assoluta without sweat, slipped discs,
Prima ballerina assoluta,
They claw her with their glances

White cat
    White as a tutu,
White cat with the lemon drop eyes,
    Upstaging
She earths them with every *jeté*
Needs no massage, no practice *barre*,
They soil their toe shoes in slopping tries

While her paws white point,
They can flex and stretch, strain and sprain,
    And never be a white cat dancing

White demon
    Pavlova cat,
You think the world owes you a living,
You hunger strike for delicacies,
Must you *prima* about
    Belittling Madam's pupils?
You cat you
Cat

Mae Winkler Goodman

IMAGE IN A MIRROR

What is this image in the clouded mirror
    mocking the contoured cheek the startled eyes
that pierce into themselves with less of terror
    than with the sharp reluctance of surprise

seeking an answer they can never give
    bridging the vision to a deeper seeing,
trying to trace a single sign of love
    between the prismed and the outer being

moving beyond the flesh, the tractile mouth
    whose words are glass, whose syllables are sand,
to trick some meaning from the fleeting breath
    or grasp the gesture that eludes the hand

and never, never breaking through, or crossing
    each into each, stripped naked to the bone
we do not recognize in the brief passing
    the dim, distorted image is our own!

Ryah Tumarkin Goodman

SILENCE SPOKE WITH YOUR VOICE

Silence spoke with your voice
As you slept.
Silence kept
Your singing voice
Locked in the cell of sleep.
Yet when you woke
Your orchard voice
Was warm as summer seas,
And silence, cold as a crow
On the bough of night
Perched on your spray of speech.

Rachel Graham

NEW HAMPSHIRE FARM WOMAN

You stand atop your hill
with blue sky elbow-near,
and toe aside a cloud
to see the valley clear.

You find a pasture wall
that offers you a chair,
and tilt a gentian cup
filled with mountain air.

You talk with migrant birds,
give repartee to brooks,
find granite strength of soul
in all the woodlot nooks.

You look from your tall hill
far down, and wide, and up,
and find that hilltop Hands
have filled your altar cup.

Lillian Grant

LINES WRITTEN IN A MAUSOLEUM

Though I have given
flesh and bone
a rectangled
house of stone

And named you on
the unhinged gate
occupant
of this estate

I know right angles
cannot bind
the vast circumference
of your mind

Nor symmetric
stillness prove
the finality
of love.

Adele Greeff

SONNET XI

Is God invisible? This very room
Pulses with chairs and tables, and with books,
Mouthed by the shelves perhaps in silent doom
'Tho ready for a spirit glad to look,
To hear with vision message on a page;
Is God, then, visible?' Oh surely, not
Only visible; man's myopic range
Is much too narrow to encompass God;—
God is; the full abstraction that is real;
Whatever is, is real without a doubt;
The forms, the force; as thought, and flapping seal,
And plus and minus numbers, and lips' pout,
And any juggler brought into the act;
God's all of this, God's everything, God's fact.

Brenda Heloise Green

NEW ENGLAND IS NEW ENGLAND IS NEW ENGLAND

Is seacoast fog, is starfish caught
    In sandy kelp, is measured tide,
Is mansard roof and widow's walk,
    Is inland roads that turns aside

To lag by elm and lilac bush,
    By stony brook and berry patch
With bloom of sun on every bush,
    Is saltbox roof with flowered thatch,

Is old maid in ancestral home,
    Is Pilgrim's faith and patriot's blood,
Is Transcendentalism's spark,
    Is Walden set in solitude,

Is rebel heretic, is tale
    Of figurehead, is enterprise
Of clipper ship and whaling boat,
    Is poet's glimpse beyond the rise

Of Amherst hills, is Sabbath bell's
    Clear tone, is steepled town that sleeps
In legendry and elm-tree shade,
    Is cemetery grass that keeps

My father's ashes company
    While seasons pass, is grave of one
For whom I keep a lover's grief,
    A lover's sentiment, is tune

Of bygone spinning wheel, is pride
    In daily stint and homely chores,
Is treasured worth in old antique,
    Is homespun virtue that endures,

Is stubborn strength in old stone wall,
    In barn, in hillside's granite core,
Is granite marker on man's grave
    And granite in man's character.

Lisa Grenelle

DUEL IN THE PARK

When did these gray ones
select this sagging bench
on which to balance their chess board?

Did anyone see them come?
Are they the same two
who were here last year?

Black moves . . . shadow
of predatory fingers
poise above the White Queen.

Sun hovers low over taut
shoulders. Perambulator
and poodle depart.

A small squirrel surveys
possibilities.
Lovers linger. Silence stiffens.

Pawns are taken. A Knight exchanged
for a Bishop. Onlookers drift off,
others take their places.

When did the game start? Will it end soon?
Are these the same men
who played here last year?

R. H. Grenville

PAWNSHOP WINDOW

In boxes lined with faded satin
Medals await their tardy heroes,
Gilt and glory equally tarnished.
Ballet shoes, suspended by their laces,
A Buddha, brass lids closed in contemplation,
Ignores the worldly stare of a box camera
And the sensuous nearness of a Spanish fan.
Elephant book ends of bogus marble
Strain to hold closed an ancient Bible
Lest its tomblike covers
Gape to release the living Word.
Pins, combs, necklaces and signet rings
Lie tangled in a tray. Assorted watches
Declare their blatant ignorance of time,
And all wait in a kind of dead patience,
Like prisoners in an oubliette,
For the incredible word, the reprieve,
The sweet ransom,
That by some strange miracle
May reach them yet.

Willard M. Grimes

PIAZZA DI SPAGNA

Here Keats and Shelley heard
Cascade of music on the Spanish Steps,
Bearing the fragrance of a thousand flowers,
Tinged from the palette of the sunset sky.

Cadence of waves with ever rising beat
Flowed past their windows to the Square below,
Submerged the fountain and lifted the stone boat
Till stripped of weight it rode the vibrant crest.

How brief the voyage! Yet Shelley brought
Fruit from the far Hesperides;
Keats wrote in water that engulfed the world.

Amy Groesbeck

MOMIST

Seemingly as other men, yet always
Somewhat uneaseful with them, as if cold
Gathered in angles untouched by his roundness.

Adoring and adored by women, whose quick sense
Answers the hunger of the uncut cord
Indifferently as mistress, wife or friend.

Sun lost: colorless under the moon
He slumbers between pale mountains curled,
Comforted, warmed, remembering the womb.

Alida Carey Gulick

ON WAKING

Rose in the breast
Unfold in this day's unfolding.
Hold, petaled nest,
The Focus of all beholding;

That through the diurnal line
Nested and nest combine,
So that full circle spun,
Focus and rose are one.

Louise D. Gunn

CONVERSATION WITH RAIN

That night, when I woke suddenly, was sweet
With wet earth; it was raining,
Summer rain beating gently on the tin roof.
I thought as I listened, *This is peace.*
But the rain replied, beating, beating,
On the roof, *For the time being, peace:*
For the time being. Then the clock
Chimed the hour. It was four,
Four o'clock. Quiet again
Save for the rain, dwindling away now,
But whispering still. *Only*
For the time being, peace.
The rain stopped.
The wind rose a little
And the fragrance of the honeysuckle vine
Crept in through the window on the wind;
And I thought, *This night is peace.*
But the rain started up once more,
For the time being, for the time being,
Peace.

Lawrence Gurney

NEVADA

1.

Like snakes of golden autumn fire
    the alder creeks
    run up the dark pine mountain.

2.

Scarves of rain hang over the desert,
    but do not reach the ground.
But from the distant Sierra
    the Truckee runs by full and strong.

3.

The great bronze swimmer leaves the skies;
    now I can see the pebbles
    at the bottom of Heaven.

Maude Miner Hadden

CREATIVE FORCE

How do you know it is time to bloom,
    Lovely magnolia tree?
Your waxen blossoms touched by rose,
    With infinite delicacy.

How do you know it is time to leave,
    Scarlet tanager,
The palm-fringed shore for New England woods—
    A singing traveller?

There is something within that urges us on,
    Called by whatever name—
Nature, instinct, creative force,
    Fanned to a living flame.

Oliver Hale

WHERE UNIMAGINABLY BRIGHT

My least height flowers late with buds
not opened yet upon the sun;
I feel them as late summer broods
on barks which autumn winds have won.

Am I not soil as well as branch
as you are branch and soil of me?
My growths shall find me fast and staunch
as are your roots within my tree.

The great Tree has a myriad stems,
its bark is stars, its bole the dark
between the stars' millenniums;
is not my star my bole and bark?

Thou far Titan, desirest thou me?
Spread Dove whose feathers weight my days,
Death's iron bird nests in my tree
whose rust gathers to your embrace,

where unimaginably bright,
the Universes spun and spanned,
speed forth on voyages of light,
and are returned upon your hand.

Amanda Benjamin Hall

THE GREAT FAREWELLS

The great farewells and last leave-taking,
    Poor tear-drenched kiss and futile phrase,
Should be deferred till dawn is breaking
    And heaven shows bright as fields of maize.

Then, all the aching drakness over,
    The dreadful visage of the night
Cannot appall the valiant lover
    Whose heart has breakfasted on light.

The man and woman are a couple
    Sun-gilded by the Persian East;
They see the rays of morning stipple
    The earth, the greatest and the least

Of nature's forms. The blue-veined sedge
    Awakes and over sea and bar
The birds pass in a flying wedge
    As if they drew Aurora's car.

With tender fortitude he chides
    Her grief and whistles down his woe,
Then forth he sets with terrible strides—
    The woman, tearless, lets him go.

Kay DeBard Hall

DEER IN ASPENS

Day does not come with violence
Here among aspens,
But filters in,
Balancing the grasses.
Leaves, not yet trembling, are infinitely small cisterns
Not yet ready to spill their cargo to sun.

Beginning low, ascending through branches,
A yellow scarf of warblers lifts;
The shaken leaves tug like planes.

Sun comes bringing its tepees of heat and light,
And the ear throbs twice;
Once with a pulse of its own,
Again with the locust beat.

It is easier to believe here,
Easier to believe in the Absolom cry
And all biblical things—
Here where the velvet-thatched bees hum
And miracles fall easily from blunt gold beaks.

And then they come:
Not with fanfare, snapping of twig
Brittle as bamboo,
Nor scent, nor cry.
Only in this place of shadow
And of sun on the sweet-smelling leaves,
Only here do they come, bounding on cane-brake legs,
Shadows emerging from darker shadow,
Still holding sun from the leaf-dividing trees
On small poised heads between skeletal horns.

And we see their eyes,
Innocent as Christ's.

Marion Ethel Hamilton

BIRD AT NIGHT

O Bird at night, who, hearing, could forget
Your song across warm gardens in the dark?
Your voice, immortal as the young Juliet,
"It is the nightingale, and not the lark."
Yours is the strangeness of some dream of dread
Brought back from sleep, and half remembered, waking!
Your cry is deep as Romeo's with his dead,
Your cry is sharp as Juliet's, with heart breaking.
O mocking bird, in my magnolia tree,
Your song is cool as marble in a tomb;
It is as mournful as a threnody,
It is as white as my magnolia bloom.
If, at my death, I could but hear your song,
No night would be too dark, no death too long.

Leigh Hanes

OLD FENCE POST

The old fence post that tilts awry
Was never a thing to hold the eye,
Till one fine day in a nervous flit
A wren flew out of the heart of it!

A tiny hole was all I could see
But much, so much was hidden from me

That now, whenever I pass that way,
I tip my hat to a very fine day,
And an old fence post, and a little brown wren
That may any moment fly out again!

DESERTS

Deserts are more than shimmering heat and sand:
Deserts are veils that Time has slowly drawn—
The covered wagon and the waving hand,
The singing silence and the singer gone.
I never saw one with a palmed oasis
Or burning bushes that were unconsumed,
But I have seen a desert's arid spaces
Bloom like a garden when a cactus bloomed.

And once I saw a desert like the pages
Of an old letter with long wrinkled seams,
The lonely buttes were dreaming golden ages,
The dried arroyos their forgotten streams,
      And far away the antelope would dart
      In streaks of light across the desert's heart.

Phyllis Hanson

WISDOM

Nothing here is bitter
at the source:
the garment and the weaver Plato
loved still appoint

the hour.
Can it then matter that we know
untasted waters
still shall flow?

Be sure that words
we suffer to forego
impel the sterile
twilight of their birth,
and garments that have fallen
from the weaver's hands,
fold ancient pity
over new-turned earth.

Elizabeth Stanton Hardy

ECHO

Travelers who came that day to Pisa's Baptistry
Called Giovanni from a pillared shade,
Bade him come and sing.

The sweet voice of the boy rose to a stone rotunda—
Higher to a colonnaded dome.
A pause, then floating down
The clear-toned echo came.

For those listening to notes of earthly origin,
Who hear no glory in the Voice descending,
Nor whispering of wings,
The echo waits, the years close in.

Dorothy Harriman

CAT ON THE PORCH AT DUSK

Near the edge, as on a shelf,
The patient cat combines himself.
Motionless he huddles there
Before the changing light, and broods
On daylight's deep ineptitudes.

When gradually the night takes place
He rises, stretching whiskers, toes
And stepping royally, he goes . . .
Slowly the darkness slides apart
And soundless, lets him in.

Marguerite Harris

MY SUN-KILLED TREE

I see no bird arise
    from the ashes of my small flame:
No phoenix fires burn
    on my lived life's plain
Nor no fruit rots to fall
    host for a tender seed
    from my sun-killed tree.

Bud of my plunging green delight
    falls stillborn from the light-hacked root,
    denied the night's dread nourishment
    by guilt-eyed captors, heavenbent,

and yet a tilted cross endures
to mark their covin crime.

Now from my frail and faulty perch
    alas, I sullen see
    the failed the ruined angels rise
    how nearer by a universe
    to their divinity.

Gwendolen Haste

TOMORROW IS A BIRTHDAY

Eighty years ago a woman passed
Heavily from shelf to table. Winter
Was thick on the land. Through the small glass
Snow glanced at her distorted curve.
Eighty years ago pain swerved her
Foreboding the night at hand. This I know.
This is not a figure flowing up through fable.
This birth happened as I tell it now.

And as all birth this was a beginning
And an ending. She who was lightened
Of that guerdon knew no further rending
And watched few more snows burdening the pines,
Sifting upon the earth. Eyes I have never seen
Were closed. A body my memory cannot call back
Reposed. Yet this has lived with me
That she lived and was dissolved.

From that bearing came vigor, flame, and laughter,
Drawn from the robust ground by hard generations,
Pouring richly toward age—toward eight round decades
Which would make a life, the finished sound

Of them calling for soil and cerement.
Yet the full eight were not tied compactly
But jaggedly rent, and again there was a dissolving
And life stopped with difficult secret wailing.

Close to the mind, warm to the nerve,
These decades have turned, interlaced with the past,
Hard and exact with my weight when it enters the circle.
And the circle will haste and the birthdays will go.
Other decades will form. And again will a body
Be racked. There will be a dissolving. Once more bones
That tasted pleasure from this earth will lie down.
The whirl will be marred. This I know.

Fanny de Groot Hastings

LATE COMER

I am not bred and born New Englander.
These Eastern states that equally divide
Their heart between the mountain and the tide,
Seasons of cold and heat, the elm and fir,
Have yielded slowly to this listener
Secrets of stubborn stone and green hillside,
Of fur and feather and a native pride
In white farmhouses and their blue larkspur.

But only the late comer brings an eye
Mature and fresh to such a varied scene,
And only the late comer such as I
May stand on some New England village green
And being neither part nor parcel of
Its tranquil beauty know herself in love.

Sara Henderson Hay

"BOTTLE SHOULD BE PLAINLY LABELED 'POISON'"

Too powerful a drug is Hope
For constant use, and every day.
It warps the present's able scope,
It leads the wishful wits astray.

That eye which Hope has focussed far
Upon some visionary good
Is blinded by a distant star
To the small flowers of the wood.

Man builds of simple stones a palace,
The dry plain, tended, greens with grass.
Who looks the most to future solace
Will make the least of what he has.

There is a delicate balance set
Between Hope's virtue and its vice.
The man who takes it to forget
Must know how little will suffice.

THE DAILY MANNA

If suddenly, wonderfully, glittering among the leaves
The fabled, the gilded Phoenix would break from cover!
But here is only a small, brown-breasted bird that grieves
In a few plaintive notes at dusk, over and over....

Oh, if a milk-white unicorn would appear
And stamp with silvery hooves at the edge of the meadow!
But that which moves near the birches is only a deer
Dappled with light and shadow.

I wish I could take three steps into an enchanted wood!
But this is only the grove where the lovers come
At evening, the whispering boys and girls; only the valley road,
The short way home. . . .

Doris Hedges

PRAYER

O God of Goodness, Forwardness, and Fulness
Let not my feet stray from the path of nature
Nor my heart and soul from contemplation of the heavens.
Keep Thou my mind alive and ever searching
And my eyes open to the glow of beauty.
Help my strength that it may flow outward
And return from conflict unvanquished and undimmed.
God of all strength, keep me strong.
God of light, terrify me not by fear of ultimate futility
But let me hope one day to gaze unblinded at the sun
And sing my song of joy in perfect purity.

Pauline Henson

ON THE EDGE OF THE COPPER PIT

The shovel-gnats gnaw at the open wound,
And the drill-bugs bore,
To lay their eggs of explosives where
The earth bleeds ore.

The truck-flies swarm the clock around;
The worm-trains crawl;
And I'm but a breath on the steps of Heaven—
If I'm at all!

Helen Rowe Henze

ETRUSCAN WARRIOR'S HEAD

Out of the terra cotta still a voice
Two and a half millennia ago
Speaks with Etruscan accents' meager choice:
"I know what beauty is, I know, I know."

Dust on the chariot wheel, the turning post,
Sweat on the horses' flanks, the cheering throng,
Goblets of Massic wine, the feast, the toast,
Dances of nymphs and satyrs and a song.
These empty eyes once looked on life, look yet;
The moldering dust within the funeral urn
Once speared a Marsian boar through twisted net,
Once wooed a maiden on a couch of fern,
Once threshed the Libyan wheat from golden field,
Once sailed Icarian seas through wind and storm.

O flesh, whereof this image lies revealed,
What triumph did you know, what rose, what thorn?

Moss Herbert

A GENTLE PARK

If I deny my kinship to a man,
I lose my immortality. We are
Grounded in the same center which I can
Dismember at my peril. Falling far
To finitude's defeat in victor's rise,
I pit almighty self against a world
Of mighty selves, in whose vain might life dies;
But knowing how together we are furled,
Admitting I am weak, I multiply
My strength, by what immensities I join,
To strength's perfection. Listen! What if I
Stand small upon the earth in darkness? Coin
Of earth's rich coin and brother to the dark,
I walk forever in a gentle park.

Miriam Hershenson

LOVE POEM—1940

Meet me tonight as usual at nine—
Love me between a bombing and a broken sunrise
Under clandestine trees in a secluded park.

For tomorrow we are encased in rigid fence;
Signs saying "Keep off the Earth,"
"Don't trespass here;"

For tomorrow our private tree shields a public gun.
Each bench that held your taut warm breath
Will hold men mating there with death.

However you may yearn for your dessert of moonlight
Seeping through trees tall as newsreel redwoods,
These spears of light cannot protect you,
These soothing hands of light will never
Massage oblivion into your bones.

Agnes MacCarthy Hickey

OLD ESSEX DOOR

The casual glance on me
Apathetically
As deer at the moon's round ring,
But, though an humble thing
What honour I have known!
To how much wisdom grown!
What happiness I've seen!
In what dire moods I've been!

I know sharp stabs of rain
And foraging and strain
Of winds! But in each bout
I shouldered the invader out!
Long winters now I know
The caressing feel of snow
And never would I miss
Young Day's awakening kiss.

How gaily wide I swung
With Life! ... But thrice, Death hung
His drear, desolate wreath ...

And Birth ... What narrow things
Doors are, that a Soul's wings
Must fold to stoop beneath!

Lois Smith Hiers

ON LAYING UP TREASURE

Out of the wild sweet grape, I have trampled a wine
Colored with sun, cooler than mist-blue air;
I have brimmed me a cask with fire from the free-
    swinging vine,
Essence both tart and sweet. I shall drink what is
    mine
When the branch of the grape is bare.

When the wind is a shriek in the hollows, a shout
    on the hills,
And the old, old sorrow of snow is a blight on my
    land,
I shall be warmed with the warmth that the grape
    distills:
Fullness of flame, flow of shadow that fills
My cup with the grape's blue blend.

All have not wisdom. All have laid by for tomorrow
No certain sweetness, nought for a shield but the
    shape
Of the beggared bough, the white of remembered
    sorrow;
In a season of snow, they shall batter my door to
    borrow
A sip of my wild sweet grape.

Hyacinthe Hill

OLD EMILY

Emily wandered through town and folks said that she saw
what was not in that place at that time or what couldn't be seen;
on cloudy days, the sun; on "scorchers," rain;
butterflies among snowflakes and wine in empty barrels.
She saw strawberries in jewelry boxes and feathers in ferns.
When I was a boy she was my favorite friend.

Her daily thin repast was a holiday feast.
We wondered that she kept so well and rosy.
She thought she lived on manna, nectar, ambrosia.
Any dry crust to her was angels' bread.
"Who feeds you, Emily?"
                              "The One Who feeds the birds."

Every stray mongrel was a fabulous beast or
of extinct species so rare it needed her care.
Each kitten was a princeling in disguise.
A cobweb on a hedge was a fairy's curtain.
She looked through it and saw the little eyes.

She knew the first name of every passing flower
and every bird's address. She found a clock
without any hands but with a strident alarm.
She said it told the hour for the planet Mars
and woke a Martian up. She didn't mind
winding it for him. (He hadn't time.)

She found a scarlet stone upon the beach
and said it was the ocean's heart, and each
evening she stood and watched from a hilly height
the sunset glow upon a distant village.
She never grew weary of the sight. There were

"houses with golden window-panes out there."
When I was seven she was my dearest playmate.

Once I visited her little "nest,"
furnished with odd discards she had gathered together.
Such "treasures" the neighbors had thrown away she repaired,
and cleaned and waxed and thanked them for their "gifts".
We had lunch under the cherry tree in her yard.
I climbed to the top and shook the dinner down.
But she said we mustn't eat until the plates
were laid on her favorite cloth and everything
was neat. She made a bouquet from dandelions
and a blue jay's feather and set a place for the squirrel.
She said if we sang our grace we would never quarrel.

No one wanted her taken away. She was gentle
and harmless (but then you could never really tell!
and the children preferred her foolishness to school
and they seemed to believe her lies so perhaps it was well
it was done). I wasn't around and I thought she'd enjoy
the adventure, "Off in a pumpkin coach to follow the sun"
but when I learned she died in captivity, I remember
it rained and I cried and daddy bought me a gun.

Robert Hillyer

EPPUR SI MUOVE?

Although it may appear archaic
My cosmic system's Ptolemaic,
The earth for center, round which run
The circumnavigating sun,
The stars, the galaxy, the moon,
The planets, in concentric tune
To music of the spheres, that plucks

Notes in the theme of *Fiat Lux*
From every heavenly body bound
In counterpoint of radiant sound,
To merge in silence at the end,
Just as in white all colors blend.
And since I know I see but darkly,
I quite agree with Bishop Berkeley—
All is illusion—and I'd therefore
Choose the illusion I most care for.
     Nowise, so it seems to me,
Is happiness or dignity
Advanced by thinking earth is spun,
A mote of dust, around the sun
As sly Copernicans attest
From facts illusory as the rest
And in observed results more dreary
Than any other cosmic theory.
     Ah no, we sit, the earth and I,
While day and night go wheeling by,
The focus of attendant spheres
And keystone of the arching years.

THE BATS

These caverns yield
But vampires upside down.
Better the field or town
Than exploration such as this.
These creatures of antithesis
With webbed unfeathered wings
Will shrink away from our electric wink
Lest they be dazzled to the dark of things.

Through stalactites
Of lancets in reverse
Their muffled flights rehearse
A foray on the world of sleep.

These are our underdreams that keep
Our secrets from ourselves,
The lark become half rodent in that dark
Wherein the downward mountain climber delves.

Seal all, before
In ragged panic driven
These nightwings pour to heaven
And seal us from our natural sun.
Of two forbidden trees, there's one
Untampered with till now,
Where throng, with their inaudibly high song,
The bats headdown from roots that are its bough.

THE RELIC

A murmuring in empty shells
Recalls the ocean's undertone,
But not a wisp of music dwells
In this small skull of dulcet bone—
A thrush's skull, miraculous
Amid dead leaves and threads of ice,
This delicate contrivance was
The sounding board of Paradise.

Beneath the tree lies music's skull,
The tree a skeleton of spring,
And both, perhaps, are beautiful
Though leaves and thrush no longer sing;
But, growing old, I have a reason
For wishing some divine delay
Could hold a song beyond its season
And hide the thrush's skull away.

Sophie Himmell

IN THE MONTH OF GREEN FIRE

Let us remember the yellow
Dusk-surfeit of linden and yarrow,
Wood sparrow.

Let us scoop heavy honey of yarrow,
The tart, heavy sweet of October,
Let us remember.

In the cruel brisk month of green fire,
The green high gold, the lovely,
Let us pause gravely.

Let us pause gravely and ponder
On the ripe rich season of valour—
The cargo of color.

Let us remember the yellow
Dusk-surfeit of linden and yarrow,
Wood sparrow.

Katherine Thayer Hobson

DUALITY

Love, I should be content
to share a dream forgotten, born afar,
of ever-new desire, not passion-spent,
the ecstasy and not the aftermath

of human intercourse. Vibrating, fleet
our hours are winged with joy, soar down the path
of heaven almost like a God whose feet
leave stars as foot-prints—I would kiss each star
while haunted by a thing I never see.
The book whose pages never feel my touch,
your early-morning face, reality,
the thousand routine tasks I cannot share;
the tired impatience of a weary day,
small, vexing duties, economic care,
both gain and sacrifice to mark the way
which holds at once so little and so much.
And in my blood dead women stir again,
those endless generations who have spun
both swaddling clothes and shrouds for all their men,
fed them and warmed them, worn both yoke and crown
in endless labor, and with a strange desire
I long to serve you too by stooping down,
to tend both heart and hearth with primal fire.
The roots of life are deep and dearly won.

Phoebe W. Hoffman

PEDRO

Vivid, alone, against the wide expanse
Of ocean, he bends with hollyhocks, sweet peas.
Patient as time he hoes as in a trance,
Or stakes up plants in the perpetual breeze.
He never raises pondering eyes to look
At sea or mountains. Unconscious of the din
Of rollers on the rocks his pruning hook
Makes little swishes as he stoops to thin
Dead flowers. No joy in his fingers

Or happy smile at seeing small plants thrive;
Impersonal as in a factory he never lingers;
Six days a robot, Sunday he comes alive.

Like the frail fly that hatches out in May
Each week he lives one brief and glorious day.

Joyce Horner

PUBLIC HOLIDAY: PARIS

In the picture the people stroll and stroll all day
By walks and lawns, *allées,* by pair and pair,
Or families in bouquets, contained and gay.
The clouds fly out like flags on the volatile air—
I have seen it a hundred times and wished to be there.

There with them in a radiance of parasols
With sky between, ambience of summer flowers
Where Idleness flutters her sleeves and strolls and strolls
By lake and sail, where sunflakes scatter in showers
And a rose and violet shadow marks no hours.

Now I am there, lit by their idle light,
One with them, held in the day's glass
Among the spikes of scarlet and flecks of white.
Still beyond reach the holiday people pass.
I am a patch of darkness on their grass

That moves——for I must rise and go away
Now, while their voices ride on the air; alone,
While the brilliant children run in the fountain's spray;
Before the gathering sun sinks like a stone,
Before the man with the blown balloons goes home.

Frances Minturn Howard

NARCISSUS IN A COCKTAIL GLASS

Sipping judiciously, he saw come near
His own true image, blurred yet growing clear

As in a crystal ball; saw knowledge pass
Into the pointed triangle of glass,

And as two mirrors split the truth between
What is revealed, and what remains unseen

Perceived himself, while seated in his chair
Standing apart; his half-self wavering there

Unjoined and disembodied; he could feel
It waiting like a dog to come to heel,

Threaded by breath upon him; in a pause
What he had been regarding what he was,

And for one second closed his eyes to savor
His new omniscience in its full blind flavor.

Sleep came instead, in a three-cornered skull
Shaped much like death's, and oddly beautiful.

HERON IN SWAMP

Had I not seen him by a swerve of eye
In movement as his natural element,
Air plastered to his wings, thin falls of sun
Cascading down his breast, legs locked in flight,

I should have thought him reed, so pure he stands
Frozen in silence; bird into vegetable
Transforms hard fact to fluid miracle;
So thinks himself a reed that reed becomes.
If there's such sanctuary in belief,
I'll trust the verdict of the hoodwinked eye;
Know, if I clap my hand,
One reed will stay, though all the swamp fly off.

Grace Clementine Howes

WIND OF THE PRAIRIE

Blow, blow over me, sweet-scented breath
    of the prairie summer.
Fill me with perfume of thorn-flower, blue
    grass and sunburned loam,
Here are the peace and the strength of wide
    spaces, lonely and splendid,
Here where the blackbird and meadowlark people the
    plain shall I make my home.
Their song for my twilight and dawn, the voice of the
    stream for my noon,
And your strong music, plowing these billows of grass
    in a far green tide.
I shall drift on this ocean unafraid and exultant,
    make welcome all weathers,
The will of the wind for my pilot only, the stardrift
    my compass and guide.

Dorothy Hughes

THE DUSTING OF THE BOOKS

With every movement, the soft particles
Invade us. We are dry, and the dust smells
Of its neutrality. The clean books flash
In the afternoon, they leap from me like fish.
I watch you seize them, shelving them again,
Rebuilding the familiar diagram.
There they stiffen, the light gone out of them.

We move through our round with the gravity
Of dancers, and I can remember how
In other places, coupled in some chore
Without words, I have felt this before
(Cutting or carrying, breaking or seeding)
That we do homage and our rituals bring
An identity and a leveling.

I hear you through the thunder of recall.
Through the cold clangors of Burnt Njal,
Syllables of war, through the lonely furor
At Amherst, the tune of a blue guitar,
The cadence of your tread is heard. The Sidhe
Are hosting—Ever between them and me
I hear you walking, enchanted and free.

The light is emptied now, the dust drifts down.
The grey cloths lie collapsed, and the moth-motion
Ceases. We wash our hands. Once again
Between us the fracas of speech breaks out,
The mannerly word hiding its wilderness root.

Ted Hughes

THRUSHES

Terrifying are the attent sleek thrushes on the lawn,
More coiled steel than living—a poised
Dark deadly eye, those delicate legs
Triggered to stirrings beyond sense——with a start,
    a bounce, a stab
Overtake the instant and drag out some writhing thing.
No indolent procrastinations and no yawning stares,
No sighs or head-scratchings. Nothing but bounce and stab
And a ravening second.

Is it their single-mind-sized skulls, or a trained
Body, or genius, or a nestful of brats
Gives their days this bullet and automatic
Purpose? Mozart's brain had it, and the shark's mouth
That hungers down the blood-smell even to a leak of its own
Side and devouring of itself: efficiency which
Strikes too streamlined for any doubt to pluck at it
Or obstruction deflect.

With a man it is otherwise. Heroisms on horseback,
Outstripping his desk-diary at a broad desk,
Carving at a tiny ivory ornament
For years: his act worships itself——while for him,
Though he bends to be blent in the prayer, how loud
    and above what
Furious spaces of fire do the distracting devils
Orgy and hosanna, under what wilderness
Of black silent waters weep.

WITCHES

Once was every woman the witch
To ride a weed the ragwort road;
Devil to do whatever she would:
Each rosebud, every old bitch.

Did they bargain their bodies or no?
Proprietary the devil that
Went horsing on their every thought
When they scowled the strong and lucky low.

Dancing in Ireland nightly, gone
To Norway (the ploughboy bridled),
Nightlong under the blackamoor spraddled,
Back beside their spouse by dawn

As if they had dreamed all. Did they dream it?
Oh, our science says they did.
It was all wishfully dreamed in bed.
Small psychology would unseam it.

Bitches still sulk, rosebuds blow,
And we are deviled. And though these weep
Over our harms, who's to know
Where their feet dance while their heads sleep?

Jeremy Ingalls

MY HEAD ON MY SHOULDERS

In that day I had hoped for a pair of boots to guard my feet
    on the terrible trek.
I had hoped for a knife cutting again and again with courage.

When I had shot a bullet what had I left to defend the children?
A knife will do also to cut down trees for shelter.
A pair of boots and a knife and my head on my shoulders.

All my life I have been storing not books nor cut stone,
    not disk nor paper music;
But memory, memory. While you live—I have told
    my children—
You will have so much no more than your head has room for.
Store memories a great storing. The ripening dark within
Will nourish fruit come honey-sweet with wisdom.

The sudden fire, the necessary flight
May burn my boots or lose them. Our needed haste forget
Even the knife so long beside me sharp in sheath.
My head on my shoulders, my heart for love shall serve.
Though boots, though knife shall fail us, fear no death.

Sulamith Ish-Kishor

WAR

Two bloated bodies in rotted rags
Spoke to each other on island crags.

"I say, you floated from far away!"
"The storm was swift out of Suda Bay."

"I batted for Oxford; we didn't win
That year." "I played the violin."

"Roast beef was good, and I liked it rare."
"I liked schnitzel, and Münchner beer."

"I say, what watch was the last you stood,"
"I, on the *Bismarck.*" "I, on the *Hood.*"

Two bloated bodies in rotted rags
Stare at the sun from island crags.

Catherine Haydon Jacobs

SECRET

We are the only ones who will remember
    We are the only ones who have ever known
How far this Autumn is from last November;
    We two, alone.

Wind, and the bitter taste, the disillusion
    of courage, whittled thin, the dulling pain
Of questioning what was right, the heart's confusion,
    Frost and cold rain.

Today the meadow glistens green at dawning,
    And every step is firm beneath the sun.
The world is beautiful this autumn morning;
    We two have won.

Josephine Jacobsen

THE ANIMALS

At night, alone, the animals came and shone.
The darkness whirled but silent shone the animals:
The lion the man the calf the eagle saying
Sanctus which was and is and is to come.

The sleeper watched the people at the waterless
    wilderness' edge;

The wilderness was made of granite, of thorn, of death,
It was the goat which lightened the people praying.
The goat went out with sin on its sunken head.

On the sleeper's midnight and the smaller after hours
From above below elsewhere there shone the animals
Through the circular dark; the cock appeared in light
Crying three times, for tears for tears for tears.

High in the frozen tree the sparrow sat. At three o'clock
The luminous thunder of his fall fractured the earth.
The somber serpent looped its coils to write
In scales the slow snake-music of the red rip globe.

To the sleeper, alone, the animals came and shone,
The darkness whirled but silent shone the animals.
Just before dawn the dove flew out of the dark
Flying with green in her beak; the dove also had come.

Grover Jacoby

JUXTA

A well of freshness
Overflows among the skyscrapers.
The trees in billowy interruptions
Of all this precise geometry
Are carrying on—
Their verdant vague remarks
Announcing Nature's presence,
While somewhere
In a roomful of busy typewriters
She moves about—
A spring gale
Eddying amidst the scrap iron.

Robinson Jeffers

SIGNPOST

Civilized, crying how to be human again: this will tell
    you how.
Turn outward, love things, not men, turn right away
    from humanity,
Let that doll lie. Consider if you like how the lilies grow,
Lean on the silent rock until you feel its divinity
Make your veins cold, look at the silent stars, let your eyes
Climb the great ladder out of the pit of yourself and man.
Things are so beautiful, your love will follow your eyes;
Things are the God, you will love God, and not in vain,
For what we love, we grow to it, we share its nature. At length
You will look back along the stars' rays and see that even
The poor doll humanity has a place under heaven.
Its qualities repair their mosaic around you, the chips
    of strength
And sickness; but now you are free, even to become human,
But born of the rock and the air, not of a woman.

RETURN

A little too abstract, a little too wise,
It is time for us to kiss the earth again,
It is time to let the leaves rain from the skies,
Let the rich life run to the roots again.
I will go down to the lovely Sur Rivers
And dip my arms in them up to the shoulders.
I will find my accounting where the alder leaf quivers
In the ocean wind over the river boulders.
I will touch things and things and no more thoughts
That breed like mouthless May-flies darkening the sky,

The insect clouds that blind our passionate hawks
So that they cannot strike, hardly can fly.
Things are the hawk's food and noble is the mountain, Oh noble
Pico Blanco, steep sea-wave of marble.

THE ANSWER

Then what is the answer?—Not to be deluded by dreams.
To know that great civilizations have broken down into
        violence, and their tyrants come, many times before.
When open violence appears, to avoid it with honor or choose
        the least ugly faction; these evils are essential.
To keep one's own integrity, be merciful and uncorrupted and
        not wish for evil; and not be duped
By dreams of universal justice or happiness. These dreams will
        not be fulfilled.
To know this, and know that however ugly the parts appear the
        whole remains beautiful. A severed hand
Is an ugly thing, and man dissevered from the earth and stars
        and his history . . . for contemplation or in fact . . .
Often appears atrociously ugly. Integrity is wholeness, the
        greatest beauty is
Organic wholeness, the wholeness of life and things, the divine
        beauty of the universe. Love that, not man
Apart from that, or else you will share man's pitiful confusions,
        or drown in despair when his days darken.

Christie Jeffries

LONE HUNTSMAN

Lone seas are ominous,
The untraveled road
Whispers of evil;

Lone trails forebode
Danger, and he
Who follows no train
Nor hunts with his fellows,
Courts safety in vain.

But his the delight,
The incalculable treasure
The lone huntsman wins;
His the full measure.
Who rides unattended
By kinsmen or friends
Is lord of the quarry
When the chase ends.

Oliver Jenkins

MERRY-GO-ROUND

Brightly colored for a new season—
Black, sorrel, white, and dappled—
Awaiting their first riders, the horses
Pose in motionless flight, hoofs up,
The glossy reins looped to poles,
The embossed saddles, the chrome stirrups
Catching the glint of morning sun.

Soon the motor will start, the music begin,
Playing a medley from another season,
And the horses, neither gaining nor falling back,
Go galloping in circles of time,
Heads thrust forward, manes flying,
Carrying us giddily away and over
The bright, green terraces of summer.

TIME OUT

We shut them out, the houses,
The roads, the sails going by,
Lying here encircled by dunes,
Sand and grass, square of sky.

No feared encounters here, no
Marking time, running away;
An end now to fixed alarms,
To the partitioned day.

Once rise, leaning on elbows,
Even a moment out from cover—
World suddenly at arm's length,
And the spell's over.

Leslie Nelson Jennings

BELDEN HOLLOW

If ever you should follow
The half-lost road that leads
Down into Belden Hollow,
Ending in grass and weeds,

Look for no habitation
That stood its ground somehow
Against a desolation
Pushed back by axe and plow.

This land was not worth taking
From trees too thick to fell,
From stones too hard for breaking,
From seeds that throve too well.

Here, where the woods surrender
To underbrush and vine,
Wall-builder and fence-mender
Dispute no boundary line.

Earth quietly possesses
More than a scythe can reap,
Where wind-sown wildernesses
Keep what is theirs to keep.

Cullen Jones

NOW THAT THE FLOWERS

Now that the flowers are gone, and the wind
Runs up and down hill calling for the last
Bloom to surrender, shivering, I find
Myself recalling voices from the past:
"Sleep by the fire, old man; smile as you dream;
Know that this whir is but the breath of leaves
Rustling to rest; know that the winter's scream
Is not earth lamenting, and no bud grieves."
And shadows rising from my memory's frame—
Towering roofs, outrunning thought, the power
Of season, storm or light or sound or flame—
Rechant their old psalm to the faith of a flower:
"Nothing is dead, my child; nothing is dying;
It is only the wind that you hear sighing."

Mary Hoxie Jones

THE FOUR DEER

The four deer we saw in the early morning,
    Tails up, skimming over the frosty pasture,
Were they aware in their urgent running
    Of the hunter, hidden and waiting, gun poised on
                                    their rapture?

Who takes care of deer in the early winter,
    Leaping the fences which separate meadow from meadow?
What will save them from the desire of the hunter
    Standing waiting, part of the sycamore's shadow?

Where are the deer we saw? Who knows, far safer
    Than we who watched them running into a cover.
We, who had known their danger, found a swifter
    Hunter beside us when the morning was over.

Barbara Leslie Jordan

DESERT SHIPWRECK

I am adrift in a desert where too much sun
Leaves me parched and faint from swimming a sea of light,
I will sink in these arid swells, I will be spun
Like an empty shell to the cool, dim shore of night.

I am becalmed in a molten current of sand,
Huge combers of rock surround me, upthrust and stark.
Tossed within dusty squalls in a waterless land,
I search the sky for the first, faint promise of dark.

This solar tide will ebb at dusk and I will reach
The clouded coast of evening where I will lie
As still as any shipwrecked sailor on a beach,
While overhead the far, uncaring stars wheel by.

Hannah Kahn

TO BE BLACK, TO BE LOST

Ask night how it feels to be dark,
To be pitch, to be black, to be lost . . .
Ask winter the feeling of cold,
The bitter taste of frost.

Ask day how it feels to be light.
Exposed so that all may see
Through the sharp lens of the sun
The glare of intensity.

With fears that torture the dark
And days that are rimmed with pride,
Ask me how it feels to be both
Exposed and doubly denied.

Douglas V. Kane

WESTERING

The westering pennon of the sun waves toward California,
Where the sky is a blue helmet upon the heads of mountains;
The manzanitas sentinel the trails, with glazed leaves
Eyeing vacuities; and the winds are dry swords
That cleave away fungi clinging from the cities.

Up, up fly the peaks, floating in the hot air,
With ridges redwood-green, and trails scratchingly defined
Against the sheer slopes to the forest ranger's eyrie
On Tamalpais—where birds pecked their morning bread
From the toss of that single watcher of fires,
Who peers toward Hamilton on the Peninsula,
And Diablo in the East, where the volcanic grape yields
Blond or garnet wine. On Lookout Point,
Where the rail leans against the emptiness
Of two thousand feet, and sturdy rock forms a nook
From the winds—there, O crusader of heights,
Sit and dream into the blue flame that roofs the day!
Ride bodiless through breath of conifers
Into the holocaustal sun, and with renewed, emblazoned wing
Hover, phoenix-free, above the deep Edens of the valley.

Milton Kaplan

THE CIRCUS

The circus was never meant for children:
They believe too firmly to tremble as
The acrobat, suspending chaos, grasps
The outstretched fingers of redemption.
Success for them being foreordained,
They look away, unsatisfied,
Lured by the clamorous blandishments
Of paper monkeys dangling on sticks.

Only their parents lean forward, transfixed:
Believing in gods but knowing gods can fail,
They focus passion on the serpent tricks,
Intent upon their spangled deities
Resisting the temptation of the fall.
And in their seats they swing ambivalent

In close communion with the timed trapeze,
Dreading and yet half-hoping for mischance,
Waiting for the instant when the hand will slip,
The wish just missing the receptive grip,
The dazzling body plunging down to burn
Upon the pyre of horror-kindled eyes
In ancient ritual of sacrifice,
While high above, the restless children dance
Across the tightrope of their unconcern.

Norma Keating

NEVER, NEVER CAN NOTHINGNESS COME

Never, never can nothingness come,
Even destruction leaves a wake of spurs,
That golden, sparkling atomic dust of hers
Is the first-born seed of a new star's riding;
Atomic dust like a golden nut
Hiding a kernel of mind and heart,
Rich in orchards, old lanes and trees,
Old arts, old wisdom, solved mysteries,
Packed in a seed, hurled into space
This, then, would grow a giant race;
Never, never can nothingness come
Without the crackling of a great blade's spark,
Lighting the all too obvious dark;
With etheral dust, translucent-white
One cannot breed the infinite night;
Pour no worry in the new world's making
Consider a host of giant's raking!

Joseph Joel Keith

IN THE FIRST HOUSE

In the first house (still it is painted white)
petty thieves were locked up in small cells:
rooms; food and diners left alone;
silenced, a Testament to be read;
forbidden, glad books on shelves.

In the first house, god sat on his throne.
Penitents walked meekly toward the Chair;
waited long to be spoken to;
ordered, we sweated and with dry throats,
we managed to speak to father There.

In the first house, righteousness in rage
placed his felons (scrappers) behind bars.
Almost we felt the Vast Breath down our necks
as we reached across the dark to raise the blind—
we never did; we had no right to stars.

Martha Keller

DEADFALL

What the wind harried, the fire worried,
What the fire worried, the flood caught.
What the flood carried, the snow buried.
What the snow buried, the wind sought.

The snow was a shroud and a flurry of fog,
A cover of cold and a smother of sleep.

Are they branches or bones by the mouldering log,
Where the hemlocks are bowed with the quiet they keep—
By the track, by the trace that will never be found,
And where death is a mound that the wind drifted deep?

The rain was a wrack and the rain was a roar
Where the wall of the bank had been worried away.
Are they branches or bones by the sink, by the shore
Where the current swings slack and the waterweeds sway—
By the track, by the trace that will never be found,
Where the deadwood is drowned and a body would stay?

The fire was a flame and a flicker of smoke,
And it hissed in the grass like the tongue a snake.
Are they branches or bones where it scattered and broke
Like a wave, as it came with the wind in its wake—
By the track, by the trace that will never be found,
Where a rattler has wound what the creepers will take?

The wind was a hush and the wind was a cry,
As high and as wild and as black as the air.
Are they branches or bones in the tangle of sky
Bent down by the brush and the tamaracks there—
By the track, by the trace that will never be found,
Where the wind-beaten ground is as black as his hair?

He followed the deer, but he never came home.
He followed the deer, but he never came back.
Like a print in the snow, he was vanished and gone,
Like the froth, like the foam where the current is slack,
Or the leaf of a tree when the branches are blown,
Or an ash in the air—without trace, without track.

> *What the wind quickened, the fire blackened.*
> *What the fire blackened, the flood held.*
> *What the flood sickened, the snow slackened.*
> *What the snow slackened, the wind felled.*

Mary Kennedy

THE UNFORTUNATE MOLE

In the night the agile mole
Seeking for a water hole
Behind his sensitive pale hands
Skillfully advancing,
With his pointed scholar's nose
Curling eager for a drink
And his monkey-fashioned toes
Pushing him too near the brink.
Reckless, swift, his spirits lift,
Quivering in his sightless face
As he nears the cool wet place.
Small and soft and trusting
From the hard earth thrusting,
Poor blind mole to tumble down,
To fall so far and then to drown.
Drowned alas! in a midnight minute,
Reaching the pool he fell right in it.

Who now on the yielding surface lies,
Earth-conscious face turned to the skies,
Soft fur and fine, disheveled, wet,
His gentlemanly hands astonished yet.
The long meek fingers elegantly spread
Protest the indignity of being dead.

Mourn an instant this mechanism wasted
With so much of his small life untasted.

He was grey, slender, quick, clever,
Neatly, excellently put together.

He knew the feel of friable earth,
He could test for clay,
For dirt or gravel,
Could make a road on which to travel.
He knew the nature of rock and stone,
And dark days and nights endured alone.
He could nibble roots,
And gather fruits,
And provide for the future of son and daughter,
But little or nothing he knew of water.

Alas!
The unfortunate mole!

Blanche Whiting Keysner

OLD RIVER ROAD

The willows are taking the old river road,
The willows and grass are growing
Where buckskinned hunter and trapper strode
To follow the river's flowing.

So deep is the bed of the old, old trail;
There otter and mink were hiding,
And the hillside echoed the bobcat's wail
When the pioneers came riding.

The deer came down to the river to drink,
They sniffed at the tracks of the cattle,
And fled when they heard at the water's brink
The sound of a wagon's rattle.

The broadaxe glittered above the road,
The woodland echoes rousing,

And the oxen bent to a heavy load
Of fresh-hewn logs for housing.

The long years wove, on Time's slow loom,
Pale grief and joy and daring;
The last homecoming—and bride and groom
Who rode to a gay infaring.

The old river road has served her day,
We leave her now to her dreaming;
The new road bears her burdens away
On shoulders broad and gleaming.

With hum of motor and whirl of spoke
The winds of speed are blowing!
The old road served for homecoming folk,
The new highway's for going.

Kenton Kilmer

YELLOW

Green are the tussocks of the marsh-grass springing,
Pale green the sickles of the sweet-flag blades.
"Green, green, green," as the Spring goes singing,
Yellow, yellow, yellow, falls the sunlight in her glades.
Yellow on the maple buds and yellow on the hazel,
Yellow in the little suns that blaze upon the lawn.
Breezes blow the saffron from the hanging, swinging catkins,
Yellow stands the noon sun, and yellow spreads the dawn.

Red and white the roses that deck the way of Summer,
Deep green her shadows in mossed and leafy wood,
But Summer stands in sunlight, in yellow, yellow sunlight,
Her feet in yellow buttercups, her gold hair daisy-strewed.

Yellow on the corn-silk and yellow on the hay field,
Yellow on the little waves that leap along the rill.
Dusty go the bees, buzzing-bright with yellow pollen.
Yellow lies the storm-light across the shining hill.

Scarlet stands the sumac and crimson glow the oak leaves,
Purple springs the ironweed above the stiff brown grass,
Blood-red the berries that cluster on the fences,
But yellow flare the poplars as candle-flames at Mass.
Yellow glows the great moon, swinging over tree-tops,
Yellow stand the corn-stalks and yellow heaps the corn,
Yellow on the hillside the goldenrod is blowing.
Soft through mists of silver the yellow light is born.

Blue-cold the shadows and pale the drifted hollow,
Silver-pale the sparkle of moonlight on the snow,
Dark green the hemlock with night-enfolding branches,
But yellow, yellow, yellow is the sunlight's glow.
Yellow lies the broad path, with jagged, rippled edges,
Of light across the snow crust, and on the frozen lake,
And yellow, yellow, yellow, in thousand starry sparklings,
Looks up into the yellow sun each mirror-yellow flake.

Ethel King

WOOD MUSIC

The trees learn music from the birds they hold,
    And song becomes a part of branch and spray.
    No listening leafy grove could hear each day
    These notes and not remember that bright gold.

Such fortune is stored deep against the cold
    Of winter with its silence darkly gray—
    Safe in the tree's heart carol, hymn, or lay,
    Seraphic measures never turning old.

And when the trees are felled and cut to give
    Rich wood for flute, bassoon, or violin,
    Therein is found once more true melody.

The tones of thrush and philomel relive
    As tree-born instrument's soft discipline
    Releases all the pent-up harmony.

James H. Koch

TO A YOUNG LADY SWINGING UPSIDE DOWN ON A BIRCH LIMB OVER A WINTER-SWOLLEN CREEK

Sun's snow, conversing, lowly slides from limbs,
Undoes his morning craft and doing dims;
While chatters blood, chased, its merry steam
Spring we topsy-turvy, taunt bravely the stream,
A perspective world apart, world warmer than there:
Hangs, unshorn, summer kindling, your hair,
Oh Louie, Lou lovely, alone my Lou,
Sing Lou, my Louise, my love.

Sheer witchery your possum's postures make
The artless tracery of your figured wake,
Oh, Louie, Lou lovely, alone my Lou,
Sing Lou, my Louise, my love . . .

Graceful marsupial, in mortal wiles untaught,
A rhythm's maker catch, by words uncaught.

Fania Kruger

PASSOVER EVE

Beside his wife at Passover in spring
Jacob sits on pillows like a king.
Elijah may appear with flowing hair
To lift the dark and sing away despair.
That holy sage who utters truth in jest
May enter in the guise of unknown guest.
A cup of wine for him, and goblets too
Are set for absent ones. In sorrow's hue
Jacob, on such symbolic night of song,
Recalls his boys, slender and brave and strong.
His wife beholds the five dark handsome faces
Above the festive table's empty places.

As *Matzos* lie uneaten, candles sputter:
What says the wind that whispers in the shutter?

The mother speaks: *"My prayer flies back and forth;*
Our boys lie east and west and south and north.
Each one has fallen in an alien land.
Prophet Elijah lift your holy hand
In succor ... give us faith, dispel our fear
Our sons no longer sit beside us here."

Then suddenly the darkening shadow falls—
Upon the board, the floor, the dusky walls.

The Seder table lengthens and grows wide;
The sons come in and sit on either side;
The sons come in, as tall as pines are straight,
Elijah leading them. And from each plate
They lift the brimming goblets. Then like wind

Their voices echo, deep yet strangely thinned:
"Forever keep the vow: That men be free
Like rain which gives sustenance to a tree.
That pestilence and sword be gone this hour;
The air be sweet with peace, the hedge in flower."

While Jacob chants the psalms, the candles sputter
And winds are whispering in every shutter.

Maxine W. Kumin

HALFWAY

As true as I was born into
my mother's bed in Germantown,
the gambrel house in which I grew
stood halfway up a hill, or down,
between a convent and a madhouse.

The nunnery was white and brown.
In summertime they said the mass
on a side porch, from rocking chairs.
The priest came early on the grass,
black in black rubbers up the stairs
or have I got in wrong? The mass
was from the madhouse and the priest
came with a black bag to his class
and ministered who loved him least.
They shrieked because his needles stung,
they sang for Christ upon His cross.
The plain song and the bedlam hung
on the air and blew across
into the garden where I played.

I saw the sisters' linens flap
on the clothesline while they prayed
and heard them tell their beads and slap
their injuries. But I have got
the gardens mixed. It must have been
the mad ones who cried out to blot
the frightened sinner from his sin.
The nuns were kind. They gave me cake
and told me lives of saints who died
aflame and silent at the stake
and when I saw their Christ, I cried

where I was born, where I outgrew
my mother's bed in Germantown.
All the iron truths I knew
stood halfway up a hill, or down.

Joan LaBombard

THE SIBYL

Power lies in my hand
To rear the olive grove,
The grey-leaved, sacred tree
Where hawk and adder move,
The emblematical
Of feather and of fang.

If I lift my wand
Carved of the olive wood,
A woman-headed serpent
Doubles its golden tongue
For evil or for good
Whereof I speak.

I raise the marble column
By the wine-dark sea,
A raging, changing sea
Where all is tossed, or spume:
Out of my sea-dark word
The pillar stills in time.

I hollow the sea's shell
For sound to gather in,
The oceanic music
Clanging its bronze bell
Foams of my white hands
Which mold its song.

I wait in the dark grove,
Power leashed in my wand,
A hawk gripped on my shoulder,
My serpent wreathed and twined
For the prophetic wounding;
From trance I strike.

The column, the white shell
Flame on the olive tree;
Past all seas' estranging
The sunned form will be,
And on my eyelids blaze
Acanthus and grape leaf.

Frances Stoakley Lankford

REQUIRED COURSE
"Between the animal lost and the angel unfound"
                        —Carleton Drewry

Translation is man's deep, continual task;
To this the most unlikely scholar bends

Early or late. His rustic questions ask
A classic meaning. All his need extends
Beyond the native idioms of dust
Toward an eternal diction. Slow of pace
The groping work goes on, — *fear* into *trust*,
Pain into *mercy*, *penitence* to *grace*.

Assiduous his shadow leans, depending
Upon the Light in curious joy, in loss
Less vivid now, transmuting and transcending —
(Notice the prefix, *trans*, across, across . . .)
A gulf that narrows toward the coast of day,
Whose language he would live, upon the way.

Clifford James Laube

AT THE BATTERY SEA-WALL

From inland ledges I had dreamed this bay,
    Guessing its glamour with a boy's surmise;
Now at the sea-wall, leaning toward the spray,
    I store the living harbor in my eyes.

Is this the brine that broke in amber foam
    Against the cleave of Verazzano's prow?
Are these the roads the *Half-Moon* dared to roam?
    Where are the Nyacks and their kinsmen now?

Behind me rises tiered, colossal steel,
    Terraced, and plumed with bannerets of steam;
Before me ferries glide and lighters reel
    And tugs go throbbing by, and sirens scream.

An old tramp freighter slinks in, weather-stained,
    Scaring the sea gulls with an angry snort.
O sight more fabulous than I had feigned!
    I am a stranger in an alien port.

Norma Lay

SEA SONNET

Tell me today, when all my tides are gone,
when on each desolate shore no waters play
salty with substance, no rock pools contain
sea urchin, starfish, sea anemone —

whisper a dream of wide galactic tides
that sweep this planet sky, this buoy blue-curved
set in a stellar seaway, where it guards
a channel every venturous mind has loved.

Tell me again of those who heard a bell
that eased their darkness, those who listened close,
who found the clear harmonic interval
beyond the bounds of silence, of discourse.

Tell me I say, who contemplate, aghast,
sky bells now silent, and the channel lost.

Laura Lourene LeGear

UNBRIDLED NOW

My slain! Oh silver-hoof! Oh clover breath!
Sleep, proud-limbed Nahla, rest, my smoke-pearl mare,
Who staunchly fought against the stallion Death,

And know what dust has thorned such ripe despair.
Lie gently in your blanket for a tomb,
Oh, loosed of halter, who were wild and fleet!
Cloud-meadows tempt with oats and lotus bloom,
As purple clovers fade beneath dim feet;
From fields of blue run nickering home to me,
Dark nostrils wide with breath earth-winds deny.
Canter to drink under the coolest tree
Near lakes of Paradise where hoof may lie,
Unbridled now, to lip eternal grass,
A shadow grazing, let my courser pass!

Wake, Nahla, cavern night is arched and young,
Await me there, though cosmic horses neigh!
Unleashed, the Dog Star springing, froth on tongue,
Routs packs of comet hounds that leap and bay.
Teeth flashing, when you raced with lunging Time,
Ears flattened as we sped against the sand,
who slept to moons and muted pastures' chime,
Your forehead starred, a pearl against my hand.
No lover's arm can check this racking ache,
While death is urging, spent and hoofless gust,
No cloud of sorrow's arrows, sharpened, break
Swift pace, nor mix your dust with gelding dust!
We rode like spirits—we shall ride again—
Head bent, hair loosed now mingles with your mane.

Louise Leighton

Time is a fox on quick, velvet feet
and I ride after . . . ride after . . . after.
It fled from me one vernal morning,
sinuous and still, over a lime-green hill
among the lavender shadows of birch trees
curving between the white bloodroot
and the pink anemones.

It is late, I said,
and the fox has fled.

It fled through the columned white light of noon
and hid awhile in the grain,
the shining field flowing
like water in the sun
and the song-sparrow's notes were blurred
with the redwing's rolling chord
as I streaked through
trampling the butterfly weed and the meadow rue.

Afternoon . . . and far across the valley
the hounds were crying;
the hooves of my steed made a thudding sound
on the harvested ground;
they swished through the tall marsh grass,
imprinted the moss
and shook the wintergreen bells
in the wildwood aisles
and the darkening dells.

Where is my quarry now?
Far ahead . . . over the brow . . .
beyond the quick-snatched breath of the rose
as faint the laughter of children grows.
Morning . . . pillared light . . .
revelation of the night . . .

Reluctant now for the flesh is worn,
the wind-rubbed eyelids weep
and the trails are steep,
I ride after . . . I ride . . . ride
. . . the fox is faster.

At the wall of the sky
it will vanish then . . .
vanish . . . because it had never been.

Cornel Lengyel

FOOL SONG

Lean in the greenhood of my fearful years,
Lost in the world's dust fallow I lay,
Dreaming of thunder, hopeful of rain,
A boy in December, an old man in May.

Gone the loud thunder, gone with the rain,
A lightning-struck branch now burns to an ember;
Lost in the world's dust lightly I sing,
An old man in May, a boy in December.

Adele Levi

THE DEATH OF FRIENDS

These being the haunts of those
who now speak
with the grave speech of mountains,
how shall they recede from the landed rock,
being tideful of memory
as the low sea is with her weed-nets
pulling upon the shore.

The shining of the live ones,
and now this dragnet hair,
these shapes of driftwood
tossed in tunnels of hereafter.

In the uncrossed air of tomorrows
we lean forward like lost birds
with a bird's feeling of time:
an endless treetop shelving leaves
in a pond of sky.

Now the dead bury us
with their final falling.

Elias Lieberman

NOTATION IN HASTE

Miss Brown, before these walls unquote
A phrase of fate and crush us both,
Please take a note to Me Inside
Dissatisfied.

I am the man on a curtailed budget,
Entrepreneur for a plastic gadget
Made to suit either giant or midget.
Radio and television
Shepherd the crowd to the right decision
And hundreds of infidelity stations
Clutter my folds with public relations.
(My analyst patiently smiles, repeating,
"If you enjoy it, keep on bleating.")

But what am I doing and where am I going
At a pace that is always *frenetico,*
Molto, molto frenetico
To a goal beyond my knowing?

Where are the signs at the intersections?
Followed by creditors ever dunning,
I must get there, running, running
Faster, faster, ever faster
Playing the game of follow-master
Straight to the edge of the next disaster.

Where should you file this? Come, Miss Brown,
Smell the smoke? There is time to burn,
So say the clocks around the town:
I am the Whom It May Concern.

CLASSROOM IN OCTOBER

There is a hush this golden afternoon;
Even the master blinks at Cicero
While trudging up a mountain path in June.
Through open windows oak and elm trees show
Their dreams in color. Grasshoppers recite
Inconsequential themes in praise of song
And youth; they hint the sum of all delight
Is witchery that cannot last for long.

His mind is not upon the third declension,
Nor will he play the sleuth for any case;
Her lipstick flouts the noun that seeks attention;
She is engaged upon another chase.
When Pan in whimsey blows his woodland flute
No ablative is ever absolute.

Carolyn Wilson Link

ELEMENTS

Air, which is not anything,
Bears feathered or metallic wing
On nothingness, or wantonly
Levels a house, uproots a tree.
Its light unconscious rhythm can
Defer mortality in man.

Fire, hardly more than flickering air,
Man's dear companion and his care,
May slumber on the hearth as tame
As if it never had been flame,
May serve and solace, biddable,
Or leap with crimson fang to kill.

Water, too weak to stand alone,
In falling will demolish stone,
Or turn the dynamos which move
Comfort and culture in their groove.
Water, no less than fire or breath,
Is sovereign over life and death.

For each its human counterpart;
The mind, inferred, the fluctuant heart,
The channeled will; these blent together
And multiplied, create that weather,
Invisible, invincible,
Wherein, self-prisoners, we dwell.

Gordden Link

ARTIST AND APE

I stand before your cage to make my sketch,
catching in line and shade your jungle look,
your hate of man, your willingness to play
his little game for food and drink, your hope
that someday he will lose his wariness
and come too close. I make my pencil move
in ways I do not altogether fathom
and here on paper see your fingers tight
around steel bars you someday mean to bend.

Your eyes upon the paper somehow show
fury and fright and lust that were not there
before I started work. The sketch takes shape
limning a creature (the idle thought occurs)
with more of man in him than many men
my pencil knows. And suddenly I want
to tear it off the pad, to make confetti
against the wind, to sow a thousand parts
of paper ape upon an earth that spawns
too many apes already. But art or the Devil
lurking behind the bush prevents the gesture.

And anyway the sketch is good . . . too good.

I look into your eyes once more and wonder,
should I say "Thank you, Ape," for posing well,
for showing me the depths to which man sinks
or whence he came? Or should I turn away
as if you were a model paid to stand
twenty minutes while my pencil made
mock of the paper's virgin unawareness?

Those deep-set, beady surfaces give stare for stare;
my spine feels the little mice of history
run up and down with frozen feet. I shrug,
try not to shudder, then twist around and jot
the date in lower left-hand corner.

                                              A pause.
What title shall I write across the top?

The picture, lecherous and frightful, names itself:
boldly I scrawl the descriptive phrase—"Self Portrait."

Katharine Day Little

HAZLITT SUPS

After a soiree, with his dark head bent,
     Hazlitt went chatting in a note
     to a friend—We supped (he wrote)
and a lady said: Miss G.
(Don't you see, Mr. H. don't you see?
     I'm sure you agree)
     looks prodigiously
     like a tree?

So they supped on grilled bones
     with for ladies a bowl of pale syllabub;
a barrel of oysters was broached,
     Marsala flowed, beer—Hazlitt's deep tones
diapasoned the cheer. Ah, but she, but Miss G.
her looks, were they arch,
     did she shrink, did she prink,
was she ash, was she larch,
did she sway like a poplar or royally soar
like a pine, stand foursquare like an oak?

Were her curls copper-bronze like a burgeoning beech,
    did her silken folds droop like a willow?
was she maidenly slim and white as a birch,
    did she rest one suave foot on a pillow
moss-green? Ah, we're left in the lurch
    for miss G. never spoke, simply she
looked prodigiously
like a tree.

Hazel Littlefield

NOT FOR ITS OWN SAKE...

Not for its own sake has the wild rose blown
Or mountain crumbled into fertile fields;
Far greater than itself the ocean yields
A timeless testament and every stone
Cries, "Read me and discover the unknown."
All nature is a sacrament designed
For man's ascent from brute to God, and mind
Confirms the purpose of our blood and bone.

We are no longer mocked by midnight stars
That melt into the morning like pale dreams;
Into our minds have flashed the mighty gleams
Of thought, concepts of law, that make us kin
To Him, the source of law beyond the bars
Of finite space and mortal discipline.

Edna Livingston

A QUESTION

I wonder if, when Galatea woke
And found the blood new-coursing in her veins,
She sensed the meaning of those growing-pains —
And what she said the first time that she spoke:

And if, as ivory changed to blood and bone
She felt a slight premonitory chill
Or questioned fearfully the voltaile
New unfamiliar dream, the veiled unknown.

When Pygmalion, clasping life he had designed,
Found Galatea breathing 'neath his touch,
Did she know she ned not fear him overmuch —
And turn to him and be of womankind?

Edith Lodge

SONG OF THE HILL

Here
High on the hill
I have studied the quiet way
Of the stone
And all that is still
And a year goes past like a day . . .

Here
Taught by the deer
And the lizard, where shadows are long

I have learned the attentive ear,
The breeze and the leaf and the bird
Are a song for the quiet to hear
The high sweet timeless song
That only the quiet have heard . . .

Alone
In the indigo shadows
As long and cool as the trees
A year goes past like a day
High on the hill
Here . . .

May Carleton Lord

OLD MAN WITH A MOWING MACHINE

He comes, the old one, his shabby cap askew,
and two sturdy roans to mow the meadow lot.
Bindweed and Queen Ann's lace, the porcelain blue

of chicory, sway and bend in a grave gavotte
before the scissored steel.   The stricken grass
lies silver-green like waves the sea forgot.

No breath of air is astir.   Like molten brass
the sun swims in the sky.   Blackbirds scream
their taunt against heat like fluid glass.

The old man rests and lets his tired team
stand in the shade of elms along gate-bars.
He claims no power to evoke a dream

or pluck a handful of ebullient stars;
he merely mows and leaves no unsightly scars.

Louise Louis

THE WOUNDED

Was it a dream? The Books were men . . .
Matthew, Mark, John — all soldiers bridging a gap,
walling up a void, stretched out
trying to be floor, circling the place
where he lay legless, it seemed,
bodiless maybe, dreaming surely. . . .

A chorusing of voices kept swelling
to a dissonance.   The singing
made the titles on the men blur
as sea-plants wrinkle in a pool
troubled by a pebble.   But he read
as far as John before he closed his eyes.

When last he looked
the men were a pile of charred chapel;
but far down the road a tall stone stood. . . .

Gertrude May Lutz

PRISONER OF WAR

Their eyes had known the quiet color blue —
hushed quality of silence held in sky,
or in still pool wherein their faces lie
under a film of shining thin as dew.
Blue was room-quiet walls, a subtle sense

of everness, the tickless clock unwound.
Then distances . . . fading with wings of sound
their cobalt feathered dream of permanence.

Now blue is coldness, shape of tear and tear;
small sob of loneliness blown from a horn;
quick stretch of eyelids in a face's turn,
or sudden fingers at the nape of fear.
But blue could be ink-rounded words of tryst
that say he is returning out of mist.

At first there had been letters — oblong shape
that brought proximity — a brief reprise
to memory: crossed "*t*"s and dotted "*i*"s—
angle and curve patterned with stubborn hope
signed with the aching stillness of a name.
Then through night violent skies of red and red
dark shadows hurled their beaks toward each bed
that sagged with nightmare blind and lost and lame.

Return the dream! Sing, birds, to sound of feet
running the morning path! O loud as drum,
thunder the heart to zigzag pendulum.
Heart and clock, beat calendar: complete
the tick and tock of why and where and when . . .
Behind bruised eyelids, start the years again.

Gloria MacArthur

PHINEAS PRATT

This luxury they call the Flesh
I had withstood for forty years
And looked on them as womanish
Who peeked at Magdalenes, no peers
Had I in hardening to stone
The sybarite that clothed my bone.

I did not even suffer spring,
The aromatic laurel leaf,
Or any other tender, young
Intoxicant to play the thief
And rob me of my godly treasure;
My loins were girded against Pleasure.

And now beneath this wanton grass
I life discomfited, I weep
That abstinence has led to this
Uneasy sleep that is not sleep
Nor succor for the Flesh denied
Nor worth the forty years I died.

Sister M. Madeleva

BALLADE ON ESCHATOLOGY
(For the Hero of the Habitually Relaxed Grasp)

Detachment is a virtue, teachers say.
Then let me practice it without regret.
What do I hold beyond this short today?
What cherish that I shall not soon forget?
These small things upon which my heart is set
Are matters for a heart's relinquishings.
One ultimate matter do I cleave to yet;
This, I shall not forget the four last things.

Remembrance, in a thief's unnoted way,
Filches from me with neither leave nor let
My thousand petty deities of clay.
Perhaps my eyes are still a little wet;
Perhaps my heart may still a little fret.
Detachment is the stuff of sunderings.
Time, so they tell me, is a brave asset.
And I shall not forget the four last things.

Your voice, your eyes — or are they blue or gray?
The day we said good-bye, the day we met;
Hills we have walked, birds, flowers, our work, our play; —
Memory, how do you aid me and abet?
Time closes round me with impalpable net.
I'll not advert to clay or crowns or wings.
I have no thing to lose, all things to get,
For I shall not forget the four last things.

Envoi

Lord, though by mortal tyrannies beset,
Immortal freedom in my wild heart sings.
A pauper comes to pay a pauper's debt.
God, I shall not forget the four last things.

Eugene T. Maleska

ASSEMBLY: HARLEM SCHOOL

"My country, 'tis of thee,
Sweet land of liberty . . .";
Now listen while the echoes of that word
Are frozen in the air.
Be glad the quavering notes are heard
From lips that do not wear
As yet the the lines of hate and disbelief,
From childish lips that ring
With words as waves will pound a reef
In rote.

"Of thee I sing."
Be glad no sullen face is slowly turned
Your way to question why.

Be glad the meaning is not burned
In every heart and eye.

"Land where my fathers died!"
Beneath the lash's hundredth stroke,
The hobnails of the conqueror.
"Land of the pilgrims' pride!"
And did they hear the chains that spoke
Already down this savage shore?

"From ev'ry mountainside
Let freedom ring!"
. . . Yes, let freedom ring;
Oh, let it ring!

Margery Mansfield

BLESSING MRS. LARKIN

A blessing on you, Mrs. Larkin, for planting my trees!
May I, in turn, doctor this cherry and this peach
Through drought or winter killings. Of these many seedlings
May one survive that other eyes may drink the green!

I know, Mrs. Larkin, you never thought to plant for me.
Mrs. Larkin, we do not know our comings and our goings,
But our times are a winter requiring all the virtues of trees.
I needed a lesson or two in giving, from the maples
— Sweet sap uprising, shade, the flaming bouquet in fall,
Boughs cast for any to gather, on frosty nights — whatever
The maple gives, the maple would give to all. But more,
I needed a lesson in hoping, from the hemlocks,
Wearing their green all year, and pointing straight to the skies.
Where will we match, for skyward reach, the clan of pines?

Mrs. Larkin, I do not know your comings and your goings,
Nor mine — but should a wish have power, you dwell serene.
And may I also live beyond my poor intentions,
And see them branching, turning into trees!

Silvia Margolis

NEVER ASK ME WHY

Keep your copper coin, save your cup of wheat.
Hide your farthing candle, hoard your hempen sheet.
Or dole them to the beggar crying in the street,
Hungry as a hunter after bread and meat.
Give me only dreams, not a crumb to eat.
Give me only fancies. I have leaden feet . . .
But never ask me why.

Give me only fancies, any one you can spare:
Dreams no longer useful, dreams no longer fair:
Raveled as a frenzy, tangled as a snare;
Such as vendors would not peddle in the square.
Such as tinkers would not trouble to repair.
Let me, let me have them. Pity my despair . . .
But never ask me why.

Drag them from the dustholes backward in your brain.
Snatch them from your towers toppling with disdain.
Wring them from your ballads, all the bootless train.
I will hold them dearly as a cloud of rain,
As a drenching cloudburst to a parching plain.
Let me, let me have them, I would live again . . .
But never ask me why.

Ann Mars

SHADOW

"Come and you shall see'
(a voice of dread proximity).

As I turned, I saw a shadow.
"Take an ax (it said) and kill."

So I went and felled a tree
(image thus struck down in me);
mortal, demon or divine
I could not tell, and whether mine.

So I smashed that horrid face
that had stepped into my place,
and I found *myself* a shadow
with no body on a meadow.

Starting from an unknown place
I fell into immortal space.

Lenore G. Marshall

INVENTED A PERSON

Invented a person named I:
Out of use and disuse
And the antique child who watched the new moon in the sky,
And a foot in the antique grave,
Out of faces cast off by mirrors eyeless under light,
Out of love and excuse

In need, on the screen of a dream:
The target of blow, the chosen of healing and love,
A marvel of fate!
Most trapped, like the wind in a trap
Sweeping forward and out, most curbed like the sea
Storming breakwater walls to the bay, like a bird that must
     break for the sky
Through all space winging straight

Longed to be:
     Invented a person named I
With a place of its own
A certain thing to be done,
And in fear for that one.

Anne Marx

THE LACEMAKER (VERMEER)

In a world of orange serenity
she plies her bobbins, weaves her thought,
confines it to warm privacy.
Bent upon work, she looks secure,
concerned with colors to be matched.
Adventure, vari-colored,
curving in her lap,
holds no allure.
Das Ding an sich is all of life,
a task to be dispatched.

John Masefield

JUNE TWILIGHT

The twilight comes; the sun
    Dips down and sets,
The boys have done
    Play at the nets.

In a warm golden glow
    The woods are steeped.
The shadows grow;
    The bat has cheeped.

Sweet smells the new-mown hay;
    The mowers pass
Home, each his way,
    Through the grass.

The night-wind stirs the fern,
    A night-jar spins;
The windows burn
    In the inns.

Dusky it grows. The moon!
    The dews descend.
Love, can this beauty in our hearts
    End?

LOLLINGDON DOWNS
XVIII

Night is on the downland, on the lonely moorland,
On the hills where the wind goes over sheep-bitten turf,
Where the bent grass beats upon the unploughed poorland
And the pine woods roar like the surf.

Here the Roman lived on the wind-barren lonely,
Dark now and haunted by the moorland fowl;
None comes here now but the peewit only,
And moth-like death in the owl.

Beauty was here, on this beetle-droning downland;
The thought of a Caesar in the purple came
From the palace by the Tiber in the Roman townland
To this wind-swept hill with no name.

Lonely Beauty came here and was here in sadness,
Brave as a thought on the frontier of the mind,
In the camp of the wild upon the march of madness,
The bright-eyed Queen of the blind.

Now where Beauty was are the wind-withered gorses
Moaning like old men in the hill-wind's blast,
The flying sky is dark with running horses
And the night is full of the past.

SONNET

I never see the red rose crown the year,
Nor feel the young grass underneath my tread,
Without the thought, "This living beauty here
Is earth's remembrance of a beauty dead.
Surely where all this glory is displayed
Love has been quick, like fire, to high ends,
Here, in this grass, an altar has been made
For some white joy, some sacrifice of friends;
Here, where I stand, some leap of human brains
Has touched immortal things and left its trace,
The earth is happy here, the gleam remains;
Beauty is here, the spirit of the place,
I touch the faith which nothing can destroy,
The earth, the living church of ancient joy."

Madeline Mason

JANUS

No two eyes gaze alike,
Each face has double stare:
Two meanings and two thoughts are there,
Unreconciled.
The face is multiple.
Turned this way, it may chart
A patient calm, a kindly wit,
Turned that way mirror passions that portend
The foe beside the friend.
Then since each man is dual,
Half kind, half cruel,
What wonder that the world divides
And cannot hold one pattern,
Honor or shame?
Half wild, half tame,
What wonder that we war,
Split as we are in twain,
With cloven core?

Marcia Masters

IMPRESSIONS OF MY FATHER
I. COUNTRY WAYS

Either to keep the thinking in,
Or scrutiny out,
Your face was shaded on your saunters by an old green hat,

Sumac color, good for wind and rain
Or the deep woods
Where the sun struck silences.

Little, not always welcome,
I was awed by the weight of your spirit,
As I was by depths in the forest,
Whose gloom had a magic;
And I dared not follow; morning took you:
I heard the twigs snap, boughs bend with your will.

In the orchard you were quite different:
Under the affable shadows
That loitered with pleasure around the pear trees,
You roamed, telling funny stories
Of Gerophiculus, beast of your own invention,
Or tales of the prairies, land of your parents, and grandparents.
Sometimes, you threw back your head, and looked at the sky—
But only the crows went by, rusting the air
With a sound of something forgotten.

You loved that country:
The childish grasses,
And the oaks, making huge statements against the clouds;
The fruit trees, busy with growth, were yours,
And the garden where raspberries grew—
Warm as a woman's hand.
And when sun on the dunes flung down its final sermon,
You returned from the woods, and the orchard,
And the house on the bluff, streaming with sunset and welcome,
Swooned like a Rhineland castle;
Slowly, the pines drew night up the banks,
The silence of books settled over the hills.

Florence Ripley Mastin

RETURN TO SPRING

Now on the verge of spring the icy silver leaf
Is dimmed with gentler rain. The austere field withdraws
its snow. Little by little the plum tree is less brittle.
The ancient cherry bends again but does not break.
Earth is aware as one who dwells no more alone;
For there are whispers now: in deepest night the bough
is listening, and the ground listens but makes no sound.
Beneath the frigid stone there is no stir, and yet
Something is whispering . . .

A man has never met the hour when on his sight
The greenness falls, and yet he feels it in the swell
Of buds along the river; rising in a faint
Blue mist upon the hills; pausing at the sills
Of frosty windows. Then more quickly than the thought
Of it, the green is caught out of the sun's pale yellow
By a forgotten willow . . .

What then, forsaken heart, have you no secret part
In the returning spring? Wear you beneath your stone
No similar, strange dust that will, as blossom must,
Unfold? Must bone on bone build only grief on grief?

As surely as the leaf, you shall return to green.
You who perceive this thing, you shall return to spring.

Alice Clear Matthews

OF THE MATHEMATICIAN

Enamored so of form, of calculation,
Of permutation past the finite rim,
Of lines bisected farther than all seeing,
The proved, the humdrum could not compass him.
His boast, no obfuscations dimmed his sight—
Only his ear was never tuned to changes
The word is capable of, the infinite
Pattern of truth the poet rearranges.

Margaret McGarvey

D-DAWN

Father, sitting on the side of your startled bed,
May I have your attention, please?
This is not the morning you stopped short in a corridor
And thanked God on your knees.

> *The hospital walls dissolve in joy,*
> *The sun shouts as it rises:*
> "The Johnsons have an eight-pound boy
> Exceeding all surmises!". . .

Morning comes early when a child is small—
A nudge from Heaven or a sparrow's cheep,
And he is off to find a dreamed-of ball
Rolled to him down the corridors of sleep . . .

> Has Santy come yet?
> *No, Dear, not quite.*

(Shall we let him go in?
Wait till it's lit)...

You saw him yourself?
What was he like?
Did he really bring me
A big boy's bike?...

No Dear, not Christmas—
But the day selected
For you to be brave—
Braver than expected!

Mother, still awake when the frightened whistles blew,
This is not the morning of the Boy Scout Hike;
Lie still, lie still, there's nothing you can do
Except to pray a while if you should like.

The bedroom walls dissolve in pain,
The sun shrieks as it rises:
"The Johnson boy's in danger now
Exceeding all surmises!"...

He sprints across the still-cool lawn,
Behavior sewn upon his chest;
A skinny, brown, and freckled fawn
Who's passed the Scouts' initial test ...

Mom, if I'd a needle
And some coarse thread,
I could sew it on
Like I saw Fred.

Mother will sew it, Don,
Mother will press it ...
Does it hurt much?
Mother will dress it ...

Mother will die for you—
You know that is true—

Now, Mom, that's something
You no can do!

Young Man, waiting in the pale Channel dawn,
Waiting at attention for the signal to fly,
This is the morning for which you were born,
This is the morning on which you shall die.

The shores of home dissolve in mist,
The sun booms as it rises:
"The Johnsons have a hero now
Exceeding all surmises."

Morning comes early when a child is gone—
(Surely by now his plane is in the sky.)
Will he take cold there in the Channel dawn?
Will he be lonely when he comes to die?...

This is not the morning
Of the Sunday-School picnic.
This is not the morning
Don gets his degree.
This is not the morning
He might up and marry
Betty Ann Smith
Or Little Nancy Lee—
Nor is it the morning
You lit his First Tree . . .
This is the morning
For which we've been waiting,
This is the morning
Of praying and hating—
This is Invasion Morning!

Phyllis McGinley

JOURNEY TOWARD EVENING

Fifty, not having expected to arrive here,
Makes a bad traveller; grows dull, complains,
Suspects the local wine, dislikes the service,
Is petulant on trains,
And thinks the climate overestimated.
Fifty is homesick, plagued by memories
Of more luxurious inns and expeditions,
Calls all lakes cold, all seas
Too tide-beset (for Fifty is no swimmer),
Nor moving inland, likes the country more,
Believes the hills are full of snakes and brigands.
The scenery is a bore.
Like the plump, camera-hung, and garrulous trippers
Whose company henceforward he must keep.
Fifty writes letters, dines, yawns, goes up early
But not to sleep. He finds it hard to sleep.

MY SIX TOOTHBRUSHES

Against the pure, reflective tiles,
Northeast a little of the shower,
Gaudy as crocuses they flower.

The colors vary: but the styles
Are recommended and didactic
(Some Fuller and some Prophylactic.)

I cannot, it is strange, recall
When impulse sent me forth to buy
These gauds, or where or even why.

But here they dangle on my wall,
Symbols of vanity and hope.
I watch them shimmer while I soap

And am astonished, more or less,
Discovering how has lived in me
Such rage against mortality

That I this morning should possess
Six, six! and all set dense as thistles
With tough, imperishable bristles.

Polychromatic, they confront
My startled, half-abluted eyes.
Do these, I think, epitomize

The frivolous trophies of my Hunt?
Is my one Creed, my guidestar polar,
In corpore sano, sana molar,

Which has no care for kind or witty
Or learned ways or actual grace?
Disturbing. Well, in any case,

At least they do look rather pretty
Hanging redundantly in files
Against the cool, reflective tiles.

Gladys McKee

SPRING CELLAR

This was the color of coolness,
Where the quiet, crystal spring,
Silvered over the cellar

To keep what we would bring,
Cream and fresh-churned butter,
Milk in a deep brown crock,
Carefully we would place them
On the wide, the violet rock.
Man since has invented devices
That are miracles set apart,
But none that a child will carry
Long, long years in the heart,
For this was the texture of coolness,
Hill quiet, shade and water,
A sheltered ledge of violet rock
And one bewitched granddaughter.

Harry M. Meacham

TO A YOUNG POET

Read no more of cantos Pisan,
Cerebration out of season.
Put aside your blue guitar
And sing me songs of things that are.
Hoi polloi will never care
For Alfred and his thinning hair,
Or phlebas, sinking in a sea
Of brilliant ambiguity.
No! Let me hear a whippoorwhill,
See moonlight lying on a hill,
Feel loveliness in simple things;
The lake, the sky, and flashing wings.

You light the light in lover's eyes,
And let the doctor etherize.

Gerard Pervin Meyer

S. T. COLERIDGE DISMISSES A CALLER FROM PORLOCK

"What's new?"—What's old? what's anything
until you sing it?
What brings you here
unless you bring it?

I dream myself awake each day.
I might as well.
Let doers do big things: I say
if you can tell
what in the end you do, let me
say what I can begin to be.

Go, leave me be!
Do thus and thus.
There's only room in poetry
for one of us!

William Millett

I AM HAM MELANITE

the one they hunt by night
        the one that hides beneath briars
sutured tight as
stitches in a wound . . .
        i see the flat faced moon
as a sterile compress

on a lacerated sky—
    i shiver and the willows
stand nude in the snow   waiting—
    i hide in woods   dark woods
and hear the drums of animals
    and their secret dances . . .
God: listen to those shouts
    listen   as my eyes roll
    suspended from a thin wire—
listen to the Klan searching
for my paralyzed scent:
        they come rope drunk
        faces wrinkled
        gloves wet with fear
looking like cellophane on fire

    i am Ham Melanite and

i feel my blood
    dropping   dropping
on two lead palms—
    a large ball of silence
is choking me
with a hooded weight
dark as a tar paper bag
    and something makes
round cold circles
above my shoulders—
    my brain splashing pain
through brilliant lights—
    the lights melting
like a castle of sand
as the great basic face
of death lifts before me saying:
        Christ is everyman's skin
        you will be with him tonight . . .

Marianne Moore

O TO BE A DRAGON

        If I, like Solomon, . . .
        could have my wish—

     my wish . . . O to be a dragon,
a symbol of the power of Heaven—of silkworm
size or immense; at times invisible.
        Felicitous phenomenon!

TO A CHAMELEON

Hid by the august foliage and fruit
       of the grape-vine
       twine
           your anatomy
               round the pruned and polished stem,
                 Chameleon.
              Fire laid upon
          an emerald as long as
        the Dark King's massy
     one,
could not snap the spectrum up for food
       as you have done.

Harry Morris

GIROD STREET CEMETERY: NEW ORLEANS

The dead here look upon the light from caves
Of the sun no longer tended; broken tombs
Of brick and mortar crumble into shallow graves,

And false spikenard bleeds crimson droplet dooms
That fall into the cracks from which they grow

But rouse no passion in the stilted dust.
The walls about the crypts hold into breath
The living, and bright emerald lizards encrust
Grey stones that mount the sentinel to death.
The bones are white that never challenge snow.

Black happy children have their blind affairs
With laughter and discovery among
The rubble of their ancient games and cares:
Carruth, D'Aquin, Leroux—frail names once sung
Past time—are trod on in their overthrow

Or dispossessed from narrow beds of clay,
Pre-empted from the least they've ever known
By tired drunks who sleep as still as they
But do not suffer pillage of the stone,
Forever certain if forever slow.

James P. Mousley

PRAYER

God of light and blossom
grant me creation

the starred night is above
the moving grass beneath me

Lord Who taught the Greeks to love
be with us

young men walk on the grass
their eyes are staring

lead them to gaze O Lord
on light and blossom

the Greeks gaze from their graves
young men are walking

teach me to sing of Thee
God of Creation

the starred night is above
the moving grass beneath me

Paul Scott Mowrer

MOZART'S GRAVE

None walked behind that shoddy rain-swept hearse;
None waited in that mud but those who dug;
Dumping this one more body with a shrug,
They filled the ditch, and gave the rain a curse.

His loved ones far away, no priest, no friend—
Most lonely fate! But was not living worse,
Faint-praised and underpaid, a pauper's end,
Whip-lashed to death by toil, and empty purse?

A soul all music, gentle, gay and wise,
A prodigy of genius, a pure spring
Of harmonies and heavenly harp-singing—
How should men know an angel in disguise?

Christ died between two felons. Mozart lay
With twenty poor, anonymous as they.

Frank Mundorf

LETTER FROM A STATE HOSPITAL

Have you noticed the docile appeal
of a man never good to look at until he is old,
wandering with great slowness through yellow gardens?

As a young nurse in this place of whitened age,
it is natural I should have my favorite patient.
He is small and clean-nailed and remembers nothing,
and in his vagueness is a sort of dignity.

His eyes have forgotten any look but that of the mild.
At parties he sings old tabernacle hymns,
and his humor is the humor of small towns.
The nurses plant lipstick on his bald, guileless head.

Today I learned something of his past,
and I have found that I am not yet beyond shock.
He wanders with great slowness through violet gardens,
and I marvel at men never gentle until they are old.

REMEMBERING LINCOLN

That wooded face of cliffs and shadows
and unexpected light,
face of strong young rivers
and Springfield and Bull Run and Gettysburg—
it knew so well, that face,
the cold of pain.

Those oak-fingered hands,
hands of the axe and gentle awkward longing

and books beside a plough and a check made out
to A Colored Man With One Leg—

They knew so well, those hands,
the feel of fear.

He tried to smile the moods away,
to herd despair
into his secret corrals.
He knew, as lesser men,
that laughter climbs like smoke into the world,
and tears creep inward, drying on the heart.

Francis Neilson

EUGENIO PACELLI
(Pope Pius XII)

Upon himself a miracle he wrought,
Not once but many times in his career.
He rose to life and shunned days' ending bier,
And added to his span when time was short.

A glowing mind with fervent hope for all—
That God's own justice should be done on earth;
That war should end, and nevermore be dearth,
And days of anguish pass beyond recall.

God's love he gave to folk of every tongue,
To be emblazoned from all towers and spires.
Its rays into the darkest night be flung
To light again hope's everlasting fires.
His birthright name Pacelli will be sung
In glad Te Deums by celestial choirs.

Paula Nelson

THE HOUSE

The last chair finally was carried out
To join the others on the wagon piled;
These rooms, where once home-makers stirred about,
Were empty. In the front yard weeds ran wild
And fences sagged. Some shabby flowers remained,
Ghosts of a garden, even the neighbors' pride.
Cracks gaped, the peeling walls were mildew-stained;
Wind in the eaves disconsolately sighed.
Strange to remember how the windows glowed
With lamplight in those years when we were part
Of this loved place. It seemed that every road
Found ending here. This house took to its heart
The love we gave it, and returned us more.
What is there left to salvage now? No crust
For any mouse; no supper waiting for
A hungry child. The signature of dust
Is over all, and spiders spin away.
Yet something lingers in the mind beyond
The reach of time, destruction and decay—
Unbroken that immemorable bond,
Which can survive each crumbling sill and beam.
Tear down the house, let every landmark fall!
We who were happy there will keep the dream;
We who have shared so much can still recall!

Starr Nelson

THE WHITE RAINBOW

When his bones are as seaweed, when his sweet tongue
    is parched

Unto madness, and the salt-glazed eyeballs for the last time
From raft, or coral reef, or rock, search rime
Of seas or centuries, O God, let there be arched
Over the blue-black ocean's dolorous thunder—
Over Bolerium's waters rolling cold,
Over the split sea-chest and the broken hold—
The lunar rainbow bridging death and wonder.

For under that undinal curve Night's arteries
Swell with white ships moving in gauzy shrouds
Through clouds of sea birds white on glimmering seas,
And dolphins like new moons in water-clouds,—
And men halloo across the waves who sang in their
        drowning breath
"Let him who may sight glory before death."

Louise Townsend Nicholl

CREATION

This was the first world, where the wild dove cries
And waits for no reply,
And if it sounds like mourning, it is not,
Only the pulsing of creation's throat,
Laying a steady groundwork of pure tone,
Layers of darkness pressed into one note
From which the daring daylight lifts its arc.
This is the first world, which the wild dove paves
With perilous stone,
And it will sound like mourning when he cries
And waits for no reply.

Medora Addison Nutter

MOUNTAIN CREED

This is the place I love. Here I belong,
    On this high hillside farm I thought I owned
Until I found it was the farm owned me
    And rights I took for granted were but loaned.

These mountains are a very part of me;
    These rocky pastures and this stubborn soil,
These woods that won't stay cut, these crumbling walls,
    Mean more to me than unremitting toil.

For here I find, not loneliness but peace;
    Here silence is transmuted into song;
Here grief forgets to twist the tired heart—
    This is the place I love. Here I belong.

Katharine O'Brien

SPRING SONG

By April mist
be not misled
or the first green fist
in the crocus bed.

Spring's not about
until the day
an old man's out
scuff-scuffing his way.

His cheeks gone white,
his knuckles like stones,
his skin drawn tight
hugging his bones.

His coat too big,
no shape to his hat—
he cares not a fig
for trifles like that.

There's a glimmer of pride
in his watery eye,
a triumph to guide
his footsteps by.

In the warmth of the sun
aches melt to a splinter,
for he diced and won
with old man winter.

O bobolink cheer
O rivulet sing
the joy to be here
for one more spring.

Rose J. Orente

THE MASTER CITY

I have loved large cities, capitals of the world
That bedded my pain and transferred me like baggage
From stations of hope to inns of loneliness. In each
I have dreamed and died, following unfamiliar streets
    with certainty.

The cities were old. Rivers changed their courses,
Volcanoes spread their ash and lava over my antiquities,
Slums fell down and vast foundations underlay the giant
        pinnacles
That cut through clouds. Language was confused
But I knew my way among the strangers and their foreign
        tongues
For my love was eternally the same.

                                        I loved my loss
Or better yet, my search for its rewards. We sought each other;
Our beacons penetrated fog and night; space crumbled and
        there was no time.
My youth went on forever, renewed in incarnations of futility.
Without fear, I could not dare, I thought; without loss,
        I could not repeat
The rituals of life; without a boundary, I could not explore.
I left my striving everywhere, that were I to return,
Longing would reach out to me and keep me safe. Then where
        I went,
Direction was all the same and the cities followed me.

When I was alone forever, and it was late, I passed myself
Upon the path and saw my face by the spark of the tracks
        that never met.

I shall never go back nor journey again, I know,
Except to the sources of my fate. My wanderlust has aged,
        grows cold,
Though I hear the cities cry and call: *Come home.*

Cities I have reached by sea, waiting at the end of rails,
My loves to whom like monstrous bird I soared, I answer: *No.*

My lanes of aspiration draw together, converging
At the apex of my soul and my City teams with life,
        coming to meet me
As I travel forward. City of response, Queen of my crying,

Answer me now: Who is the architect of your splendid
Sprawling isolation, your coming in and going out?
Your pulse is mine, traffic coursing from hub to suburb
And never too small, you receive the wanderers who dared
    and were denied,
Who search no welcome nor invite rebuff.
Here among the ancient landmarks, those that sent me forth,
That finally recalled my dedicated passport, I stand recharted
To bewildering simplicity. Blundering through the toppled
    houses,
I start again, to build, to stay.

Jennie M. Palen

EARLY DUTCH

Manahatta . . .
    A lovely name, he thought, and a lovely island,
    lemon-lime in the filament of spring.
    Only an arc of birdsong on the stillness
    and curve of wing.

    Clucking among the stones, a brook, translucent
    through leaves like moons, through fluttering scarves
        of trout.
    Beyond the dogwood's crucifix a rabbit
    skittering in and out.

Manahatta . . .
    A velvet word, he thought, and a velvet island,
    like yielding moss, like lace on a fluted beach.
    A singing word in the mouth of a salty river
    far from an old world's reach.

    Here I would live forever, said Van Twiller.
    Time does not move here, only the sun and sky.
    Here I will drift through time like a lazy swimmer
    and cities may pass me by.

Winthrop Palmer

ARLINGTON CEMETERY
LOOKING TOWARD THE CAPITOL

This is not all I would have said
To the long line of upright marble dead
With your gilded dome hanging overhead,
Not alone in their name have our sons died.

To-day the river contains their field and trees.
The oak in scarlet, the willows in silver and green
Attend a small parade of civil mourners
Who claim from death a lover, a child or a man.

Wispy and travel-stained the dingy creatures
Pretend they would recover some cherished body
From your anonymous fame. Their shuttered eyes pray.

Mortals go blind to see an angel.
Human sight comes short, looks sharp, stays earth-bound,
Lights up the cavalcade, the Great Gate and that dome;
Not man, not God, only Rome.

Maurice E. Peloubet

THE ETERNAL KINSHIP

The moon silvers the bay, she waxes, she wanes,
The waters move in steady ebb and flow,
Whether in calm or storm. Drawn by her chains

She holds the tides in check or lets them go
Far up the beach, to pull them back once more.
Though the surf beat or hurricanes may blow,

Still the rough waves, obedient evermore,
Follow at last nor can they break the tie
That holds them to the margin of the shore.

Order is here and peace and something high—
The link between the sea and earth and sky.

*   *   *

The water of the sea is blood, it brings
Rhythms that live within us all. Can we
Set man apart from any life? All things

Are one at last, but man, imperfectly,
Trying to learn, still classifies, divides,
Seeing the difference, blind to unity:

For peace and truth are one. Eternal guides,
Christ, the Arabian, Moses, Buddha, teach
The eternal kinship that we know abides

Between all men, that live in God's great reach,
The life, the force, that binds us each to each.

Edmund Pennant

LOST EXPLORER

The infusorial earthmounds of the Upper Amazon
waylaid his most earnest dreams and captured them,
whispering auras of momentous meaning
in a relic of genesis hidden in the jungle.

The eye of God scans a generation and falters,
finding here and there recruits for the cast of His intentions;
scorning the tipsy fears of the callow and the diffident
who dare to ignore a visitation, or deny it.

Then in small men an endowment of courage
seizes the one great Demand of a lifetime
to fling off the familiar hobbles of humility
and solo on wings made of maps and desire.

The plane gnarls the air, leaving a backwash of silence
that settles on the earthbound a pall of self-pity;
for they feel the eyes of the wing-borne on their nakedness,
on the dribbling termite-steps of their retreating.

He is gone—many years. Those who watched him depart
ask warmly of each other, with unashamed triumph:
Still no word from the Amazon? Have the ants left no clue-fall?
No talisman, tongue-sinew, signet-ring? Nothing?

Marie Tello Phillips

SORROW

All the glorious Spring makes me color blind.
I have loved to sing . . . song is hard to find
When loss and loneliness are portals of the mind.

Hope and joy have fled . . . left but memory.
Beauty offers bread . . . flat and stale to me
And salted by my tears for what can never be.

Sorrow makes me dumb, I must try to pray
Though my heart be numb . . . I must live today
And find my solace following the Master's way.

Dorothy Cowles Pinkney

DAME LIBERTY REPORTS FROM TRAVEL

Sit tight, little hills, little valleys.
    Little towns, sit dark.
Pull in your steep gray gravel slides,
Cover your glenside treefalls from
A tent-slit glitter of nomad's eyes;
The dandelion digger's come;
She looks for her remembered mark
On stone and crossbar. Litle homes, sit dumb,
    Sit dark.

The dandelion digger's shawl
Blows ragged over the pasture wall;
Her swart skin dusted damp with earth.
Blade worn nimble and handle of horn
Heavy with hieroglyphic symbol,
Bends to the bitter weed of dearth.
Sit dark, little houses. Little towns, sit tight,
Lest you should know her, have her in,
And sit up listening half the night
to coarselipped tales of where she's been
And violent accusations flung:

Where is the mill? she'll whine.
The miller, what of him,
Who ground so salty fine
His wildwind shriek: *Born free?*
The baker, where is he,
Who hid the brown buck slave,
The day the Law came through,
Deep in his oven? What
Of resolute wives, green boys,

Armed to the teeth? Is this
Safe semblance all you've got
Left of the lively villages
        I knew?

Look in my face! Its sparse,
Hawk-ruthless stubbornness
Was your maternal source;
Nor were you all I bore!
Poorer than you were once,
Diggers of acorns, strumming
Bold chords of devil-may-care,
Behind me, from a younger pair,
Ebullient hordes break thoroughfare;
Prepare to join; prepare
To own your wilderness heritage,
Or else beware, beware!

Sit tight, little homes, sit dark.
Pull in your neat No Trespass signs;
The dandelion digger's come;
She looks for her remembered mark.

She knows it's there, it's there.

Sylvia Plath

TWO VIEWS OF A CADAVER ROOM

I

The day she visited the dissecting room
They had four men laid out, black as burnt turkey,
Already half unstrung. A vinegary fume
Of the death vats clung to them;
The white-smocked boys started working.

The head of his cadaver had caved in,
And she could scarcely make out anything
In that rubble of skull plates and old leather.
A sallow piece of string held it together.

In their jars the snail-nosed babies moon and glow.
He hands her the cut-out heart like a cracked heirloom.

II

In Breughel's panorama of smoke and slaughter
Two people only are blind to the carrion army:
He, afloat in the sea of her blue satin
Skirts, sings in the direction
Of her bare shoulder, while she bends,
Fingering a leaflet of music, over him,
Both of them deaf to the fiddle in the hands
Of the death's-head shadowing their song.
These Flemish lovers flourish; not for long.

Yet desolation, stalled in paint, spares the little country
Foolish, delicate, in the lower right hand corner.

HARDCASTLE CRAGS

Flintlike, her feet struck
Such a racket of echoes from the steely street,
Tacking in moon-blued crooks from the black
Stone-built town, that she heard the quick air ignite
Its tinder and shake

A firework of echoes from wall
To wall of the dark, dwarfed cottages.
But the echoes died at her back as the walls
Gave way to fields and the incessant seethe of grasses
Riding in the full

Of the moon, manes to the wind,
Tireless, tied, as a moon-bound sea

Moves on its root. Though a mist-wraith wound
Up from the fissured valley and hung shoulder-high
Ahead, it fattened

To no family-featured ghost,
Nor did any word body with a name
The blank mood she walked in. Once past
The dream-peopled village, her eyes entertained no dream,
And the sandman's dust

Lost luster under her footsoles.
The long wind, paring her person down
To a pinch of flame, blew its burdened whistle
In the whorl of her ear and like a scooped-out pumpkin crown
Her head cupped the babel.

All the night gave her, in return
For the paltry gift of her bulk and the beat
Of her heart was the humped indifferent iron
Of its hills, and its pastures bordered by black stone set
On black stone. Barns

Guarded broods and litters
Behind shut doors; the dairy herds
Knelt in the meadow mute as boulders;
Sheep drowsed stoneward in their tussocks of wool, and birds
Twig-sleeping wore

Granite ruffs, their shadows
The guise of leaves. The whole landscape
Loomed absolute as the antique world was
Once, in its earliest sway of lymph and sap,
Unaltered by eyes,

Enough to snuff the quick
Of her small heat out, but before the weight
Of stones and hills of stones could break
Her down to mere quartz grit in that stony light
She turned back.

Jenny Lind Porter

IN THE BEGINNING

In the beginning, when green came on the pasture,
And on the meadow, and on the farthest hill,
When the dew first fell on the morning's cheek,
    And the warmth began, and the chill,

We do not know whose eyes came first, whether it was the mole
Or leopard's ancestor, or the great-great-grandmother
Of a magpie who first wondered at the rain;
    We do not know how it was with our first brother,

How he felt the soft earth breathing beneath his feet,
Nor whether he fixed with holy stare
The world's first ant—red, bustling creature,
    Who was doubtless too busy to care.

How he couched himself, how the vines grew tangled,
How the ape swung screaming and was grown to fear,
How one eye first in secret watched another,
    Nor who it was let fall the world's first tear.

In the beginning, green came on the pasture,
And on the meadow, and on the farthest hill,
And the dew first fell on the morning's cheek,
    And the warmth began, and the chill.

Star Powers

HARVEST TIME

Feed
Upon anticipation as you sow the seed.
Glean
The freshness of the seedling's growing green
Flood
Your eyes with promise from the pregnant bud
Gain
Awakenings from little drops of rain
Groom
The finest field to yield propitious bloom
Cull
Your fruit, discard the shriveled hull.
Toll ...
The reaper comes to gather in the prime.
Soul,
It is the season, it is harvest time!

Benjamin Sturgis Pray

MOTORCYCLE

Astride on steel
youth storms the street
with four-point feel
of hands and feet
on speed and noise
and every pound
in two-point poise
of wheels on ground.

Through prim, sedate,
suburban quiet
he plunges straight
his rampant riot
and steers a force
that blends the scope
of lion, horse,
and antelope.

Christina Rainsford

SHADBUSH

In woods still winter bare,
Dark and unpromising,
The shadbush stands in gleaming white
Heralding the spring.

All the sombre woodland
Is lighted with its bloom—
A tall candle burning
In a shadowy room.

Elizabeth Randall-Mills

CROSSING THE COUNTY LINE

I crossed over the county line,
To my own returned today;
Instantly the wind had taste
And light was sudden out of clay.

The fields no longer sleeping by,
Arose, announced their state of corn;
And the orchards that were thinned
Told me which trees the winds had shorn.

Sun had cracked the grassless ground
But new foliage newly served;
There had been rain—gullies were clawed,
But the grave mound more softly curved.

The ways of growing and of dying,
Learned within loved boundary,
Sealed me silent, and with a worn
And clear embrace took charge of me.

One need only—to abide,
To stand upon my land alone,
And at this starting point of truth
Await a widening of the known.

Henry Morton Robinson

SECOND WISDOM

Corn does not hurry, and the black grape swells
In the slow cadence of all ripening things;
Wise pumpkins idle, and the deep lake dwells
In peace above her unimpetuous springs.

What most unhurried, most full-flavorous is:
The earth turns slowly and the tide stands still
For him who surely claims, as truly his,
Firm fruitage that no hasty blight can kill.

And we who flung ourselves to sudden wars
And would not wait for quick scars to be healed—
We must recall shrewd pumpkins and slow stars
And be as wise as lilies of the field.

NOVEMBER FUGITIVE

Were I the red-brushed fox, I should go warier
    In dawns like this (when shriveled leaves cry riot
To the beagle's ear) than when the tufted wood
    Lay ankle-deep in quiet.

Were I the whirring grouse, I should fly cunninger
    On noons like this (when barren boughs uncover
Plumes to the marksman's eye) than when the bush
    With fruit was berried over.

Were I the fugitive heart, I should run wearier
    On nights like this (when cheeks are nipped by sleet)
Than ever I ran when summer was my hunter
    And loneliness more fleet.

Paul Roche

COURAGE FOR THE PUSILLANIMOUS

O you are a rajah in your rage
    or so could be
    if you could rise up from those cowering rags
Of huddled personality.

O you are a tiger that could pace
    with unblenched eyes
    if you could gaze full at your manhood's grace
Take it all and not despise.

O you are perfect in your stripling's plumage
    of bold disdain
    if you could only whip that cold poltroon
    stammering within—
To suffer and give pain.

Liboria E. Romano

LYRIC BARBER

The poet honed
his phrases on
whetstone
to make them sharp
against a critic's
carping.
Day in and day out
he split hairs
perfectly.

For bread this brave
bard also gave
a clean-cut shave.

Nathan Rosenbaum

PICTURES AT AN EXHIBITION

Here is Israel
As one man saw it with his eyes and his brush
And his love for the ancient land of his people,
Reborn like a phoenix from the ashes of history
To live in the future with the greatness of the past.

Like a magnificent mural of many designs,
The paintings emblazen the room with a vivid beauty,
Bringing a new excitement to the occidental eye
Turned from the familiar street to this flame of new life.

Here are the cities, white on white, mounting the plains,
Or rising beside the waters of an ancient sea,
White as hope is white, as faith is white;
And the villages set like jewels between the prongs of the hills,
Or dotting the sands of the Negev like visioned oases.
Here are the gardens with a riot of zinnias,
Scarlet like dreams of glory and triumph;
And the fertile fields, green and abundant,
Sown with the seeds of labor and devotion.
And here are the mountains holding the weight of centuries
Upon their bent and weathered shoulders,
Rising in the distance towards the vast horizons
Lit by the torches of fabulous sunsets.

And here are the people—the miraculous people of Israel—
Eternal as the land of their fathers is eternal.
The Sabras like the bitter-sweet fruit of a new race
Sprung from the loins of a land once old and barren,
Now rejuvenated with new vigor and fertility;
And the children like opened buds on a flowering tree;
And the survivors of the ghettos of many cities,
Redeemed and assembled through the sacrifice of their
      brethren
To breathe the air of freedom under their own skies.

This is the adventure of a soul in a land of antiquity,
Finding expression through paint upon canvas.
Here is the alchemy of art that brings to this room
The face and the spirit of Israel.

Allison Ross

GAME OUT OF HAND

Heavy heavy lies over our head
the towering tree of smoke
blossoming with ten thousand skulls
and every skull alike.
O what shall we do to redeem it, Lord?
What shall we do to redeem it?

We'd fell the tree—but it will not fall!
nor subside to an unsplit seed . . .
Must we crawl on all fours to Neanderthal?
Or dance till the last tune's dead?

Heavy over our head the tree!
The roots deep in our heart
suckle themselves on our freezing blood
and riddle our brains to dirt.

Swing low Thy Grace and lift us high
clean from the stifling smoke . . .
Ten thousand ways to come to Thee
and every way alike:

Swing high ourselves above the tree
and rise to heaven—but
all powdered rust lies charity
our only chariot.
O what shall we do to redeem it, Lord?
What shall we do to redeem it?

David Ross

I AM YOUR LOAF, LORD

I am your loaf, lord,
Enlivened from the dust,
And by your leavening
Grow on immortal yeast.

Father and fondler
Of my nameless loam,
By your loaver's grace
I golden to my name.

Rounding to my life,
I am born believed,
And through my psalming grist,
My lord, you are achieved.

When you unloave me
Piecemeal, grain by grain,
You must for your self-sake
Account for me again.

When crustfallen I lie,
Unnamed and lost,
Your palms bereaved of me
Will itch to knead my dust.

For we are twined as one.
Of each other never free.
I am your life, lord.
Shall you wash your hands of me?

NEWS REEL

The eye drags all of winter
Through the bone, and we are
Theatre to this death.
Also in dreams
The lens remembers,
Taking death into focus.
Reel on reel
The eye records the shape of agony.
The one death, masked in the many faces.
Here in close-up
Is the steel's odyssey
Embarked upon the flesh,
And exploding at each port of call.
Reel on reel
Bombs decide the weather,
And make a winter in the blood.
A mother burying her child,
Cries to the gunners,
"I come only with my tears,
And these few flowers.
Why are you afraid,
Is my sorrow a gun?"
Reel on reel
Men dissolve in terror,
And we who are assigned to life,
Are theatre to this death.

Larry Rubin

THE EXILE

Our house had wings for children, chandeliers
That tinkled in the wind, moroccan tiles
Tiny enough for hopscotch. We planted strings
Where nasturtium vines could creep in flaming piles

Of salmon, pink, and rose. Like little suns
They peeped in at the picture window; all
Was pastel. Scarlet and magneta came
Later, deeper dyes, not petals spilled

From lilliputian vines, but lip-rouge
On my sister's ancient face. She fled
Her wing, laughing on a stranger's arm.
The white she wore was like a windless cold.

THE LESSON

I was stung by a man-of-war
When I was four;
It spun purple tentacles about my thigh,
And though I cried
I saw its glistening Portuguese sail——
A sac of poison, acid with majesty.

I know royalty
When I see its barbed embroidery—
The formic wine within the purple grail.

THE ADDICT

I saw him lying there—my father—with eyes
Of frosted glass, waiting for some warmth,
His eighty hours of crawling whiteness over;
Like a man who has wintered in hell, he wore his skull
As though it hung by a hollow needle of ice.

I stood, waiting, watching him within
A cold chamber of my heart. His sheets
Stretched like glaciers; one false move
Would open a crevasse, spin his skull through caves
Where all the needles cracked like stalactites.

And so I waited. For hours I gripped the rim
Of those white wastes, gazing at the precipice
As though it were my own. And then the eyes
Jerked softly, choking through the frost
To mine. I saw my father's eyes were warm.

Virginia Russ

THE SHAPE OF AUTUMN

Along Highway 40, blare
tall trucks laden with harvest:
Crates of pears plucked
From sun-curve of hill slope or
alfalfa-scented valleys.

Watermelon smell of lake dusk,
star-shimmer of shore waves,
green-dew flecks of clover mornings, blend
in fecund mold of blunted heat.

Careening trucks bear summer
in a myriad mellow bites:
Faintly russet, leaf-shaded,
promising October gold.

Now is summer oldering,
oak-apples all fallen; . . . Buck-
eye trees lift rose-ashen branches
towards yellowing gourds of hills,

And crows,
on black sickle wings, are calling, calling, . . . towards the soon
pumpkin moon.

Ethel Green Russell

LETTER FROM THE VIEUX CARRE

If only I could send you one small slice
Of this old Quarter, what would you discover:
A bit of balcony where memories hover,
A scheming harlot's tooth as cold as ice,
Lost Lady's ghost denying her Lord thrice
And thrice again with her illicit lover,
A parrot's beak or the stubby snoot of a plover,
A pirate's dagger and a pair of dice?
Or would you find a Rose-of-Montana seed
Whose parent twined about the iron lace
To shield a patio's inheritrix?
Or would you find an Ursuline's hallowed bead,
Or come upon the Savior's imaged face
Lost from a kindly padre's crucifix?

Sydney King Russell

DEATH WAS A WOMAN

He had not reckoned on a visitor—
The day was desolate, the skies were bleak;
When he beheld a shadow at the door
He sat immovable and could not speak.

Death was a woman full of charm and grace
And not a monster avid for her prey
And when he saw the beauty of her face
It took his breath away.

I. L. Salomon

SONG FOR THE GREENWOOD FAWN

The greenwood fawn at the hidden brook
In the green green wood, O lovely!,
Shudders a fly off her dappled coat
And watches a leaf, light raft afloat,
Skip and swirl to the edge of the pool,
Where the shadows of stone are shaded cool,
Nor ever moves on her hornèd hooves
In the green green wood, O lovely!

The greenwood fawn sees her own shy face
The silver water mirrors,
And the water washes her black furred nose
As a dragonfly in emerald clothes
Darts from a branch to a stunted hedge
And swoops past a shrub to light on a ledge,
Where a trout shoots by, sleek submarine,
Dark green against the summer green,
And the fawn never moves on her hornèd hooves
In the green green wood, O lovely!

O the greenwood fawn 's a statue of bronze,
Yet quivers like a stricken
Warm live thing as the uncoiled spring
Of terror makes her quicken;
Caw-caw echoes the caw-caw cry.
A black bird warning peril 's nigh,
And the fawn's white tail is a little white broom
Dusting the door to a ferny room
In the green green wood
In the green green wood
Of the greenwood fawn, O lovely!

Helen Salz

LATE

An embassy of doves
hovers over the river
    over the tangled shores.

But the mustang-hearted
have made a final departure
    and the eagles have fallen—

Winds charge at the trees
    of yesterday
blow sand from the almost-graves,

while the village is a pail
    of spilled water.

Oh embassy of doves
    you are late
flying!

Arthur M. Sampley

THE DEFENDER
(After Toynbee)

Between the fosse and inner wall
He lunges forth and parries well
The thrust he may not live to tell
As if he did not know that all
Within the stricken citadel
Today must stand with him or fall.

You would not know to watch his stance
That he could see beside his foe
The inner self he did not know
Engaged with him in lethal dance,
And he must give and take the blow
He aims and parries in a trance.

From turret holes they watch him smile
As patches on his shirt show red;
Their mute, white faces, like the dead,
Gloam down upon his memory while
The words the enemy has said
Well from within him and defile.

They see the sharp tip of his sword
Strike flesh; they do not see him blench
And take the desperate inner wrench
From which the swift blood must have poured.
He gives the wounds which he must quench
With blood that he cannot afford.

Now steadily he rains the blows
From which he is too brave to shrink,
And he has little time to think
Why thus so ill the battle goes,
But stoutly at the outer brink
Defends the fort he overthrows.

Carl Sandburg

LITTLE CANDLE

Light may be had for nothing
or the low cost of looking, seeing;
and the secrets of light come high.
Light knows more than it tells.

Does it happen the sun, the moon
choose to be dazzling, baffling?
They do demand deep loyal communions.
So do the angles of moving stars.
So do the seven sprays of the rainbow.
So does any little candle
speaking for itself in its personal corner.

LITTLE GIRL, BE CAREFUL WHAT YOU SAY

Little girl, be careful what you say
when you make talk with words, words—
for words are made of syllables
and syllables, child, are made of air—
and air is so thin—air is the breath of God—
air is finer than fire or mist,
finer than water or moonlight,
finer than spider-webs in the moon,
finer than water-flowers in the morning:
    and words are strong, too,
    stronger than rocks or steel
stronger than potatoes, corn, fish, cattle,
and soft, too, soft as little pigeon-eggs,
soft as the music of hummingbird wings.
    So, little girl, when you speak greetings,
when you tell jokes, make wishes or prayers,
    be careful, be careless, be careful,
    be what you wish to be.

ON A FLIMMERING FLOOM YOU SHALL RIDE

Nobody noogers the shaff of a sloo.
Nobody slimbers a wench with a winch
Nor higgles armed each with a niggle
    and each the flimdrat of a smee,
    each the inbiddy hum of a smoo.

Then slong me dorst with the flagdarsh.
Then creep me deep with the crawbright.
Let idle winds ploodaddle the dorshes.
And you in the gold of the gloaming
You shall be sloam with the hoolriffs.

On a flimmering floom you shall ride.
They shall tell you bedish and desist.
On a flimmering floom you shall ride.

May Sarton

CONVERSATION IN BLACK AND WHITE

At first we sat imprisoned in this place
Where snow was falling, curtains fell to screen us,
And neither of us had a human face,
The falling snow lay silently between us.

We had no features; like two floating moons,
One black, one white, we had to strain and peer
Across a shifting, thick, ambiguous gloom,
Wanting to tear it open and see clear.

But who could summon a single word so warming
It might green over the snow-battened ground,
Or make clear daylight shine through all the harming—
And who would dare to touch the tribal wound?

Bring me your bitterness, and I will give
My guilt. Until these two have been exchanged,
Symbolic tokens between alien princes,
Still the snow falls, and still we are estranged.

But who could risk the heart out of the skin?
Then anything seemed possible but lies.
It was: cry out or stay locked up within
The moonlike faces without human eyes.

We had to risk more than we could afford,
More than men summon easily so soon,
As if I were your secret self, my lord,
And you my secret friend, no stranger moon.

And then our human anguish did look through,
The wounded at the wounded, open, stared;
The morning of the world was not more blue
Than the one world-embracing look we shared.

George Brandon Saul

SPRING SONG

In a net of mist the moon depends on the wood
Where the sap hesitates
Beneath the rustling memory of winter's hood
And the druid fear that waits
Deep in primordial caves where sighs the cautious blood.

This is no new despair to the passionate heart
Whose furious being shines
Only within that element can impart
Persistence through the tines
Of fluid agony by strange incorporate art—

The flaming bath love's salamander needs:
Inurement grown to be
Seasonless law of being—pain that seeds
The single ecstasy:
The rose forever doomed to globe but as it bleeds.

Frances Higginson Savage

DUCK IN CENTRAL PARK

How sweet to wear a shape of snow
Impervious to cold and heat
And, decorously calm, to go
On golden webs for feet—

To drift or dawdle on a pond
As lightly as a summer cloud,
Ignoring skyscrapers beyond
The curious human crowd—

To dibble-dabble in the stream
A smooth, exploratory bill,
Or turn aloft a tail of cream
And feed, head-down, one's fill—

Or waddle in a proud parade
Of feathered kinsmen, single file,
Maintaining, both in sun and shade,
The semblance of a smile!

George Scarbrough

BIRTH BY ANESTHESIA

The white pinnace on lactic waves
Skirted another coast as Lady Anne,
Swimming in the direction of seal island,
Looked for a calf.

　　　　　She came to a mountain:

In the mid-sea a mountain without shores
Shook the soft water to a low crying
As of calves mewing in bright weather
Somewhere in the wild unlull of ocean;
A mountain without trees suspiring
In sun the sound of leafy fathoms,
Waves rearing, beating, dying
In the one word: ocean, ocean.

A rudeness in catapulted coral
Threshed its own being to worlds
Scarlet and gilled on the breathing reef,
And the wind ran in first lungs
Deeper than fish circles as down
From the depth a sun fell to the surface
Under her, glowing, as Lady Anne
Sought by the rocks her harbor. O
The pure red opalizing the mother blue
This primal voyage, and the soft journey!

Now the captain with glass, squinting,
Shouting, inquired the pausing swimmer
What daily run of seal? what hour?
What hump? what mountain, the calf called
Coursing the fierce water
                        But sleepy,
Sleepy beyond the height of tides,
Drawling to herself some mother advice
Learned among potatoes and pumpkin rinds,
Riding a hallo of foam
Through the absolute beauty of the sea,
To the cold corridor and her son's blushes,
The Lady Anne came home.

Marjorie Somers Scheuer

THE FOX

The fox
like a coil of tawny rope
unwinds swiftly
down the grassy slope,
sunset bronze
autumn wood
framing his solitude.

Suddenly
he slips into a hollow
while warmth of wood
and the sun follow.

Samuel Schierloh

BUCKO-MATE

He was a big two-fisted brute,
Feared and detested;
Long-armed, short-legged,
And barrel-chested.

He kept a belaying pin
In his hip-pocket,
But around his bull-neck
Hung a silver locket.

So we bided the day—
Consoled one another—
When he'd gather his gear
And go home to mother.

C. M. Schmid

SYNEKDECHESTAI

She kneeled before the dead lamb weeping.
But I said:
    We know lambs die.
    We do not cry
        dead lambs we do not know.
But lambs die every day.

She kneeled and cried:
    The lamb that died today
    Was mine.

It was one lamb: it died. Tomorrow's sun
    will see another one.
You will not weep tomorrow's lamb.

She said:
    I weep tomorrow's lamb
        today.
    And all tomorrows, and all other lambs.
    I weep the dead.

Aaron Schmuller

LEGEND OF HIS LYRE

Light diffusing my likeness,
Outpouring legend of his lyre,
Mothering fiery stones and flowers
Or paradox of thundered utterance

Winging the blue sky-canvas of peace,
Or lament of reed-leaves and white lilies
Ripening, swaying neck-deep in river-water:

O mother of sword and ashes,
Of meditation in gloaming hours,
Earth of fresh sunlight gathering flotsam,
Earth of blossoming roses out of dunghills,
Receiver of delicate moonbeams stained by manslaughter,
Earth of densely-flowing sunlight and shadow,
Of mother-love, of torture-chambers and the crematorium:

How many of our days border on night,
How much of our ecstasy is punctured by tears,
How deep is the pain, the hunger, the fury
Welling the searching heart suffused with leaping light
Or visioned hope gliding on earth's overflowing granaries,
Abundant wheatfields boasting bread and fruit; and still
Children scratch earth's surface for crusts of food!

O mother of mourning and of wandering
Earth's flower-gardens, unspeakable loneliness
My soul's companion, brother to light and goodness,
O mother earth of cornlands, I have wandered under your sun
And dwelt upon your grass, cradle of darkness and light,
The moist roots touching my bare toes, penetrating
The skin's pores with earth-gladness!

I have wandered your periphery
In the past, O mother earth of flower-petals
And hungry children, and shall wander evermore;
Taking up the wanderer's staff, my massive head shrunken
To a bloodstained tear, a bitter tear,
A tear rolling down the cheek of
Long-suffering humanity!

R. J. Schoeck

HOMAGE   (Diptych, 2)

My God, the bitter-tasting mouth was me,
Myself the belling hounds, my life the tree,
Mine then the lonely cry was meant to be,
The long unhurrying chase.
                              Let me taste gall,
Make me say I am heartburn, God: God, call
Me—may I come to feel the tree, and fall
(I know my cliffs of frightful fall) the deep
Of my own mountains, but come the slow steep
Climb of my ascent: These willed, I keep;

This captive me at last has overthrown
The rebel, can enjoy dominion:

Homage I pay, my Lord, that now am free.

Martin Scholten

SOLILOQUY BY THE SHORE

There goes the dog of the mind
Scurrying away to explore
Some other pathway winding
Along a distant shore.

Recalcitrant hound, forsaking
The rich immediacies
Of summer sun and shade
With fleeting summer ease

To search, chimera-harried,
The course of a spent day—
As though truth's dusty bone were buried
Somewhere on that way!

But here the wooded lane is cool,
The leaf-framed seascape pleasant.
I shall whistle him, time's fool,
Back to the present.

Lulu Minerva Schultz

WHAT PRICE

I saw a tiny pebble fall,
Then diadem
Of wispy dandelion puff,
Blow from its stem.

The flinty stone caught fast in earth—
Contented lay,
The dandelion's phantom cloud
Blew far away.

A pebble holds eternity
In quiet gain,
But O the lure of chancing winds
Outriding rain!

Anne Sexton

KIND SIR: THESE WOODS

Kind Sir: This is an old game
that we played when we were eight and ten.
Sometimes on The Island, in down Maine,

in late August, when the cold fog blew in
off the ocean, the forest between Dingley Dell
and grandfather's cottage grew white and strange.
It was as if every pine tree were a brown pole
we did not know; as if day had rearranged
into night and bats flew in sun. It was a trick
to turn around once and know you were lost;
knowing the crow's horn was crying in the dark,
knowing the supper would never come, that the coast's
cry of doom from that far away bell buoy's bell
said *your nursemaid is gone.* O Mademoiselle,
the rowboat rocked over. Then you were dead.
Turn around once, eyes tight, the thought in your head.

Kind Sir: Lost and of your same kind
I have turned around twice with my eyes sealed
and the woods were white and my night mind
saw such strange happenings, untold and unreal.
And opening my eyes, I am afraid of course
to look—this inward look that society scorns—
Still, I search in these woods and find nothing worse
than myself, caught between the grapes and the thorns.

Charles Shaw

DISSEMBLER

In a corner
of the little room
that occupies my heart
I hide yesterday's sorrow
and slip on
a mask of smiles.

Later,
when they have gone, the scoffers,

I hasten to my sorrow
and clutching it in eager hands,
take it out
for a private airing.

Elizabeth Alsop Shepard

WHITE FOX
(Japanese Painting by Mori Ippo, 18th Century)

Suddenly,
out of the faint gray smother
enveloping all,
he is there,
the white fox,
whiter than the snow.
His full brush curves like a royal plume.
Black points mark his face,
delicate as tips of frozen grass
emerging from snow.
Aloof, remote,
essence of the snow,
the wilderness,
his coming is vanishing,
silently,
mysteriously,
into the faint gray smother
enveloping all.

There was emptiness.
Now—moving,
hidden,
aware,
there is life.

Ruth Forbes Sherry

PROMISES.

O, fastidious mind, gorging on absolutes, remember;
    How green Cambodian jungle crept up the stair
    of templed Angkor Wat, sealing all flesh
    in web of arrogant spider, binding
    the ritual lamb in lianas of mangrove.

    Remember Atlantis, engulfed by heedless waters
    that levelled the mullioned tower
    of the Princess, greening with slime
    the lanes where her chariot lurched;
    rotting the hero halls—porches for octopi.

    Remember Pompeii, her people flicked
    by Vesuvius' fang, caught like children
    playing at *statues;* her promises spitted
    like moths on the half-buried wall;
    her lovers welded in death.

    Remember Nineveh, sin-lost in sifting,
    drifting sand, the coins on her harlot ankle
    bruised in bright dust; her rubbled altars
    asylum for virulent viper
    and cursing rock.

O, fastidious mind,
    time is a bracelet for the wrist;
    a footfall in Argolis; a lullaby in a Mongol Inn,
    Lacrima Christi quaffed in a cloister;
    quicksilver quail in a coppice.
    Time is mountain's promise and sea's contract.

Grace Buchanan Sherwood

AFTER LAUGHTER

Laugh now but by tomorrow you may weep;
When these new fences crumble you may look
For the old, sturdy stones you scorned—they keep
Safe borders where the new ones failed or shook
To rubble—watch for fashions in this laughter
That wreck a house to the last splintered rafter.

For this is made of pride, quick to deny
Time-tested values as quite out of date;
This scornful mirth is texture of a cry
Of sharp rejection, rushing on its fate.
After these sounds by sound of sobs are drowned,
Faith's mountain spreads its roots beyond this ground.

Gene Shuford

HARVEST

In the night the man could hear the wind walking.
It tramped big-footed across the earth, talking
To itself and muttering like the rolling thunder of drums,
Its voice striking the dark and bounding like plums
That arc down a roof in a summer hail
Of bright burst red, missing the pail
Of some small boy, and, lying in the grass
Half-hidden, purple slowly into death
Where wasps come and bees drone in the breath
Of the glutted afternoon, and know dying.

But I was talking of the wind that night
(Long after the plums had lost the light)
Stalking upon his roof, beneath his floor,
Of the sound of the wind's grief beyond his door
And out in the trees where the plums still were falling
And of how the wind walked about, calling,
Telling the plums not to drop from the sky.
It was well that the man could understand
The anguish of the wind above the land
And why it wept in the grass where the plums were lying.

It is not easy to cease to be a stone:
This is what the man thought alone,
Lying at his window and watching a distant star.
And having climbed as high as a tree and so far,
Having climbed there with infinite pain,
How simple, he thought, to spill to earth again.
Plums are nothing the wind can carry far;
Fallen in a bright red hail to the ground,
They lie like the dead and make no sound,
And like the quiet dead they make no crying.

He wished he could not hear the wind that night.
He stopped his ears and, waiting for the light,
Could not shut away the wind's grief.
For the wind bears easily a seed or a leaf
But not the fall of ripened fruit to earth,
And bears not death so well as the pangs of birth.
Farmers, he knew, enjoy the sound of harvest,
But a poet feels the pain of fruit falling
Keenly as the wind, or as the last bird, calling.
No farmer, he turned in the dark and lay there, sighing.

William Vincent Sieller

WINDMILL ON THE CAPE

How long this giant hugged and spanned
Great arms around the ocean wind,
I do not know nor do I care
To tally time or measure air.

The silver-shingled, weathered tower
Has long upheld a restless flower
Whose graceful petals, patterned-four,
Fan in a circle oar by oar.

No knight has tilted at the mill
Whose fortress holds a sandy hill;
But wind, quixotic in its dance,
Has tried for conquest more than once.

Jocelyn Macy Sloan

ELIZA TELEFAIR

Wearily, still in her dressing gown,
she walked on the beach shortly after dawn
through tremulous stillness. Heat had grown

with the flowering night. *I'll go to the pier.*
Locusts thundered, "Beware, Beware!"
A shy grouse jittered, "Don't go too far."

Coiled bright-eyed in the sun-drenched brush,
"Let her alone," a grass snake hissed.

She wandered across the lake-lapped stones,
over quartz shining fishes' bones
heaped in their graveyard. "Here she comes—"

the bittern quavered. The black bass swung
in a shoreward arc, the seagull hung
from his sky trapeze as she moved along

into beckoning day. Newly begun,
no longer enwombed, she was bird and sun,
she was earth and water and fish and stone.

Nothing, yet all, she went down the pier,
wrapped in her glittering shroud of air.

Florida Watts Smyth

GREEN MOUNTAIN BOY

That's Ethan Allen on the monument
some say, and then there's others say it ain't.
Now Ethan Allen never looked like that,
officer's dress coat and sword and hat.
He carried a tomahawk and wore the thing
that came the handiest; but I can't bring
myself to saying that ain't Ethan there,
looking at Equinox. He's got a stare
like Ethan must'a had. They dressed him up,
that's all. It's him, standing there with his back
to the Congregational Church and the old clock's chime;
stubborn as stone and set to wear out time.

ETERNAL CONTOUR

It's hair and dress, framing old portrait faces,
that make them strange. Today, without the laces
and velvet, on a crowded taxi seat,
I saw a Rubens puffing out his full
red cheeks at traffic jams. Crossing the street,
a dark-haired girl on the hazardous walk to school,
with Botticelli smile, long-limbed and slight,
fixed her eyes on the changing traffic light.

Daniel Smythe

FROM MY THOUGHT

In the rain's push and the wind's hand,
The earth repeats in gales of sky.
It speaks in accents of the land,
And partial paragraphs am I.

I am the mist, the seed, the sod,
The wind in moccasins of light.
My way is dawn and flower and pod
And pouring waterfalls of night.

From my thought are the streams of spring,
Or summer crashing on the field;
Of what cicadas pulse and sing,
I am the music that they yield.

From darkness plumed with all its stars,
Or clouds descending to the day,
I am the wings, the spores, the bars,
The stone and marsh and leaf and spray.

George P. Solomos

WISDOM OF THE GAZELLE

1

Sophia, her age between
My eldest brother and
My eldest sister, is dead.

When I, then, was a child
Small enough for a carriage,
Sophia rolled me around;

She, instead of the others,
Rolled me up rolled me down—
Rolled me to Swinnerton Street.

At the corner, after dark,
Sophia upturned carriage, and me—
When I was still small.

2

Not long after this
Sophia took to ironing
My uncle's best shirt.

I stood watching
(A glass of water in my hand)
And I stood sprinkling.

When the sleeves were done
And the water was gone,
In my hand Sophia ironed
Until the iron was red.

3

When my age was eleven
And Sophia was older
I hid from her between two clocks.

I sat drawing pictures,
"From Me to Sophia" a gift—
Of Antelopes of Chickens
Of two-headed blue Giraffes.

When I was discovered
(Not a word was said):
The clocks began singing
From behind my head—

And in my hair
Three splinters remain
From a dining-table-chair
Sophia had broken.

When my age was eleven
Sophia was bolder;
I sat drawing pictures
Which were never seen.

4

One summer I had gone away.
But Sophia was taken elsewhere,
By Greyhound bus, for reasons
Which were not known to me.

I returned early in autumn.
But Sophia did not return at all,
In September, for reasons
Which were not known to me.

5

A series of visits began:
My father took me by the hand
To Sophia each Sunday—.

Packages I brought:
Chocolate bars, sandwiches
And de-nicotinized
(As she advised) cigarettes.

She showed me her hair
Cut short like my own
(But her yelling was bad).

6

A second series relayed:
Alone, I did I cottoned my ears,
Bach: *Afternoons At Four*

I would visit Sophia
In the long corridor
Which led to halls.

She showed me her wrist
With silk-worm-gut sewn
(And some years passed).

7

When lavenders bloom,
On a board I noted was listed:
No Visitors Allowed
For empty her room.

A tear from the canthus drop
But not of despairing
For marked me and scarred me
The words of the dead.

Of Sophia, of rolling
Of ironing, of clocks—
The wisdom of the gazelle
Remains in my head.

Walter Sorell

ALL THAT MATTERS ...

I

All that matters is she,
he said, and his chalice was heavy
with his great dream.

II

The dream trespassed reality.
(Or invaded reality his dream?)
She is an island in the ocean
of time, he thought. I can see
her soul dance on her skin.
I can kiss the hem of heaven
on her lips, I can touch
the wisdom of God in her palm.

III

And she made him walk
between winter and spring,
on the thin edge of the horizon,
beneath the shadow of her smile.
To him, she was everywhere
like a grand illusion,
on the seven seas of hope,
in all four corners of resignation.
And the sun of his love
frightened her into the shade.

IV

All that matters is I,
she said. Her smile turned inward
and her hands held on to herself.

Woodridge Spears

RESTORATION

New season brought sure the visible good,
At first the simple, alternate, starry leaf
On winged rough bark of liquidambar wood
In fields cut-over and assigned to grief.

Here yellow, red, and orange turned to bronze,
And brilliance of the aromatic axe
Told the adventure of his overt dawns
Cleanly whose purpose was the edged facts.

Told severance in fine, told what was here
Apparent antecedent to the keen
Stroke, linking, aimed at order, bright in air,
Told how he was the shaper we had seen.

He was a shaper of the morning bronze,
And it was he. Who would traverse the year
For us and leave earth shining in its bonds?
It was a thrust of light restored him here.

Lawrence P. Spingarn

MUSEUM PIECE

These are the signs in which my days endure:
A riddled statue with her nose knocked out,

The profile classic and the marble pure.
This irreligious goddess of my doubt
Is not time's slut to wither or grow stout:
Her smile is silent and her glance secure.
But I, being mortal, pause and twirl my hat,
The cool custodian fevered by a stone,
His blood adjusting to a habitat
Warmer than any house of flesh and bone,
His tongue a lunatic in monotone,
His muscles flabby and his arches flat.
Her smile is silent . . . This I shall repeat
Till repetition dulls the fondest ear.
Her sorcery is graphic and complete
Which renders form in statuary dear
To me, the Jason of a latter year
Piling the golden fleeces at her feet.

George Starbuck

BONE THOUGHTS ON A DRY DAY

Walking to the Museum
over the Outer Drive,
I think, before I see them
dead, of the bones alive.

How perfectly the snake smooths over the fact
he strings sharp beads around that charmer's neck.

Bird bone may be breakable, but
have you ever held a cat's jaw shut?
Brittle as ice.

Take mice:
The mouse is a berry; his bones mere seeds.
Step on him once and see.

You mustn't think that the fish
choke on those bones, or that chickens wish.

The wise old bat
hangs his bones in a bag.

Two chicks ride a bike,
unlike
that legless swinger of crutches, the ostrich.

Only the skull of a man is much of an ashtray.

Each owl
turns on a dowel.

When all the other tents are struck, an old
elephant pitches himself on his own poles.

But as for my bones—
tug of a toe, blunt-bowed barge of a thigh-bone,
gondola-squadron of ribs, and the jaw scow—
they weather the swing and storm of the flesh they plow,
out of conjecture of shore, one jolt from land.

I climb the museum steps like a beach.
There, on squared stone, some cast-up keels bleach.
Here, a dark sea speaks with white hands.

Pauline Starkweather

TWO MOUNTAINS MEN HAVE CLIMBED

1.
SINAI

The good flat earth ... and not so very high
above it, heaven fitting like a dome,

hole-pricked and set with stars . . . from time to time,
a new star blazing forth to prophesy
of royal birth or that a king must die—
all this men knew. They knew and feared the name
of that dread mountain that was Yahweh's home.
They knew enough to hide when He went by.

All this they knew—had they not eyes for proof?
Could they not hear great Yahweh in the storm?
But someone dared to climb His holy place;
somebody stuck a finger through the roof.
Lo, he that climbed the mountain knew no harm;
and he that pierced the dome found only space.

2.
PALOMAR

A billion light years . . . if an ant could see
each mote that drifts above a canyon, still
with but an ant's eyes, would he see it whole?
Could he conceive a canyon? Nor do we,
O Palomar, find in your nebulae
one shred of meaning if there is no call,
no footstep echoing there; but can you tell
if there are voices in eternity?

"And Enoch walked with God, and he was not". . .
Enoch is all that matters, Palomar.
If, at long last, you peer beyond the brink,
beyond the shining of the farthest mote,
will you then find where God and Enoch are?
The answer may be nearer than we think.

Edward Steese

TENTH REUNION

Here now once more I lie
On the cool turf at last,
After such stress as I
May name my past:

Illusioned still, untired,
But older far
Than, with their hopes still fired,
These youngsters are.

How strive they still to do
What I with ease
From my past days renew
While envying these!—

Seeing their eyes so bright
In all things young,
Their step and spirit light
And the Will strong,

Leaves me awhile to muse,
Content my lot,
And scorn the world's abuse—
As they dare not.

D. B. Steinman

BLUEPRINT

He saw it clearly and clairvoyant bright:
Twin granite pylons of majestic rise,
Founded on rock beneath the water swirl;

The lofty cables, spun of cold-drawn steel,
Cutting the sky in parabolic arcs—
A lyric pattern etched against the blue.

The spell of Euclid sang in his design:
The wizardry of radiating stays,
A geometric web to hold the stars;
The titan uplift of the singing strands;
High Gothic portals framed in stone—all these
He traced in blueprint, accurate as truth.

This magic he had made, though in the end
He did not live to see the caissons down.
The shadow of a fear that builders know
Was myth made real: 'A bridge demands a life.'
He paid the toll, the world his legatee:
His work, his dream, bridging the span of death.

Candace T. Stevenson

PUBLIC LIBRARY

Room after room, table after table,
reading lamps push up green shades
planted with regularity
like trees in a nursery.
Mandible eyes devour the printed page
as caterpillars consume the shining leaf.
Eyes advance, waver as they feed
upon the rich succulence
of words.

Helen Frith Stickney

HABITUE

Always he sits in his accustomed place
Beside the window, second from the right,
Sipping a glass of wine with lingering grace
Or with extended fingers poised to light
The smooth Corona—seasoned devotee
Following the whispered word, the sidelong glance,
Fused in a lavish room's identity,
A constant symbol amid transcience.

Here is a figure coolly set apart,
Whose look is veiled with boredom and hauteur;
Exempt from toil and the aspiring heart,
He views a vivid world as though it were
Merely a garnished menu to explore,
And life, the throb of a revolving door.

Libby Stopple

CALVARY

A mother wept: where were You, God,
The day my brave boy died?
God answered: where I was the day
My Son was crucified.

Charles Wharton Stork

A BRONZE STATUETTE OF KWAN-YIN
(The Chinese Goddess of Mercy)

Look at her, calm and benign,
    Her little hand raised to bless!
She seems not so much divine
    As a model of courtliness,

With her smooth hair built in a pile,
    Plump cheeks and birdwing brows,
Full lips hinting a smile,
    But no more than good taste allows.

The silken grace of her gown,
    Casual and yet discreet,
Looping so amply down,
    Enfolds her from breast to feet.

Lady, whatever our creed,
    We trust you with heart and mind.
How, to our anguished need,
    Can you ever be less than kind?

George Strong

THE EPIPHANY

The real was always something that came out of streets—
Jostled in crowds—
Until we found the steps that led
Into the groined forest.

In that place—stopped by the silence—
Each face was something special,
Hushed,
Humbled in earth—
And all the choked thoughts of innocence
Rushed into feeling.
In that strange place I was released—
Into your hands
Delivering the heart of me.
I could be perfect, thinking,
And when I knelt
It was to be forever kneeling.
To kiss your feet
Was nothing wrong—
To love the altar rail
And the red carpet of your blood,
The bell that beats my heart,
The small oak door that is a secret
In the wall—
In that great space our sins are nothing.
Only the men who preach
That come between us,
The iron shadows passing—
Cast from the street—
Processions of dark Matthews
In the light.
Why can't the priests be lovers?
Why must the distances grow ever greater
That go up to heaven's reach?

But now the host is gone,
The crowd coughs—is sanctified—
And shuffles feet,
Goes down the formal steps
Into the business of the street—
Outside
I saw again the common face
And heard the ordinary speech.

Julia Hurd Strong

SON AND SURF

I take him down upon the beach
And watch him hesitantly reach
The scallops of the shore.
The ripples that he goes to meet
Erase the imprints of his feet . . .
He ventures one yard more,
And now he's ankle-deep in sea!
A wave moves on determinedly
And bathes his legs knee-high,
While seaweed that the surf washed in
Tickle-scratches at his shin.
He stands quite still. And I,
Remembering, can almost feel
The sea sand sucking at his heel.

THE HUCKSTER'S HORSE

His well shaped ears were chestnut brown and they
Stuck up like pins run through the braided hat
That shaded him, as down the alleyway
He walked from gate to gate. The huckster sat
With broad patched breeches on the wagon seat
And hawked commercials, while the housewives ran
To stand bareheaded in the August heat
And measure snap beans in a granite pan.

The huckster's horse was neither dull nor slow
But patient, with his energy reined in
By strict obedience to the stop and go
Of his profession. But no discipline
Could check the tail, fly conscious and alert,
That switched his slim legs like a hula skirt.

Jesse Stuart

HEART-SUMMONED

Sometimes in bonnet that she
    used to wear,
And faded dress by wild-rose
    brambles torn,
She moves so lightly on her
    path of air
As she returns, a mother
    to her son.

She does not knock nor does she
    come within
To tell me who her new
    companions are:
She vanishes upon her path
    of wind,
Accompanied, perhaps, by
    cloud or star.

A. M. Sullivan

MONUMENT

It was a mischievous wind that pushed him; a murderous gust
    that jarred young Jan from the scaffold.

He teetered and swayed a hundred feet from the river over
    weirs of iron and concrete.

Jan clawed at the wind but the assassin slipped through his
    fingers and raced down the catwalk.

Jan reached for a cloud, for the horizon's thin line, for the
    wing of a gull that learned on the air.

The river paused at the cofferdam, fumed at the gorge, and
    boiled through the tunnels of iron,

And a thousand men at their jobs saw a shadow that
    brushed the wires and rigging.

Jan fell like a tumbling mallard, splashed in puddles of concrete,
    a spine of steel in his liver.

Jan's hat was a trophy of thieves, tossed and spun in gullies
    of air, white buttons dancing in sunlight.

But Jan was smothered unseen in a vomit of stone that poured
    from the lip of the flume,

And the lime in his bones was one with the lime that came from
    the heart of the mountain.

Water and blood were welded to stone as the breath of Jan
    rose high in a rainbow bubble,

And the bubble burst with the loosened spirit that raced from
    darkness hardening around him.

The rigor of death was matched with the rigor of stone ere they
    found Jan's hat by the river.

Rivers have flown by the tombs of the kings: the Nile,
    Euphrates, the Tiber, Yangtse, and Thames.

No king has a tomb so great as the tomb of Jan who was hurled
    from his throne by knaves of the wind.

Rich is Jan in the vastness hovering about him, the starry vault
  of the hills, the cool lake pressing against him.

No ghoul shall enter his tomb for the Union card, the pocket
  knife, and the new St. Christopher's medal.

No roar of the water in the turbines shall rouse King Jan
  in the solemn depth of his slumber

No wail of the ghosts in the windy gorge shall probe to
  the ears that are sealed with the weight of a stone,

His mouth is gagged with the silence till the blast of a
  trumpet high on the ledges of heaven.

Pounds the tombs of the world into dust and loosens the dust
  of Jan who sleeps with his back to the river.

Hollis Summers

VALENTINE

She is like pearls, of course, and rubies, and other
Extravagances, including dahlias and Venus;
She's a compendium of loveliness
Sufficient for my knowledge of the genus.

Still, loveliness has always been a bonus
For the loved as much as for the lover,
Before and during and after all. This
Is a fact I was delighted to discover.

And knowledge, such as loveliness disperses—
Despite what men including me have said—
Is frequently insufficient for a body
Which also includes an organ called the head.

Considerate of myself, male, I
Would dwell on flamboyancies. But unsheathing
Vanity a moment: she is a house
And food and the simple act of breathing.

FAMILY REUNION

A poinsettia petal drops. The rain pastes twisted flowing
    drapery
Against our Christmas windows. Our tune
Of conversation takes its key from the monotone singer
Who, before we breathed, first said, as we have said
Today for other generations, "Death has torn

Our family." We unbutton. Our digestions churn with soda. We
Eye each other, knowing soon
We can say, "Death, death has torn," of some who linger
Here among us in the tarnished green and red
Decorations we have saved from other forlorn

Gatherings of this waning clan to hang upon a frozen tree
In this hot house for Christmas afternoon.
The yellow gravy congeals on the sideboard. We breathe.
    We finger
The antimacassars and carefully count the dead.
Somewhere, surely, a child was born.

Thomas Burnett Swann

A JAPANESE BIRTHDAY WISH

I wish a cricket in a wicker boat
To swing above your hearth and sing to you
Of gardens, silverly.
I wish a pink pagoda, dwarf bamboo,

And tea-house circled by a milky moat
Where silkworms spin you mornings of repose;
And in your camphor tree,
A firefly like a little yellow rose

To make of night
A forest flowered with light.

Grace Cornell Tall

THE NEEDLE

Regard the little needle
Bespoken by the Lord:
No weighted soul can wheedle
An entry past its sword.

But he who will diminish
Himself for Love may march
In triumph through the needle's
Microscopic arch.

Sarah Wingate Taylor

WITH METAPHOR

A sculptor first in breath and blood,
intent on firm, clean-bevelled tone,
he fashions here a thing so good
the blades of Time will blunt upon.

Endowed with brief bright godhead (sand
the shifting ground he walks and shade)
he builds, lo he has scaled and spanned
Oblivion with this wonder made.

Behold his black gangs drag great rocks
slow on the blazing desert, lay
in fitted niches perfect blocks,
and he the Pharaoh of this day

to wield, decree, move Egypt. More,
his armies and his sweating slaves
are only poet with metaphor
to pile his temples, hew his caves.

He quarries in his soul to cut
the inner store of him and haul
astounding energies that shut
all time in his enigma: Small

soon and shrunken he lies hid
still master in his pyramid.

Myra Burnham Terrell

THEODOSIA BURR

Still the ghost of Joseph Alston
Wanders, grieving through your garden,
Calling sadly, "Theodosia."
All the old oaks echo, "Theo."
They remember when he brought you
Proudly to his southern mansion,
Charleston's loveliest 'first lady.'
Sometimes in the soft spring evenings,

Jasmine and magnolia perfumed,
They still whisper to each other
Of the halcyon days you spent here,
Beautiful as white camellias,
Charming all who came to know you.

Theodosia, now another
June is drenched with jasmine fragrance;
From the tamaracks and willows,
Mockingbirds, ill winds forgotten,
Fill the air with flutelike music.
No one now recalls the morning
You took passage on *The Patriot*
With your son to visit Aaron.

Was it true, as rumor whispered,
Jean Lafitte and his bold pirates,
Met your ship upon the high sea,
Took its treasure, kept you captive,
Leaving all the rest to perish?

Did you live to lose your reason,
Prisoned on some southern island;
Grieve there for your absent husband,
Mourn the little son you'd lost, or
Were you spared all this by drowning?

Dorothy Brown Thompson

AUTOSONIC DOOR

Move over, Ali Baba! Now there comes
A parallel to open sesame
And all abracadabras. Nothing hums
Our ears can hear, and it is plain to see

That nothing touched the door. And yet it moved.
"Moved, nevertheless," in Galileo's phrase,
Yet no phrase frames the magic. We have proved
The reasons, but the wonders still amaze.

Is it so strange that children in our time
For fantasy must turn to outer space?
No earthly Everest is left to climb;
A witchcraft door like this is commonplace.
So fancy hurtles blithely past the thunder
To stake the planets. Man must have his wonder.

Gertrude Tiemer-Wille

REPAST

Mice masticate from crumb to tooth,
The poor from hand to mouth;
This is the custom everywhere
From Lapland to the south.

The wealthy dine from soup to nuts,
Dogs feed from plate to pan;
Now I will tell you how I eat,
From can—to can—to can.

Eve Triem

GARDENS ARE ALL MY HEART

Gardens are all my heart,
Are my days and duties;
And my sleep at night.

Dishgarden or Hesperides,
The grassed cathedral close,
The jugwatered Persian trees.

Caved man wove the myth,
Using a thread of truth
Found on a periled path.

Man told an Eden-dream:
From a tree he came,
A daisy, his cradle-home;

A sparrow, his fountain
Ringing the latter rain
Upon his yarrow mountain.

He walked God in the green,
Imaged the pace of pain
By a serpent lure to sin.

What is sin? For the snake
Is the sign bringing back
The dead, breaking the yoke

Of the legend of loss.
What is death but a veiled place
And gate to garden days?

Gardens are all my heart,
Love's lawn, my days and duties;
Saint's grove, my rest at night.

Ulrich Troubetzkoy

OUT OF THE WILDERNESS

Out of the wilderness, ax-cleared
for the brash litter of towns,
earth puckered by the bull-tongue plow,
out of New England, Pennsylvania,
out of Virginia—
out of the wilderness of blood,
random and pedigreed,
haphazard genes and accidental names
mingling in long-boned, Indian-haired,
sad-eyed children—
out of the wilderness, out of the trough
scooped in blue mountains of Virginia,
out of the Shenandoah,
Abraham, Bathsheba and their sons,
Josiah, Mordecai and Tom,
with meal and dried beef in their saddlebags,
full powder horns and the long rifles handy,
over Boone's Trace, the Cumberland Gap,
to the Green River of Kentucky,
where innocent acres grew so tall with corn
that cougar-footed Indians could hide
waiting for Abraham—

A girl, crossing the watersheds, climbed
the passes of the mountains, singing,
singing to the baby in her arms
on the Wilderness Road,
the cruel long songs of Virginia,
the melodies as old as heartbreak but the words
already warped by distances,—
Fair Ellendor and *Barbary Ellen*—
as the memory of sea blurs in the sound of grass.

Nancy would grow up, small against the wilderness,
dark-haired like her mother's song, and learn to read,
lining the Bible out methodically.
Her roots sheared by the mountains, save that some
remnants of tales and tunes still troubled her, a scarf,
a pin, a skillet from the past.
Restless with unshaped hungers, Nancy Hanks
leaned toward the tugging skyline in the West.
This was the girl Tom Lincoln hankered for,
seeing her slim against the firelight.
He talked of cutting timber, how he'd build
a cabin of their own on Nolin Creek
among the flowering crab-apple trees.
They might have known, so many crop years more
in stony yellow clay and they'd move on,
on in the endless exodus—but then they'd take a boy,
Kentucky-born, into the wilderness.

Joseph Tusiani

ANTICIPATION

If, before being earth, the thought of sound
Was in God's mind what this near music is
In me before my love is word, I know
The joy of the creation of all things,
And can foretell the beauty of the sun.
A sudden feeling, a presentiment
Of fingers moist with laurel dew before
The green is born to make the laurel tree;
A tranquil trembling of the eyelids, won
By the splendor, before the shape of heaven—
I know what Nature will soon be, I feel
Within my heart the blend of God and man.

REST O SUN I CANNOT

O now I know: a smile
Can be the story of one who fell asleep
At the foot of the cross and woke to find
Christ risen and the nails become soft stalks.

This is the resurrection's lasting fruit—
To be part of the healed earth, and to know
That here on my same earth, next door,
The man who did not see the tempest end
Is voice of me forever. Rest, O sun,
I cannot, till I reconcile my time
With your eternal charity of light.

Stella Weston Tuttle

THE QUICKENING

Before she saw him in the wood,
saw Gabriel,
Mary stood
unbreathing, startled and aware
of something more than silence there
beneath the shadowed boughs—

of words
soft spoken as the lift of birds
through stillness
or the sudden rush
of whirring wings in underbrush.

Words like wings became a cloud
about her shoulders;
never loud
but soft as feathers are, they spread
in galaxies above her head—

she, the innocent, whose laughter
would know the weight of wings thereafter.

The slow days passed as Mary went
musing
wrapped in shy content
her grave eyes full of peace. It seemed
almost that she had dreamed
Gabriel—
had dreamed the light
which turned her tremulous and bright
that hour she learned of wondrous things
folded close
in sweep of wings.

Then summer-heavy, Mary heard
again each hushed, each secret word,
remembering
as something stirred.

Mark Van Doren

THIS AMBER SUNSTREAM

This amber sunstream, with an hour to live,
Flows carelessly, and does not save itself;
Nor recognizes any entered room—
This room; nor hears the clock upon a shelf,
Declaring the lone hour; for where it goes
All space in a great silence ever flows.

No living man may know it till this hour,
When the clear sunstream, thickening to amber,
Moves like a sea, and the sunk hulls of houses
Let it come slowly through, as divers clamber,

Feeling for gold. So now into this room
Peer the large eyes, unopen to their doom.

Another hour and nothing will be here.
Even upon themselves the eyes will close.
Nor will this bulk, withdrawing, die outdoors
In night, that from another silence flows.
No living man in any western room
But sits at amber sunset round a tomb.

THE CLOSE CLAN

Even from themselves they are a secret,
The like ones that dwell so far asunder:
So far, and yet the same; for gold is gold
In any earth, and thunder repeats thunder.

They are the scattered children of what pair,
What patient pair so long ago extinguished?
But the flesh lives, in certain ones that wind
And dust and simple being have distinguished.

Whatever these, and howsoever born,
They are the ones with perfect-lidded eyes,
Quieter than time, that yet can burn,
Can burn in rage and wonder and sunrise.

They are the ones that least of all the people
Know their own fewness, or the loving fear
Such lineage commands—that ancient couple,
And these their growth in grace's afteryear.

In them the world lives chiefly, as gold shines,
As thunder runs in mountains, and hearts beat.
They are the ones who comprehend the darkness,
And carry it all day, and sweeten it.

WHEN THE WORLD ENDS

When the world ends it is too much to hope,
And yet I do, that neither knife nor rope,
Nor sudden flame, nor worse than sudden freeze,
Is executioner. No less than these
Implacable, what if gold autumn came
And stayed till it was weary—spread the same
Cool hectic over waters and wild boughs
That now arrives but for a week's carouse;
Then winter? What if such a wonder fall
Kept on as if it were the end, the all?
What if it were, and centuries of red
So flushed each field and roof and river bed
That death itself lay down, and nothing died
Till all things did, beneath a shower as wide
As oceans of together-dropping leaves?
What if it were, and still no late reprieves
Canceled the utter end? I do not keep
That hope; and yet I dream of this slow sleep,
This indolent, this all but evermore
October such as never came before.

Beren Van Slyke

THE SHEPHERDS

Poets like shepherds on green hills
    Drowse near their browsing sheep,
Lead lambs to cover from hawks that hover
    Above the shelving steep.

Theirs is an ancient realm of words
    Where rhyme and time can turn
In mortal gesture to immortal
    Traceries on an urn;

Where creep and weep are half-asleep
    As death takes breath to bed,
Where ever has a daughter never
    Denies all she has said;

Dusk is the husk of the hazelnut sun
    Fringing the arc of the dark:
Sweet is the meat to them who feed on
    The unearthly mirth of the lark.

Like shepherds on a leopard's hill
    The poets hold their sheep,
Bell them at dawn, tell them at evening
    In what fold they must sleep.

Linda Lyon Van Voorhis

TO A HUMBLE BUG

Poor humble roach
Your plain secluded ways would seem beyond reproach
And your ancestral mother I believe
Has been declared far antedating Eve.
Unvexed by human ills and human lore
Your ranks unthinned by internecine war
Your pure communal living should succeed
For each bug has according to his need.
No bug is master, each one for himself—
None cares if he is left upon a shelf.

Isabel Williams Verry

ALCESTIS

It was lonely in the zero dark, Admetus,
not even the ghosts of flowers for company
but moving animals
invisible
plush-footed
while outside the tomb
the god of death gulped sacrificial blood.

The dead are nothing, you have said.
The pore and marrow of their god, as well,
is nothing.
Who but Heracles
could box with marsh-gas or with cloud
and buffet it to bargaining?
He caught my hand
before death's leprous love-making began
and led me to the presence of my lord.

Veiled, mute, I stand
vertical flesh
not horizontal bone
which you unrecognizing yet desire
forgetful of your celibate oath when I
(not father, no, nor mother either)
withdrew, your proxy, into onyx cold.

It was too lonely there
(sealed under midnight, fear locked in the brain)
remembering the living
ticks away
downy with sun, ripe-blooded as the grape.

I am returned, Admetus,
but instead

of that pale sister that the sculptors formed
to comfort you bereaved
you now have two
Alcestis replicas.
Nor wish nor will
can strike a fingerling of fire from one
who died for your too acquiescent sake.

George Sylvester Viereck

AFTER THE BATTLE
(1930)

I struck for what I deemed the right.
I saw the Truth. I was her knight.
My foemen, too, were thus aflame,
Blind chessmen in the obscure game
Of some malign divinity.

Now, with unfolding eyes, I see
The paradox of every fight,
That both are wrong and both are right,
That friend is foe, and foe is friend,
And nothing matters in the end.

Harold Vinal

THE QUEST

We came to the islands. We came saying:
Here there is peace, the voyage passed, gale, thunder,
The sleepless nights, the watches. Swept landward,
It was as it had been before, tall tamaracks under

A cloud-whipped sky, the vales, the estuaries,
The wild, slow summer. So at nightfall we pitched
Our lean-to by a hill; we found
Sleep in the gut of night; we stretched

Aching limbs and forgot, glad of the islands.
Occasionally there were fowl plumaged upon the streams,
Occasionally deer, but always the electric water
Broke in upon our words and upon our dreams.

We heard the dynamo sea below, we heard
Waves leaping under the night-hawk firs,
And knew there was no rest for us, that ever
We would be wanderers.

And now for a year or more we have sailed, journeyed
Upon a chartless errand, our hopes riven,
Not knowing what we seek—if it be earth
Or love or death or, beyond chaos, heaven.

William S. Wabnitz

THE HINDS OF KERRY

Past them he strode
    and through the towns of Kerry
With his stick.

They found him snoring
    when the nights were faery
Underneath a rick.

On market days and at mid-summer fair
    The worthless fellow
Was always there. Then frost came in the air
    And leaves were yellow.

They had not missed him when
    in February,
In the drear
Winter, they found him in a ditch,
    the hinds of Kerry,
Working, working near.

Charles A. Wagner

THREE CITY CANTOS

    1.

Which are the living? We who stride unyielding
    earth in engine fumes
or they who, done with breathing, bide in verdant tombs?

Which are the dead? They free to coil the seasons
    to a rung of tree
or we who, living, sense a soil we never see?

    2.

The kiss will carve the granite through and leave
    no trace of residue;
though boulder drool across the road, the
    carnal chiseling will goad
until the stone has molted crust and shaped the urging
    to the lust—
as ever the wind did love, and must!

    3.

When my poor substance thins away to gaseous
    fantasies of clay
make only grass of me, I pray:

a patch of common walking-grass for feet that once
    were mine to pass,
for lover to invite his lass;

to nourish insect hordes and herds, to implement the
    beaks of birds
with song far too profound for words.

Mary Boyd Wagner

THE LETHAL THOUGHT

The flowing robe of words you weave
    To cover up your thought,
However well it may deceive,
    Adds naught to naught.

For I have felt the angry thing,
    So deftly hid from view,
And writhed to see its lethal sting
    Destroying you.

Dee Walker

ET CETERA

Floods and gales
Denude the land,
But crabs and snails
Imprint the sand.

Geese fly South
When winter blows;

But after the drouth
A rainbow shows.

The dew on the web,
Spots on the sun,
And tides that ebb
Are silver spun.

Dice and luck,
Lovers and birds,
A doe and a buck
Never need words.

If love is king
Are kisses pure?
When is Spring?
And are you sure?

May Williams Ward

WET SUMMER

The hollyhocks are ten feet tall,
The larkspur deeply colored;
Once dried-up lakes are nearly full
And shelter half-grown mallard.

The ivy overflows its urn.
The elm which long drouth withered
Revives, and on each branch-tip burn
Bright leaflets, newly feathered.

The crows have grown not quite so rude,
The robins, fat as butter.
They chant a new Beatitude:
    Blessed be water!

Hamilton Warren

REQUIEM

Let the mountains stand forth!
Let a Northwind whip the lake waters
Till the bright stallions charge
And the blue mares shake foam from their lips!
Let the high pines roar
And the young birches crouch
And a dazzle and gleam and a shining be borne
On the breath of a wide-hearted morning!

But at dusk, when the glitter has faded,
Let the small waves remember in turquoise and rose
And sweetly, and low, her requiem sing
Who was gentle and kind
And lies dreaming
Of sunlight on viable water.

James E. Warren, Jr.

SCHOOLROOM: 158—

Why do you lean beside the window, Will?
What do you hear upon the Warwick wind?
I hear the snarling of the Thane of Fife,
the laugh of Rosalind.

Your scholars stare, and they are whispering!
Why are you smiling now? What are your dreams?
I smile at one who is clad in motley and one
who rails beside Arden streams.

The room is still except for goose quills scratching.
The heads are bowed. The scholars scarcely stir.
I cry upon Saint George before the iron
high ramparts of Harfleur.

Now Caesar's eagle leaps to Roman glory.
The boys thrill to the music of the swords.
But I am sick for Thames, for English triumph,
for salty English words.

But here is life and here is England, Will.
Mark you this lad. His face is English-wise.
Aye . . . but his hair is yellow as a Dane's.
He has a prince's eyes.

Irma Wassall

STONE FROM THE GODS

These are the words
that long ago a Grecian heard
flung from Olympus: Why
do you mourn for joy the gods deny?
For a splintered dream, a blown
frail bauble less than glass?
The gods have given you a stone,
you grieve, and you have thrown
the blue and clouded thing upon the grass.

With a rain of tears no longer drench
your empty hands, nor lift them, clenched,
toward the Mountain: Take up the stone, and cherish
it in your hands no longer empty,
and still your tears that dimmed the stone,
that its fire may never perish.

Gaze at the stone, the jewel of the mind
the generous gods have flung from Heaven, and atone
for the bitter hour that you were blind.
Then gaze again into the jewel heart,
and even in the d~~k, discover
the star within the stone.

Tessa Sweazy Webb

BRIGHT ABANDON

The hills are calling me from care and reason
Away from chaos of the city's din,
To silent beauty of the russet season,
Where smoke of Indian summer, blue and thin,
Rises from autumn's slowly dying fire.

For these, a bright abandon bids me follow
The primitive design of each proud tree,
Where I shall hear an echo in the hollow,
And learn the secret of infinity—
That only seekers find what they desire.

Now when summer's smile is sad and sober,
The linnet and the lark have made retreat;
When chestnut, oak and maple meet October
To lay their leaves of amber at her feet,
Here is an altar where the brown ash spills.

These autumn colors have a rainbow beauty
That shames the sunset, or the afterglow.
And though I hear the urgent call of duty,
I must abandon city walls and go—
For I am friend and comrade of the hills.

James L. Weil

AT A LOSS

If asked the day that this man dies,
I shall say he fell

In love with Death, and realize
The immaterial

Way she takes us—leaving presence
Of mind here no answer,

Almost an impertinence
To him embracing her.

Cecil Cobb Wesley

AS NIGHT COMES ON

As night comes on great flocks of dreams
Settle on the minds of men—
As passive as the forest-trees
Invaded by the owl and wren.

A bird as sparkling as red wine
Pauses on the dying pine.

And from the green and growing bay
A hawk drives other wings away.

A strange bird lights on the sycamore
Migrant from an alien shore.

As day comes on great flocks of dreams
Fly out toward the vastest sea
And not a twig and not a thought
Remember where they used to be.

John Hall Wheelock

THE DIVINE INSECT

Already it's late summer. Sun-bathers go
Earlier now. Except for those who lie
Dazed between sea-music and radio
The beach is bare as the blue bowl of the sky,
Where a cloud floats, solitary and slow.

And up the beach, where at mid-summer's height
One gull with occasional lurch and pause would steer
Onward his leisurely loose-winged casual flight,
Gull wings weave patterns, their noise floods the ear
Like a fugue, cry answering cry in hoarse delight.

Now on the beach there also may be found
Straddled in mimic flight, with arching wing,
Spread either way, some gull swift death has downed
There, like a tumbled kite whose severed string
Kept it in heaven by binding it to the ground.

Inland, when the slant evening sun-beams touch
Leaves, long obscured in tunnelled shade, to flame,
The divine insect, for I called him such,
Begins his high thin music. To my shame
I never learned what he was, who owe him so much.

Listening to his frail song, so pure, so dim,
I made my poems, he was mystery's decoy,
Something far and lost just over the rim
Of being, or so I felt, and as a boy
I wove fantastic notions about him.

Throughout long evenings and hushed midnights when
Grasshoppers shrilled, his barely perceptible note
Wound on like a thread of time, while my pen
Made its own scratchy music as I wrote.
The divine insect and I were comrades then.

That highly hypnotic sound opened some door
On a world seemingly come upon by chance,
But a world, surely, I had known before.
Deeper I sank into a timeless trance—
Strange thoughts and fancies troubled me more and more.

I could pass through that minuscule sound, it seemed to me,
As through a fine tube, getting smaller and still more small,
Until I was smaller than nothing—then, suddenly,
Come to the other end of the tube, and crawl
Out, into glittering immensity.

For if by travelling west you shall come east
Or, as Einstein has it, the continuum
Curves on itself, may we not through the least
Come to the largest, and so finally come
Back where we were, undiminished and unincreased.

Since then I have tried to put this into verse,
But language limits the sense it often mars—
I still believe, for better or for worse,
We look through one atom into all the stars,
In the note of one insect hear the universe.

These few green acres where so many a day
Has found me, acres I have loved so long,

Have the whole galaxy for crown, and stay
Unspoiled by that. Here in some thrush's song
I have heard things that took my breath away.

It is a country out of the world's ken,
Time has no power upon it. Year on year,
Summer unfolds her pageant here again—
I have looked deep into all being here
Through one loved place far from the storms of men.

Here often, day and night, there will be heard
The sea's grave rhythm, a dark undertone
Beneath the song of insect or of bird—
Sea-voices by sea-breezes landward blown,
And shudder of leaves by the soft sea-wind stirred.

In the jade light and gloom of woodland walks
The spider lily and slender shinleaf stand,
The catbird from his treetop pulpit talks
The morning up, and in the meadowland
The velvet mullein lift their woolly stalks.

The world grows old. Ageless and undefiled
These stay, meadow and thicket, wood and hill:
The green fly wears her golden dress, the wild
Grape is in bloom, the fork-tailed swallow still
Veers on the wind as when I was a child.

And in mid-August, when the sun has set
And the first star out of the west shows through,
The divine insect, as I call him yet,
Begins his faint thin note, so pure, so true,
Putting me ever deeper in his debt.

The old enchantment takes me as before,
I listen, half in dream, hearing by chance
The soft lapse of the sea along the shore,
And sink again into that timeless trance,
Deeper and deeper now, and more and more.

Margaret Widdemer

AS I LAY QUIET

As I lay quiet
      From weeping sore
My father and mother
      Came in at the door.

They stood in the dark by me
      Arm-in-arm,
They said, "We were young,
      We meant no harm,

"We were only lovers
      Our world went gay with
Who thought a child
      Would be fine to play with—"

But there was no word
      I could find to say
Till daylight came
      And they went away.

COMFORT

You told me Age was a black wolf that lay
To spring from the night-cave where we must pass,
A yellowing that brittled fern and grass,
A python, slowly gulping day and day,
And ice that dulled to ash the living starm
A shaming thickening fungus, that must reach
All men and women who cried each to each

"How beautiful, how wonderful you are!"
An end at best past power to sing or grieve . . .

No, no, my darling! You must not believe!
Have you not known, no thing can ever die?
Have you not seen dawns rise, new suns upraying?
Then what is evil in a twilight's graying,
What is there cruel in a sunset sky?

Dedie Huffman Wilson

SPEAK TO THE SUN

You, Voyager, with exile-heart that yearns
Forever toward the quintessential sun,
The road is bleak. It forks before it turns
To skirt the confines of oblivion.
Look only on the tall, symbolic flame
That fires the crags of midnight and of noon;
Deny the labyrinthine way you came,
Deaf to the storm of darkness, and immune.

Ignore Death's weak command, its worn decree.
Speak to the sun. Tell all the winds of dawn
That man must find his lost identity
In vanquished selves, in lives by life withdrawn:
Must be reborn and cradled in old skies
That fill with light his young and wondering eyes.

Mary Winter

BLESSING THE HOUNDS

Frosty, the bite of the autumn air
And the leaf, blood-red, on the church steps, where
The huntsmen are gathering, scarlet dressed,
Waiting to hear their good hounds blessed.

Now may St. Hubert and word of priest
Give drive and power to every beast
In the whip-held huddle that waits nearby,
With lolling tongue and shivering thigh.

Let nose be keen and limb be fleet
To follow the scent, so maddening, sweet;
And sharp the tooth for the last attack,
In at the death, the yelping pack.

But you—red miscreant, oh fox!
Small, unblessed, unorthodox,
Will need your own and the Devil's cunning
Today when the hunters and hounds are running.

LOWER FORMS OF LIFE

Who has not thought, when scuffing shells
Thick strewn upon the beach,
Of perishable bodies
That lived awhile in each?

The lime-white, spiral, fluted case,
Clean-scoured by wind and tide,
Lies comelier in death than we,
Who wear our bones inside.

Frances Winwar

AUTUMN

Now Autumn comes, the wise fool of the year
In tattered motley, in his hand the dry
And chattering gourd and on his head the sere
Pods of the milkweed, the white silk awry
Like hair thought-tangled. Up above, so near
You see the white and gray of breast and thigh,
The great V of the duck clan in its flight
To kinder suns; and on the pond's edge, still,
On one leg poised, the heron cocks his sight
For some incautious frog. Now down the hill
Comes lumbering the wagon with the hay.—
You scent, before you see, it. Slyly you
Reach out to snatch a straw, and mutely say
A wish, and half believe it will come true.

Harry Woodbourne

THE FLUTE OF MAY

In grey April when the bud rounded
Fat on the black twig,
But no bird landed,
Silent I too stood there,
Tuneless and bare,
Slapped by the cold wind
In the thin and voiceless air.

Looking about,
As an artist without tool
Craves instrument
To give his longing form,
I found a young Scotch broom,
Wind-orphaned and wind-rent,
And plunged it in the ground to root and bloom.

Like pollen raining down,
Starlight poured out
All the dew-scented night,
Yellow on brown.
By day the trees, leaf-bright,
Spread plumages of green
For winds and birds to tinkle in and preen.

The sun's red ray rouged April's bud and shoot,
And as the sprout
Of that Scotch broom tongued out,
My tongue uncurled the word
Till then unlearned,
And I began to play
The bird-sweet flute of May.

Catharine Morris Wright

HILLSIDE PAUSE

Butternut and walnut
butternut and bees;
We upon the hillside lying,
apples at our knees,
passing pleasantries—

Walnut black and heady,
Four of us together;
checked shirt on its back,
pants of duck and leather
lying indolent and slack
in the soft weather,
soft as a feather.

Look, you in pink gingham;
you in wool sleeves;
Over yonder on the hill
yonder under leaves
where the honeysuckle weaves
lies a fox, inert and still,
watching us as foxes will,
from the corn sheaves.

So we see a peace proceed;
chewing bits of pod,
scraps of bark and apple seed,
on the hard sod;
quivering as the fox indeed
and one eye watching God.

Butternut and walnut,
butternut and breath,
these are things as actual
and permanent as death;
let butternut and walnut
multiply before
other men, another day,
contemplate a war
on the hill floor—
"A late apple's good," I say,
laying down the core.

Jennette Yeatman

EXILE

I look on kingship in high pines;
I walk through park-wide gardens, grown
With white blooms rarer than the rose,
    But they are not my own.

This sun, that shreds slow morning mist
After the film of night is spun,
Stiffens my flesh with flameless cold:
    It is a stranger-sun.

Where thread-thin twigs cut black, before
The last spread of blue evening dye,
These hard, impassive stars flare on
    Out of an alien sky.

Down deepened streams, no mother nymph
Sings me warm-throated welcoming;
The bitter water that I drink
    Flows from a silent spring.

I hear no reed-drawn call, to be
One with the wheel of night and day;
While my lips thirst, on stone-green sod,
    Old gods sleep far away.

Virginia Brady Young

THE TEACHER

Writer, attend no schools,
no Summer Conferences.
Obtain your degree from the cat.
Exquisitely concentrating
he savours his meat.
O, the power in his stare!
His leap, a dagger in the air.
By instinct slow then swift,
he does not know
that Stare is from God
and Leap the Devil's gift,
but knows the taste of his meat.

Biographical Notes

ABBE, GEORGE received his B.A. from the University of New Hampshire (1933) and his M.A. from the University of Iowa (1938). He has taught at various campuses and is now Resident Poet at Russell Sage. Among his published volumes of verse are *Wait for These Things* (Holt 1940), *Bird in the Mulberry* (Marshall Jones 1954), and *The Incandescent Beast* (American Weave 1957). He has also published books of fiction and non-fiction. In 1956 he won the Shelley Award. He was born in Somers, Conn. in 1911.

ACTON, ELLEN M., who teaches English at Jamaica High School, is a painter as well as a poet. Her verse has appeared in Poetry, Poetry Review, The New York Times, etc. She succeeded Elias Lieberman as Poet Laureate of the N. Y. School Garden Association, which post she currently holds. Miss Acton was born in New York City in 1902.

AGNEW, MARJORIE L. is the author of *And the Moon Be Still As Bright*, published in 1956 by Banner Press. A West Virginian by birth, Miss Agnew was educated in her native town of Charleston.

ALBERT, SAMUEL L. is on the Board of Directors of the New England Poetry Society. Born in Boston in 1911, he received his A.B. from Harvard College (1934). He is represented with six poems in *New Poems by American Poets #2*, edited by Rolfe Humphries (1957).

ALEXANDER, FRANCES won a $2000 scholarship in Southwestern Literature at the University of Texas in 1946 for *Mother Goose on the Rio Grande*, a book of Mexican folklore in rhymed translations. Miss Alexander, who was born in Blanco, Tex. in 1888 and took degrees at Baylor and Columbia (B.A., M.A.), has also published three books of her own poetry.

ALLEN, GRACE ELISABETH is the author of a first book of poems *The Mother Beach* (The Fine Editions Press 1959). A native of St. Paul, Minn., Miss Allen attended the Finch School and the New York School of Social Work, and earned her B.S. and M.A. at Columbia. During World War II she was Assistant to the Director of Military and Naval Welfare Service, American Red Cross.

ALLEN, SARA VAN ALSTYNE, born in Philadelphia in 1905, received her B.A. from Pomona College in 1927. A member of Pen and Brush and other poetry groups, she served on the Board of the PSA for several years. Her verse has appeared in the Yale Review, Harper's, The New Yorker, and Thomas Moult's Anthology, *Best Poems of the Year*.

ALTROCCHI, JULIA COOLEY has contributed to Harper's, Poetry, and other magazines. Her published works include *Poems of a Child* (Harper 1904), *Dance of Youth* (Sherman French 1917) and several books of prose. She has received many literary awards. Born in Seymour, Conn. in 1895, she earned her A.B. at Vassar in 1914.

ALYEA, DOROTHY is an alumna of Wellesley. She is the author of *All My Argument* (1935) and *Beach Fire* (1951), and has contributed verse to Poetry and other magazines. She was born in Portland, Ore. in 1898.

AMES, EVELYN, a native of Hamden, Conn., was born in 1908. She attended Vassar College. She has contributed to Voices, Saturday Review, etc. Dodd Mead published her collection of poems *The Hawk from Heaven* (1958) as well as two books of prose.

ANGOFF, CHARLES is the author of nearly thirty books of fiction and non-fiction, including *Between Day and Dark* (a multi-volume study of Jewish life in America) and *When I Was a Boy in Boston* (short stories). He was born in Minsk, Russia in 1902 and is Adjunct Professor of English at Fairleigh Dickinson University and co-editor of The Literary Review.

ANT, HOWARD, a native New Yorker born in 1927, received his B.A. from Brooklyn College and his LL.B. from Harvard Law School. He is an attorney by profession. On two occasions he was the recipient of the PSA monthly first prize. He has also served as Discussion Leader.

ARCHER, KATE RENNIE has published seven volumes of poems, among them *Recurrent Vigil* and *Jock Tamson's Bairns*. Her work has appeared in many periodicals, here and abroad. A native of Scotland, Miss Archer received degrees in literature from Glasgow University, the Sorbonne, and Lausanne. She served as Graduate Lecturer at Dominican College for fifteen years.

ARMKNECHT, RICHARD F., born in Donnellson, Iowa in 1901, is a graduate of Rensselaer Polytechnic Institute and the U.S. Naval Academy. He served as a naval officer for thirty years and now teaches civil engineering at Northeastern University. He is the author of two books of verse.

ARNSTEIN, FLORA J., a native Californian, was born in 1885 and received her education at the University of California and San Francisco State College. She taught music and dancing for many years. In 1951 Stanford University Press published her *Adventure into Poetry*, a treatise on the teaching of poetry to children. Miss Arnstein's verse has appeared in the London Mercury, Poetry, etc.

ASH, SARAH LEEDS has contributed to many magazines and newspapers and is the author of a book, *Little Things*. She was educated at the University of Pennsylvania and taught in Atlantic City (N. J.) schools. She was born in 1904.

AUXIER, SYLVIA TRENT, a native of Kentucky (1900), holds degrees from the University of Cincinnati and Pikeville College, Kentucky. She is a high school teacher. Among her four published volumes of verse are *Meadow-Rue* (1948) and *No Stranger to the Earth* (1958).

AVRETT, ROBERT received his B.A. from the University of Texas in 1928 and in 1936-37 was Harrison Fellow in Romanics at the University of Pennsylvania. A U.S. State Department official, he served as Director of Instituto Cultural Argentine-Norteamericano in Argentina (1945-46). He is currently an English instructor at the University of Tennessee. His three published volumes include a book of verse, *The Dream Comes First* (John W. Luce Co. 1949). Mr. Avrett was born in Texas in 1901.

AYER, ETHAN began to write verse in his senior year at Trinity College and later studied the subject at Columbia. He published a novel with Little, Brown in 1951. In recent years he has contributed to the Literary Review, American Weave, etc. He has also served as guest editor of Voices. In collaboration with Alec Wilder he wrote a musical based on *The Importance of Being Ernest*, scheduled for Broadway production. Mr. Ayer was born in South Hamilton, Mass.

BAKER, KARLE WILSON of Nacogdoches, Tex. is a native of Little Rock, Ark., where she was born in 1878. She holds an honorary Litt.D. degree from Southern Methodist University. Among her nine published books are two works of fiction and three collections of verse. Her first book in the latter field was *Blue Smoke* (1919), followed by *Burning Bush* (1922), both brought out by the Yale University Press.

BALDWIN, MARY NEWTON is the author of *Here in These Hills* (Durham Chapbook 1946). Past president of the Poetry Society of Vermont, she is now managing editor of that society's magazine, The Mountain Troubadour. A resident of Montpelier, Vt., Miss Baldwin was born in Burlington. She received her Ph.B. from the University of Vermont and studied at Wellesley and at Universidad Internacional, Santander, Spain. Her writing has appeared in magazines and newspapers.

BARBER, FRANCES, born in Waterbury, Conn. in 1881, entered Wellesley but left almost immediately because of illness. She traveled extensively in the Near East just before World War I, and has devoted most of her time to Defense and Red Cross work. Brimmer Company in 1923 published her volume of poetry, *Realms We Fashion*, edited by William Stanley Braithwaite. Serious eye-trouble prevented further work for many years. Miss Barber's poems have appeared in Yale Review, Poetry World, and elsewhere.

BARBER, MELANIE GORDON, a resident of Connecticut, was born in Anniston, Ala. A graduate of Columbia University, she studied at the University of Mexico and abroad. She has contributed to the Saturday Review and other periodicals, and is author of *Peace*

— *An Ode for the Morning of Christ's Nativity*, for which Nicholas Murray Butler wrote the foreword. Mrs. Barber is a former Vice-Pesident of the Three Arts Club.

BARKER, EDNA L. S. won the PSA annual first prize in 1951, and in 1953 the annual second prize. She is at work on two books. A past president of the Albany County Poetry Society, Mrs. Barker was born in Washington, D. C. in 1890. She is now a resident of Crown Point, N. Y.

BARR, ISABEL HARRISS is a graduate of the College of New Rochelle with the degree of B. Litt. *cum laude*. She is a native of Greenville, Tex. Her *Sword Against the Breast*, a volume of poems, was published by Putnam in 1935. Among her other published books is *Jericho Road* (Baker 1948). Formerly associate editor of The Poetry Chap-Book, Mrs. Barr has contributed poetry and reviews to a number of magazines and newspapers. In private life she is Countess Aria.

BARTLETT, ELIZABETH was born in New York City in 1913 and received her B.S. from Teachers College. She taught at Southern Methodist University from 1947-49 and has been book reviewer, lecturer, poetry reader and consultant at writers' conferences. Her published works include *Behold This Dream* (Editorial Jus S. A., Mexico, 1959). She is a 1959 Fellow of the Huntington Hartford Foundation.

BECK, REV. VICTOR E. is Secretary of the Literature Department of the Augustana Book Concern. A native of St. James, Minn., he now lives in Rock Island, Ill. Among his many published works is a book of verse, *Time's Borderland* (1953). In 1952 he was knighted with the Order of the North Star by the King of Sweden.

BEHREND, ALICE recently retired from a teaching post at Julia Richmond High School in New York, her native city. After graduating from Hunter College, she attended Columbia and New York University. She has contributed poetry to Spirit, the Poetry Chap-Book, the Vineyard Gazette, and other magazines and newspapers.

BENET, LAURA is a Vassar graduate. Early in life she engaged in social settlement work, later doing editorial writing on newspapers. In World War II she was active as a Red Cross Gray Lady. Member of a distinguished writing family (the late Stephen Vincent and William Rose Benét were her brothers), she is the author of twenty volumes of poetry and prose, including a novelized biography of Emily Dickinson. Her most recent book of poems is *In Love with Time* (Wake-Brook Press 1959). She is on the Executive Board of the PSA.

BENNETT, ANNA ELIZABETH trained for her career as librarian at Adelphi College and Pratt Library School (A.B., B.L.S.) and has served in the Morristown, N. J. Library and the Brooklyn Library, among others. Her book for children, *Little Witch*, published by Lippincott (1953), is now in its fifth printing. Her poems have appeared in Poetry, American Scholar, etc. The Fine Editions Press published her first collection of verse, *Cantabile,* in 1954. Miss Bennett was born in Brooklyn in 1914.

BENNETT, GERTRUDE RYDER lives in Brooklyn, her place of birth. She holds B.S. and M.S. degrees from New York University and Columbia. She has won a number of prizes for her poetry and is the author of *Etched in Words,* published by Putnam in 1938. She won the Ficke sonnet award in 1960.

BENNETT, MURRAY made his stage debut with George Arliss in "The Green Goddess" and has appeared in many Broadway plays. A native of Charleston, S. C., he is a graduate of the American Academy of Dramatic Art. He has contributed poetry to many periodicals, including The Lyric and Voices.

BENTON, PATRICIA was born in Westchester County, N. Y. and studied in this country as well as abroad. Poet and musician, she has contributed to numerous periodicals. She is the author of *Pebbles* (Peter Pauper Press 1939), *Voices in the Willows* (Dierkes Press 1947), *The Whispering Earth* and *Signature in Sand* (the two latter published by Greenberg, 1950 and 1952).

BIRNBAUM, HENRY is a native New Yorker now resident in Wheaton, Md. He is Assistant to the Director of the National Bureau of Standards. Born in 1921, he received his M.A. from New York University (1946) and his Ph.D. from George Washington University (1953). Mr. Birnbaum's work has been published by Olivant Press: *The Simon Passion* (1955) and by Voyages Press: *Poems by Five* (1959).

BIRNEY, EARLE, Professor of English at the University of British Columbia, was born in Calgary in 1904. His writing has brought him many awards, among them the Stephen Leacock Medal for Humour (1949), the Governor-General of Canada's Medal for Poetry (1942 and 1945), and several Research Scholarships and Fellowships. The most recent of his six books is *Down the Long Table,* a novel published in 1955 by McClelland & Stewart, Toronto, and in 1959 by Abelard-Schuman, London. Professor Birney is a Fellow of the Royal Society of Canada.

BLACKSTOCK, WALTER published his first book, *Quest For Beauty,* with Dorrance in 1942 and his seventh and most recent in 1955 with Wings Press. In 1954-55 he received a Ford Foundation Faculty Fellowship for a year's study at Harvard under Archibald MacLeish. Born in Atlanta, Ga. in 1917, Mr. Blackstock holds a number of degrees, including a Ph.D. in American literature from Yale. He is currently Professor of English at High Point College in North Carolina.

BLACKWELL, HARRIET GRAY, now a resident of Florida, was born in Laurens, S. C. in 1898. She completed her B.S., majoring in music, at Columbia University in 1919. Mrs. Blackwell has contributed articles and poems to many journals. In 1954 the Dietz Press brought out her volume of poems, *The Lightning Tree.*

BLANKNER, FREDERIKA is Resident Poet of Adelphi College, where she is founder-chairman of the Department of Classical Civilization, Languages and Literatures. Born in Michigan, Miss Blankner received a Ph.B. and M.A. from the University of Chicago and a Litt.D. from the University of Rome. She has been active in the fields of music, dance, and theatre as well as in literature. Among her numerous published works are *Pirandello Paradox* (Theatre Arts 1928), *All My Youth* (Brentano's 1932), and *Art, Man and the Cosmos as Vibrational Design* (Harvard University Press 1940).

BLUM, ETTA, born in New York City in 1908, received her B.A. at Hunter College and did postgraduate work at Columbia University. She has taught in the New York City schools and is now on the administrative staff of the N. Y. C. Board of Education. Mrs. Blum's work has appeared in *New Letters in America* and in poetry journals. Her *Poems* was published by the Golden Eagle Press in 1937.

BOURINOT, ARTHUR S. has published forty books of poetry and prose, including *Collected Poems* (Ryerson 1947) and *This Green Earth* (1952). Born in Ottawa, Canada in 1893, he won the Governor-General's Award for Poetry in 1939 and was elected F.F.S.L. (England) in 1950. He has contributed to many Canadian and American magazines and anthologies.

BRADY, CHARLES A., born in Buffalo in 1912, holds degrees from Canisius, Harvard, and Le Moyne (B.A., M.A., Litt.D.) and is Professor of English and Department Chairman at Canisius College. Among his published works in prose and poetry are *Stage of Fools* (Dutton 1953), *King of the Cats* (Sheed & Ward 1947), and *The Place of the Bull* (Doubleday 1959).

BRENNAN, JOSEPH P., a resident of New Haven, Conn., was born in Bridgeport in 1918. He is Senior Assistant at the Yale University Library. Mr. Brennan has published four books, including *The Humming Stair* (Big Mountain Press 1953) and *The Dark Returners,* a collection of short stories (Macabre House 1959).

BRIGGS, OLGA HAMPEL has been appearing on radio and television for the past twelve years as book commentator for the Albany Public Library. Born in Cohoes, N. Y. in 1906, she is an alumna of The University of the State of New York. She has published in several periodicals and is President of the Albany Poetry Society.

BROCKMAN, ZOE KINCAID is woman's editor of the Gastonia Gazette of Gastonia, N. C., where she was born in 1893. In addition to winning a number of prizes for her writing, she has published a volume of poetry, *Heart on My Sleeve,* brought out by Banner Press in 1951.

BROWNELL, FLORENCE KERR studied at Columbia, the University of Buffalo, and elsewhere, and spent a year of travel abroad.

Her book of poems, *Pendulum*, was brought out by The Fine Editions Press in 1949. Born in Buffalo in 1902, she is a resident of White Plains, N. Y.

BRYAN, ELIZABETH MABEL holds degrees from Elmira College and Columbia University. She has been a newspaperwoman and an English teacher. Her poetry has appeared in Ave Maria, The Christian Science Monitor, and other media. She was born in 1886 in Elmira, N. Y.

BUTTERFIELD, FRANCES WESTGATE was born in Norfield, Miss. and has taught in schools in this country and in Korea. Her poetry and book reviews have appeared in a number of periodicals. In addition to editing two high school poetry anthologies, Miss Butterfield is the author of *From Little Acorns* (Renbayle Press 1951).

BYNNER, WITTER, President of the PSA (1920-1922), honorary member, Gold Medalist, Droutzkoy Award (1954), and author of scores of works in poetry, criticism, drama, biography, and translations from the Chinese and Greek, is a graduate of Harvard, was assistant editor of McClure's, taught at the University of California, and traveled extensively in the Orient. He was the Phi Beta Kappa poet at Harvard in 1911, at the University of California in 1919, and at Amherst in 1931. Among his publications in poetry are *A Canticle of Pan, Take Away the Darkness*, a *Book of Lyrics;* in biography, *Journey with Genius;* in translation, *The Jade Mountain, The Way of Life according to Laotzu*, and *Iphigenia in Tauris* of Euripides. Mr. Bynner, a long resident of Santa Fé., N. M., was born in Brooklyn, N. Y. in 1881.

CANE, MELVILLE was born in Plattsburgh, N. Y. and is a graduate of Columbia College (1900) and Columbia University Law School (1903). He has published six volumes of verse, the most recent being *Bullet-Hunting* (Harcourt, Brace 1960). He is also the author of a collection of prose essays *Making a Poem*, which appeared in 1953. In the same year he co-edited *The Man from Main Street: A Sinclair Lewis Reader*. Columbia University honored him in 1933 and again in 1948 for excellence in law and literature. Mr. Cane is a lawyer by profession. He was created a PSA Fellow in 1960.

CANTUS, ELEANOR HOLLISTER has done radio and platform lecture work, and has served as book and newspaper editor. Her *Color Bearer*, a volume of verse, was published in 1937. She was born in 1908 in Cedarhurst, L. I., and educated at Columbia University.

CARAGHER, MARY E. is a native of Lima, N. Y. (1890). She took her B.S. and M.A. at the University of Rochester, and has had a varied teaching career at the Universities of Rochester, Pennsylvania, and elsewhere. Her writing has appeared in a number of magazines.

CARLETON, SARA KING, born and brought up in New York City, is the author of two books of verse, the most recent *The New Country*, brought out by Bookman in 1954. Her work has appeared in

Harper's, Atlantic, and Scribner's, among other periodicals. She is the winner of several PSA awards.

CARPENTER, MARGARET HALEY is the winner of the Greenwood Prize of the Poetry Society of London and co-winner of the PSA Arthur Davison Ficke Award. In 1958 she collaborated with William Stanley Braithwaite in editing a new *Anthology of Magazine Verse*. She is a resident of Norfolk, Va.

CARRIER, CONSTANCE teaches senior high school Latin in her native town of New Britain, Conn. A graduate of Smith College, she received her M.A. from Trinity. The manuscript of her first volume of poems, *The Middle Voice* (Alan Swallow, 1955) was the first Lamont Poetry Selection. Her work has appeared in The Atlantic, The American Scholar, The Nation, The New Yorker, and numerous other publications. She was second prize winner in the PSA Annual Awards in 1948 and first prize winner in 1955.

CARVER, MABEL MacDONALD, in addition to being a poet, is a painter, and has had many exhibitions. Born in Forest, Ill., Mrs. Carver studied at the Wicker School of Fine Arts, Detroit. She is the author of two books of verse, *The Golden Rain Tree* and *Out of Asia*.

CHACE, JEAN VALENTINE was born in Chicago on April 27, 1934 but has spent most of her life in New York and Boston. She studied at the Milton Academy and is a graduate of Radcliffe (1956). In 1955 the Harvard Advocate published a poem of hers, the only one in print. She is married to James Chace, whose first novel *The Rules of the Game* appeared early in 1960 over the Doubleday imprint.

CHAPIN, KATHERINE GARRISON was born in Waterford, Conn. in 1890 and was privately educated. In 1918 she married Francis Biddle, U. S. Attorney General under F. D. Roosevelt. During 1944-51 she served as a Fellow in American Letters of the Library of Congress. Among her published works are *Time Has No Shadow* (Dodd, Mead 1936) and, most recently, *The Other Journey* (University of Minnesota Press 1959). Two of her choral poems have had performances with orchestra in Mexico, England, and the United States. She is a member of the PSA Governing Board.

CHAPPELL, JEANNETTE (Mrs. William MacKenzie Kalt) has contributed poetry to Saturday Review, American Weave, etc. as well as to Golden Quill and other anthologies. A native Chicagoan, she is an alumna of the Spence School of New York.

CHARLES, MARY GRANT was born in Boston and now lives at Covered Bridge Farm, Andover, N. H. She was, before her marriage, a social service executive, after receiving her M.S. from Simmons College School of Social Work. Her *Across a Covered Bridge* was published by Granite State Press in 1958.

CHERWINSKI, JOSEPH has been employed by the Michigan State Library for a score of years. He is active in the Poetry Society of

Michigan, and is the author of a prize-winning book of poems, *No Blue Tomorrow* (Kaleidograph Press 1952). Born in Green Bay, Wisc., he is now a resident of Lansing, Mich.

CHUBB, THOMAS CALDECOT is a gradaute of Yale, where he won the John Masefield prize in poetry. His interest in the Italian Renaissance resulted in two major biographical works, *The Life of Giovanni Boccaccio* (Boni 1930) and *Aretino, Scourge of Princes* (Reynal & Hitchcock 1940). In the field of poetry he is represented by *Cornucopia* (The Fine Editions Press 1953) and other volumes. His most recent publication is *The Byzantines* (World Publishing Co. 1959). Mr. Chubb was born in East Orange, N. J. in 1899 and makes his home in Greenwich, Conn.

CLAYTOR, GERTRUDE, native of Staunton, Va. and now resident of New York, was educated at Virginia College. She is the author of *Sunday in Virginia & Other Poems* (Dutton 1951) and is the winner of a PSA first annual prize. A poem of hers commemorating Governor Spotswood is inscribed on the bronze plaque set up on Skyline Drive. For a time she served on the advisory board of the Borestone Mt. Poetry Awards.

COLE, E. R. (Eugene Roger), born in Cleveland, O. in 1930, was ordained a Catholic priest in 1958. He is on the staff of Experiment, a quarterly of new poetry. His first volume of verse *H-Bombs in His Beard* was brought out in 1959 by Experiment Press Books. Individual poems of his have appeared in Compass, Beloit Poetry Journal, etc.

COLEMAN, LUCILE, founder of New York State Poetry Day, is the editor of three anthologies and the author of two books, the most recent being *Strange Altar* (Decker Press 1947). She is a native of New York City.

COLONY, HORATIO was born in Keene, N. H. and is an alumnus of Harvard. A retired woolen manufacturer and trustee, Mr. Colony published *Free Forester*, the first of his six books, in 1935 with Little Brown. The most recent work of his is *Young Malatesta* (Richard D. Smith 1959).

COLUM, PADRAIC was a leading figure in the Irish Renaissance, a close friend and associate of Yeats, AE, Joyce, Lady Gregory and others. He is the author of *Wild Earth* (1907), *Dramatic Legends & Other Poems* (1922), *Balloon*, a comedy (1929), and numerous books on travel and folklore. He is co-author, with his late wife Mary Colum, of a memoir of James Joyce. In 1952 he received the $5000 Fellowship of the Academy of American Poets and in 1953 the Gregory Medal of The Irish Academy of Letters. He is a former president of the PSA.

COOPERMAN, HASYE teaches Comparative and American Literature at the New School for Social Research in New York. She took degrees at Hunter College (B.A.) and Columbia (M.A., Ph.D.).

Among her published books are *The Aesthetics of Stéphane Mallarmé* (Koffern Press 1933), *The Chase* (Bayard Press 1932) and a second collection of her verse, *Men Walk the Earth* (William Frederick Press 1953). Her poem "The Mists Are Rising Now" won first prize in 1957 in the American Literary Association's national poetry contest.

CORNELL, ANNETTE PATTON was editor for three years of Talaria Books. She has contributed poetry to a number of magazines, and in addition to co-authoring a book, published her own volume, *The Forbidden Woman* (1939). In 1945 she won the national prize awarded by the League of American Pen Women for a sonnet, and in 1958 the same league's prize for a lyric.

COUSENS, MILDRED took her A.B. with honors in English at Radcliffe. A native of Portland, Conn. (1904), Mrs. Cousens has contributed to The American Scholar, The Saturday Review, and other periodicals. She was guest editor, with Jocelyn Macy Sloan, of the Spring 1959 issue of Voices.

COX, ELIZABETH before her marriage taught high school in Pennsylvania. She was born in Atlanta, Ga. in 1907 and received her A.B. from Bucknell (1929). In 1958 her poems won first and second place in the writing contest of the American Association of University Women. Mrs. Cox now makes her home in College Park, Md.

CURTIS, CHRISTINE TURNER, native and resident of North Abington, Mass., received her B.A. from Wellesley College. For sixteen years she served as art editor for Ginn & Co. In 1955 Peter Pauper Press published the most recent of her three books, *Fragile Lineage*.

DABNEY, BETTY PAGE is a teacher of high school English in Norfolk, Va., where she was born 1911. She received her M.A. from the University of Virginia. Miss Dabney's book, *The Ancient Bond*, was published by Dietz Press in 1954.

DALVEN, RAE was born in Prevesa, Greece in 1904. She is a graduate of Hunter College (B.A.), New York University (M.A. in English), Yale University Theatre (M.F.A.), and is now a candidate for a Ph.D. in English at New York University. She is on the English faculty of Fairleigh-Dickinson. Among her published books are *Poems*, 1944 (a biography and verse-translations) and an anthology, *Modern Greek Poetry*, 1950. She recently completed her translations into English of all the extant poems of the eminent Greek poet Cavafy.

DARGAN, OLIVE TILFORD published her thirteenth book, *The Spotted Hawk*, with John F. Blair in 1958. Her first book, *Semiramis and Other Plays*, was brought out by Brentano's in 1904 and taken over by Scribner's in 1906. Born in what is now Litchfield, Ky., Miss Dargan studied at Peabody College for Teachers and at Radcliffe. She received the honorary Degree of Doctor of Literature from North Carolina University in 1924. She is a charter member of the PSA.

DAVENPORT, MARIANA, now resident in Riverside, Conn., was born in Chestnut Hill, Philadelphia, in 1902, and educated at Bryn Mawr (B.A. 1925). She is married and the mother of four sons. Her poetry has appeared in the New Yorker, American Weave, Lyric, and other periodicals.

DAVIDSON, GUSTAV (B.A., M.A. Columbia University) is founder of The Fine Editions Press, editor of the PSA Bulletin (since 1949), Secretary of the Society, and Curator of its collection at the New York Public Library. He compiled *In Fealty to Apollo,* the pictorial history of the PSA, and initiated its two *Anthologies.* At one time he served as Research Bibliographer at the Library of Congress. Recipient of many awards, he is the author of half a dozen works in poetry, drama, and bibliography. Recently he completed *Principalities and Powers,* a work on angels and demons. His *Dictionary* on the same subject is in preparation. He is Senior American editor of the *International Who's Who in Poetry,* and an editor of The Book Club for Poetry. He was created a PSA Fellow at the Society's 50th Anniversary ceremonies in January 1960.

DAYTON, IRENE G., a resident of Rochester, N. Y., was born at Lake Ariel, Pa. in 1922. Married and the mother of two sons, Mrs. Dayton has published poetry in a number of periodicals. A book manuscript of hers was chosen as one of the finalists in 1958 Yale Series of Younger Poets.

DEAN, ELMA studied poetry under Lawrence Hart and Muriel Rukeyser. She is represented in *Modern American and British Poetry, Midcentury Edition* (Louis Untermeyer, ed.) and other anthologies. She won second place in the PSA annual award in 1944. A resident of Oakland, Calif., she was born in 1899 at Beaver Falls, Pa.

DeFORD, MIRIAM ALLEN has published eight books since 1931, when the Dial Press brought out her *Love Children: A Book of Illustrious Illegitimates.* Among her volumes of poetry is *Children of Sun* (League To Support Poetry 1939). Her novel *Shaken with the Wind,* was brought out by Doubleday in 1942. She is also the author of a biography *Powder of Diamonds.* Last year her *Overbury Drama* appeared under the Chilton imprint. A labor journalist for many years, Miss DeFord was born in Philadelphia in 1888 and attended Wellesley, Temple University, and the University of Pennsylvania.

DELAFIELD, HARRIET L. was born in Quogue, L. I., N. Y. in 1922. She studied singing for a time at the Mannes College of Music. For two years she served as editor of the Hampton Chronicle (Long Island) and in 1956 published a book of nature sketches, *Sea, Sand and Soil,* brought out by the Westhampton Publishing Co. Her poetry has appeared in many periodicals.

De LONGCHAMPS, JOANNE is a native of Los Angeles, now resident in Reno. She received her education at the Institut de Saint Pierre, in France; at the Los Angeles City College; and at the University of Nevada. She is represented in the 1953 and 1955 *Poetry Awards Annual*. In 1954 she received the Reynolds Lyric Award. Her second book, *Eden Under Glass*, was a Book Club for Poetry Selection (1957).

DERLETH, AUGUST is one of the most prolific of living writers, having published, to date, close to one hundred books, fifteen of which are collections of poetry. He is active also as historian, editor, book reviewer, lecturer, and directing head of his own publishing firm, Arkham House. In 1938 he received a Guggenheim Fellowship to assist him in further work on his Sac Prairie saga. Among his books are *Wind over Wisconsin, The Moon Tenders,* and *Still Is the Summer Night.* He is a native and resident of Sauk City, Wisc.

De WITT, SAMUEL A. was born in New York City in 1891 and was educated at the College of the City of New York, New York University, and Columbia University. He has published eighteen books of poems, plays, translations, and librettos. For the past thirty-eight years he has been president of a machine tool company. He once served in the legislative assembly of New York State.

DI CASTAGNOLA (Countess), ALICE FAY is the author of two books of verse, *Our America: A Symphony of the New World* (1927), and *The Soul's Quest* (1936), both published by Putnam. A native of Chicago, where she spent her early years, she is now a resident of New York. Her poems have been widely published. At one time she served as Poetry Chairman of the National League of American Pen Women, Poetry Editor of *The Pen Woman* (1948-50), and compiler of the League's *Anthology of Poems* (1951). Miss Fay is now at work on an autobiography.

DILLON, George, a native of Jacksonville, Fla. (1906), received a Ph.B. from the University of Chicago and took graduate courses at the University of Paris. His second volume of poems, *Flowering Stone*, won the Pulitzer prize for poetry in 1932. He was a Guggenheim Fellow in 1932-33 and for many years, until World War II intervened, served as editor of Poetry, of whose Advisory Committee he is now a member. In 1936 in collaboration with Edna St. Vincent Millay, he did a translation of Baudelaire's *Fleurs du Mal*.

DIMMETTE, CELIA grew up in Brookings County, S. D. She now lives in Akron, O. In 1950 her *Toward the Metal Sun*, a book of poems published that year, won the award of the Midwestern Writers' Conference of Chicago. Her work has appeared in the University of Kansas City Review, The Prairie Schooner, etc.

DORN, ALFRED was born in New York in 1929. He holds a B.S. and M.A. from New York University, where he teaches literature and composition. His two volumes of verse, *Flamenco Dancer* and *Wine in Stone,* both appeared in 1959.

DRAKE, LEAH BODINE has published *A Hornbook For Witches* (Arkham House 1950) and *This Tilting Dust* (Book Club for Poetry 1955). The second-named won the $1250 Borestone Mountain Poetry Award (1954). Miss Drake's work has appeared in many magazines and anthologies, most recently in *Jubilee,* the Atlantic Monthly anthology. She is the winner also of several PSA annual and monthly awards. Born in Chanute, Kan., Miss Drake received her education at Hamilton College for Girls in Lexington, Ky.

DREWRY, CARLETON brought out his first book, *Proud Horns,* with Macmillan in 1933, and since that time has published four additional titles, with Dutton. The most recent of these, *Cloud Above Clock-Time,* appeared in 1957. *A Time of Turning* won the 1951 Borestone Mt. Poetry Award. Mr. Drewry was born in Stevensburg, Va. in 1901 and is now a resident of Roanoke, Va. He has served as lecturer at Hollins College and has also taught creative writing at the University of Virginia.

DURYEE, MARY BALLARD is the author of five books, the first, *Avenues of Song* (1926), published by the Brick Row Bookshop. Putnam brought out *No Special Pleading* in 1940, and The Fine Editions Press her *Free Enterprise* the same year. Her most recent book is *This Instant Joy* (Pageant Press 1958). Mrs. Duryee is a native of Philadelphia and served for four years as president of the Women's City Club of New York.

EARLE, VIRGINIA was at one time a professional ballet dancer and teacher of ballet. She is a resident of Asheville, N. C. Her poetry has appeared in The Harp, Saturady Review, Commonweal, and in the Braithwaite *Anthology of Magazine Verse* for 1958. She won the PSA Annual Award in 1955.

EATON, BURNHAM was born in New Jersey in 1901 and grew up in New England, studying at the University of Massachusetts. Winner of various national poetry awards, Mrs. Eaton is a frequent contributor to periodicals. She has also published a book of verse, *True Places* (Golden Quill Press 1955).

EATON, CHARLES EDWARD at one time served as Vice-Consul at the American Embassy in Rio de Janeiro. A native (1916) of Winston-Salem, N. C., he received his A.B. at the University of North Carolina and his M.A. at Harvard. He has taught creative writing and has published three books of poetry and two collections of short stories. His *The Shadow of the Swimmer* (The Fine Editions Press) won the Ridgely Torrence Memorial Award in 1952. His *The Greenhouse in the Garden* was one of the final nominees for the 1957 National Book Award. Twelve Brazilian tales under the title *Write Me from Rio* were published late in 1959 by John F. Blair.

EATON, EVELYN has published several novels, from *Quietly My Captain Waits* (Harper 1940) to *I Saw My Mortal Sight* (Random House 1959), and two collections of short stories reprinted from The New Yorker. In 1925 Miss Eaton won the John Masefield

Award for short poems at the Festival of Arts and Letters, London. She is a Fellow of the Edward MacDowell Association. Born in 1902 in Montreux, Switzerland, Miss Eaton lives in Sweet Briar, Va. where, at Sweet Briar College, she serves as Professor of English.

EBERHART, RICHARD was born in Austin, Minn. in 1904. He received his B.A. from Dartmouth and his M.A. from Cambridge University. For nine years he was master of English at St. Mark's School, Southborough, Mass. After serving in the United States Navy, he joined the Butcher Polish Co., Boston, in 1946, and has been vice-president of that firm since 1952. Mr. Eberhart has given extensive readings from his poetry. His awards include: the Guarantors Prize from Poetry magazine, 1946; the Harriet Monroe Memorial Prize, 1950; the Shelley Memorial Prize, 1951. Principal works: *Reading the Spirit*, 1936; *Poems New and Selected*, 1944; *Selected Poems*, 1951; *Undercliff*, 1953; *Greek Praises*, 1957.

EDWARDS, JEANNETTE SLOCOMB has been Poet Laureate of the Delaware State Federation of Women's Clubs since 1948. She is a native of Wilmington, Del. and a graduate of the Pennsylvania Museum College of Art (1914) and the Columbia School of Journalism (1932). Mrs. Edwards has published two books: *Songs Against the Dark* (1936) and *Inward from the Sea* (1946).

ELDRIDGE, RICHARD BURDICK was born in Duluth, Minn. in 1891. He received his B.S. from St. Lawrence University. In 1947 Decker Press published his *Remembered Music*, a book of verse. His translations from the French, *Flowers from a Foreign Field*, was brought out in 1959.

ELLIOT, JEAN, a native and lifelong resident of Westchester County, N. Y., is a graduate of Fassifern in North Carolina. She studied at the National Academy of Design, later entering the field of journalism. Her poems have appeared in many magazines, as well as in anthologies. She is a former officer of the New York Women Poets, and has served the PSA as Discussion Leader.

EMERY, FRANCES D. has been published widely. She is treasurer of the Albany County Poetry Society. A resident of Watervliet, N. Y., Miss Emery was born in Dover, N. J. in 1907 and attended Russell Sage College.

ESPAILLAT, RHINA P. (Mrs. Alfred Moskowitz) was born in the Dominican Republic in 1932. She received her B.A. from Hunter College (1953) and is currently working for her M.A. at Queens College. Her poems have appeared in Voices, Ladies Home Journal, and elsewhere.

EVERTS, LILLIAN is a native New Yorker. Born in 1905, educated at Brooklyn College, Columbia, Middlebury, and Harvard University, she has been a teacher of writing for the New York Public Library, and a contributor to the Writers' Journal. In 1954 and 1955 she published two collections of poems with The Lantern. Farrar,

Straus & Cudahy brought out, in 1956, her *Journey to the Future*. Two long poems,*While the Past Burns* and *Lost Edition*, appeared as French Academy Award publications.

FANDEL, JOHN was the H. E. Russell Fellow at Yale (1948-49) and The Robert Frost Poetry Scholar at the Bread Loaf School of English, 1950. Later he studied at Fordham. He was born in Yonkers in 1925, received his A.B. from Trinity College and his A.M. from Middlebury College. He is now an instructor at Manhattan College. He has published several brochures. In 1959 Sheed and Ward brought out his *Testament and Other Poems*.

FARBER, NORMA was born in Boston in 1909, took her B.A. at Wellesley and her M.A. at Radcliffe, and studied music in France, Germany, and Belgium. She was awarded the Premier Prix in singing in Belgium in 1936. A concert artist, she appears as soprano soloist with orchestra and chamber music groups. In 1955 Scribner's published her book *The Hatch* (Poets of Today II). She won the PSA Reynolds Lyric Award in 1959.

FARNHAM, JESSIE, a native of Cleveland but lifelong resident of Cincinnati, won first prize in poetry in 1937 at the University of Cincinnati, which she attended at the time. Her work has appeared in The Saturday Review, New York Times, and other periodicals.

FARRAR, JANICE has been teaching for four years, and is currently a lecturer in English at Barnard College. She was born in New York City in 1933, received her A.B. from Barnard and her A.M. from, Columbia. She is now working towards a Ph.D. Her poetry has appeared in The Atlantic.

FARRAR, JOHN, chairman of the board of the publishing firm of Farrar, Straus & Cudahy, and a vice president (formerly president) of the American Center of P.E.N., is the author of three books of poetry and a book of one-act plays for children. He has also edited a number of anthologies and written short stories and essays. At Yale (class of 1918) he was chairman of its Literary Magazine. While an undergraduate, he joined the PSA at the time Stephen Vincent Benet did. During World War I he served as 1st Lt. US Air Force, and as Executice Officer, US Information, in France. In World War II he was with the Office of War Information in Algiers. In the years 1920-27 he edited The Bookman. He is a member of the PSA governing board, and one of the editors of *The Golden Year*. He was born in Burlington, Vt. in 1896.

FERRIL, THOMAS HORNSBY has won many prizes, including the Yale Competition for Younger Poets, an award by the Academy of American Poets, the PSA Ridgely Torrence prize, and the $10,000 offered in 1958 for a play in verse by the Denver Post Central City Opera House Association. He has published four books of poetry and a book of prose essays. Born in 1896 in Denver, Colo., Mr. Ferril is a graduate of Colorado College. He won the first Robert Frost $1000 poetry Award (1960).

FOSTER, JEANNE ROBERT was born in Johnsburgh, N. Y. in 1884 and educated at Boston University. She has served as editor, book review editor, and municipal housing counsellor. She has published several books, including a volume of verse: *Rock-Flowers*, and a play, *Marthe*. She now makes her home in Schenectady, N. Y.

FRANCIS, MARILYN is Director of the Phoenix (Ariz.) Poetry Workshop, serves as poetry lecturer for the Phoenix Public Schools, and recently completed a 20-week radio program of poetry readings. Miss Frances received a B.S. from Ohio University. She was born in 1920.

FRANK, FLORENCE KIPER is a native of Atchison, Kans. (1886), and an alumna of the University of Chicago. She published her first book, a volume of poems, in 1915. Her third and most recent,*The Silver Grain,* was brought out in 1956 by Bookman Associates. Her poetry has appeared in The New Yorker, Poetry, and other magazines.

FRANK, JOHN FREDERICK has been a vice-consul for the State Department, served in Army Intelligence during World War II, has taught at Penn State University and the University of Pennsylvania, and is now a Professor of English at the University of North Carolina. Born in Milwaukee in 1918, Mr. Frank was educated at Northwestern University (B.S.), Johns Hopkins (M.A.), and the University of Pennsylvania (Ph.D.). He has contributed poetry to Esquire, etc.

FROST, ROBERT, dean of American poets, was born in 1875 in San Francisco, Cal. His father, a New Englander, died when Frost was ten, and the boy was taken by his school-teacher mother to his grandfather's home in Lawrence, Mass. There he attended grammar and high school and developed a love for Latin poetry, especially that of Virgil. After a few months at Dartmouth he went to work as a bobbin-boy in a Lawrence mill. He continued to write verse, and at twenty-two, having been married for two years, he entered Harvard University in 1897, but left two years later without a degree. He then served as country school teacher, cobbler, and editor of a weekly newspaper. He received the Pulitzer Prize four times: in 1924 for *New Hampshire,* in 1931 for *Collected Poems,* in 1937 for *A Further Range,* and in 1943 for *A Witness Tree.* He was awarded the Loines Prize in 1931, and the gold medal of the National Institute of Arts and Letters in 1939. That year found him the first incumbent of the Ralph Waldo Emerson Fellowship in poetry at Harvard University. Remaining at Harvard until 1934, he has since been George Ticknor Fellow in Humanities at Dartmouth. In 1958 he received the PSA Gold Medal for Distinguished Service. He is the Society's Honorary President.

GALE, VI was born in Noret, Sweden. She has lived in various parts of the United States but now resides in Portland, Ore. Her work has appeared in Poetry and other magazines, and in two anthologies. Her first collection, *Several Houses,* was published in 1959 by Alan Swallow.

GEORGE, MARGUERITE (Mrs. Otto Rothenburgh) was born in
Little Rock, Ark. in 1898. She attended Galloway College and the
School of Fine Arts in Chicago and taught at Henshaw Conservatory
and in private schools. She is the author of one book of poems,
Wings on the Hilltop (Kaleidograph Press 1933).

GINSBERG, LOUIS is a resident of Paterson, N. J., where for many
years he has taught classes in English at the Central High School.
He was born in Newark in 1895 and received his B.A. and M.A.
from Rutgers (1918) and Columbia (1924). He has published
two books of poems: *The Attic of the Past* (Small, Maynard 1920)
and *The Everlasting Minute* (Liveright 1937). His work appears
frequently in American, Canadian and British magazines.

GLEN, EMILIE is a frequent contributor of short stories and poems
to New Mexico Quarterly, Epoch, Prairie Schooner, New Directions,
etc. A native of Syracuse, N. Y., she studied piano with Ernest
Hutcheson, attended Columbia, served as an editor for Macmillan,
as editor of Conference Trails, and editorial assistant on The New
Yorker. A book of her poems is scheduled to appear as a special
issue of Olivant Quarterly (1960).

GOODMAN, MAE WINKLER grew up on a Louisiana sugar
plantation. Born in New Orleans, La. in 1911, she moved to Cleveland, O. when she was thirteen and has made her home there ever
since. She received her education at Northwestern University and
Western Reserve (B.A.). In 1948 American Weave Press brought
out her collection of verse, *The Single Flame*. Three years later her
In Time of Swallows appeared under the Devin-Adair imprint.

GOODMAN, RYAH TUMARKIN was born in Russia and came
to this country at the age of four. She attended Emerson College.
In 1952 her first book of poems, *Toward the Sun,* was published;
a second book, *Green Applause,* is now in preparation. She has
contributed to The Atlantic, Saturday Review, and many other
poetry journals.

GRAHAM, RACHEL has taught zoology at Mt. Holyoke, Barnard,
and DePauw University. She was born (1895) in Wurzburg, Germany at the time her father was doing graduate work there. She
is an alumna of Oberlin College (B.A.) and Columbia University
(M.A.). Her verse has appeared in more than eighty journals.

GRANT, LILLIAN is a native Texan, now a resident of Florida.
She was born in the town of Marshall and educated in private
schools. Her poetry has appeared in Lyric, Voices, Kaleidograph,
and other magazines.

GREEFF, ADELE received her education at Barnard College
(B.A.), Cornell Medical College, Columbia University, and at the
School of Architecture, where she studied painting. She was born
in Brooklyn in 1911. Poet, painter and lecturer on art, Mrs. Greeff

has published one book, *Love's Argument* (Macmillan 1952), which has an introduction by Mark Van Doren.

GREEN, BRENDA HELOISE is employed as a private secretary in the Department of Psychiatry, University Hospitals of Cleveland. A native of Meadville, Pa. (1910), she was educated at Oberlin College and at Western Reserve University. Miss Green's work has appeared in The Golden Quill Anthology, Contemporary Ohio Poetry, and elsewhere.

GRENELLE, LISA is a native New Yorker and a former daily columnist with King Features. She is President of the Manhattan Branch, National League of American Pen Women, and teaches poetry and creative writing. She has published two books: *This Day Is Ours* and *No Light Evaded*. Her work has appeared in Prairie Schooner, Educational Forum, University of Kansas City Review, American Weave, Yankee, etc.

GRENVILLE, R. H. (Mrs. Frank Ernest Rowley) has been a professional writer since her early twenties. Her work is represented in several anthologies, and appears frequently in Poetry Review (London), The Fiddlehead, etc. Miss Grenville was born in Bromley, Kent, England. She became a Canadian citizen in 1925.

GRIMES, WILLARD M. is a native of Minneapolis (1890). He was educated at Harvard (A.B. cum laude) and Columbia (A.M.). From 1942-46 he served in the U.S. Army as Captain, Major, and Lt. Colonel. He has published three books: *A Few Fragments* (1937), *Veri-Tasse* (1939), and *The Unquenched Cup* (1948).

GROESBECK, AMY is the author of two books: *Tales Gay and Ghastly* (1958) and *Gull Geometrics* (1959), both brought out by Falmouth Press. She contributes to Saturday Review, American Weave, etc. and is active in various theatrical, literary and philanthropic organizations. Mrs. Groesbeck serves as Monitor of Recording for the Blind, Chairman of Skinner Memorial Drama Library at the Cosmopolitan Club (New York), and is a member of Actors' Equity. She was born in Bay Shore, N. Y. in 1894.

GULICK, ALIDA CAREY was born in Portsmouth, N. H., a New Yorker by descent. Since the outbreak of World War II, she has lived in Martha's Vineyard. She contributes to Poetry, The Beloit Journal, and to British magazines.

GUNN, LOUISE D. is a teacher of English at the Albany (N. Y.) High School, and gives courses in creative writing. Her poetry has been published in *Golden Quill Anthology* (1956 and 1959), and in *Japan: Theme and Variations* (also an anthology), as well as in various periodicals. Miss Gunn, born at Canton, O. in 1906, received her A.B. and M.A. from Albany State College for Teachers and was granted a Ford Fellowship at Columbia for 1954-55.

GURNEY, LAWRENCE holds the unusual post of Sea Serpent Observer for the Rocky Mountain Herald. Although trained in geology, Mr. Gurney has more recently been concerned with mechanical and inventive matters and lapidary work. His poetry has been published in Epos, Fiddlehead, and other magazines. He was born in Manila, P. I. in 1921 and received his B.A. from the University of Southern California (1943).

HADDEN, MAUDE MINER published her first book with Macmillan in 1916: *Slavery of Prostitution: A Plea for Emancipation.* She subsequently published two books of verse, the more recent being *High Horizons* (Whittier Books 1957). Mrs. Hadden has served as New York City's First Probation Officer, Magistrate's Court, and as a member of the Governor's State Probation Commission. She is also Founder and former Director of the Girls Service League, now serving as member of the Board. A resident of New York City, Miss Hadden was born in Leyden, Mass. in 1880.

HALE, OLIVER is a native New Yorker. He has contributed poetry to New Caravans, Poetry, and other magazines. With his wife he did research in Children's Folklore, results of which were published by the American Folkore Society. Mr. Hale is cataloguer for the Tamiment Institute Library.

HALL, AMANDA BENJAMIN (Mrs. John A. Brownell) is a native and resident of Connecticut. She attended private schools in the United States and abroad, and studied fiction and verse technique at New York University and at Columbia. She is a winner of PSA and Poetry (Chicago) annual awards. She has three volumes of fiction and six of poetry to her credit. *Frosty Harp*, a book of verse, appeared in 1954 (The Golden Quill Press).

HALL, KAY de BARD was born in Turon, Kans., but moved to Seattle, Wash. when very young. She is now a resident of Berkeley, Calif. After attending the University of Washington, Mrs. Hall engaged in the study of modern verse. Her work has appeared in Poetry, Accent, etc. She is the author of *Poems of the Sea* (Harbinger House 1948).

HAMILTON, MARION ETHEL is the author of three books of verse, the latest, *Bird at Night* (1949), brought out by The Fine Editions Press. Mrs. Hamilton contributes to Poetry, Poetry World, and other magazines. She grew up and attended school in Albany, N. Y., the family home for two generations, although she was born in Ripon, Wisc. For many years she has been a resident of San Diego, Calif.

HANES, LEIGH holds LL.B., M.A. and Litt. D. degrees from Washington and Lee Universities. He has published four books, lectures extensively, and served as editor of The Lyric from 1929 to 1949. He is a native of Virginia and practices law in Roanoke.

HANSON, PHYLLIS was educated in private schools, at Peabody Institute, and at the University of Oklahoma. Her poetry has appeared in several anthologies and magazines. In 1948 she selected and edited a volume of essays published by Putnam's under the title *Other Men's Minds.* She is a native of Virginia and a resident of Norfolk.

HARDY, ELIZABETH STANTON was born in Cleveland, O. and now resides in Rochester, N. Y. She has taught at the University of Rochester and elsewhere. She is the author of a book on poetry technique, an autobiography, and *Time in the Turning,* a collection of poems published in 1940.

HARRIMAN, DOROTHY (Mrs. Walter M. Sutton) is an alumna of Iowa State College and did graduate work at the University of Pittsburgh. She has contributed to various magazines and newspapers, and is the winner of two college contests. She is a native of Ames, Iowa.

HARRIS, MARGUERITE was born in Brooklyn and was privately educated by her grandmother, Hannah George, a Welsh preacher. She served as assistant to Sir Geoffrey Scott, first editor of the Boswell Diaries. Her poems have appeared in the Yale Literary Review. A first volume of her verse, *The Long Labyrinth,* is in preparation. In 1930 she pioneered in creating markets for contemporary American artists. She lives in New York City.

HASTE, GWENDOLEN is a graduate of the University of Chicago and a native of Streator, Ill. (1889). She won The Nation poetry prize in 1922. A collection of her poems, *Young Land,* was published by Coward-McCann in 1930. She contributes to many magazines and is represented in more than twenty anthologies. She was secretary of the PSA in 1928-29 and a member of its executive board from 1929 to 1936. At present she is secretary of The Westerners, a New York group of writers, artists, librarians, etc. interested in western history.

HASTINGS, FANNY deGROOT is a native of Tarrytown-on-Hudson and a present resident of New Canaan, Conn. Her first book *The Victory of Defeat* was published in 1912. In 1917, 1919 and 1921 William Edwin Rudge brought out her *Ten Minutes, Lesser Stars* and *Through a Glass.* A brochure, *From a Barn Window,* appeared in 1928, and another, *Christmas Poems,* in 1954.

HAY, SARA HENDERSON, the wife of the Russian-American composer, Nikolai Lopatnikoff, is the author of four books of poems: *Field of Honor,* which won the 1933 Kaleidograph award; *This, My Letter* (Knopf, 1939); *The Delicate Balance* (Scribner 1951), which won the Edna St. Vincent Millay Award; and *The Stone and the Shell* (University of Pittsburgh Press 1959). Other prizes won by Miss Hay are the John David Lietch Memorial Prize (1955) and the Lyric Prize (1959).

HEDGES, DORIS was born in Montreal and educated in private schools. She has written and given many radio talks. For her war services she was awarded several decorations. Four books of verse and three novels are her output to date.

HENSON, PAULINE has done newspaper work and taught school. Born in Sparta, Tenn. in 1914, Mrs. Henson studied journalism and education at Abilene Christian College, New Mexico University, and elsewhere. Her poems have appeared in western magazines and newspapers. She has two sons, and lives in Prescott, Ariz.

HENZE, HELEN ROWE is the author of four books, the most recent, *Arise, My Love*, brought out by Doubleday in 1953. In preparation are her translations of the complete *Odes of Horace* in the original metres. Miss Henze, a resident of Kansas City, Mo., was born in Pittsburgh, Pa. in 1899.

HERBERT, MOSS is a native New Yorker. He was born in 1914 and received his education at Columbia University. He is now columnist for a Los Angeles newspaper. He has contributed to The Lyric, The American Poet, Arizona Quarterly, and Coastlines.

HERSHENSON, MIRIAM serves as chairman of the Writers Club at Veterans Hospital in Manhattan, and edits the work of the patient-writers. She has done translations from the work of Mani Leib, the Yiddish poet, and is an amateur collector and sometime performer of folksongs. Born in New York, Miss Hershenson attended Brooklyn College and took special courses in writing and linguistics at The New School.

HICKEY, AGNES MacCARTHY is a resident of Madison, Conn. Poems from her book *Out of Every Day* (Bookfellows Press 1953) have appeared in London Poetry Review, Harper's, and elsewhere. The book is now in Braille. Her Shakespeare poem, a framed copy of which is in The Folger Library, received an award from The Poetry Review of London and was read at the Arts Theatre, London, on Shakespeare's birthday.

HIERS, LOIS SMITH is a resident of Canada, Ky. where she was born in 1910. The author of one book, *My House and My Country* (The Fine Editions Press 1958), she has won a number of awards, including the Reynolds Lyric Award, the Leonora Speyer Memorial Award, and the Norfolk Prize.

HILL, HYACINTHE has had more than four hundred of her poems, short stories and essays published. Two brochures, *Shoots of a Vagrant Vine* (1950) and *Promethea* (1957) were brought out by New Athenaeum Press and by Cameo Press (Scotland). She was born in New York City and is a resident of Yonkers, N. Y.

HILLYER, ROBERT won the Pulitzer Prize in 1934 for his *Collected Verse*. Since then he has published many other works, including *Poems for Music, The Death of Captain Nemo, The Suburb by*

the Sea. He is the author also of a novel, *Riverhead.* He is a Fellow
of the Academy of Arts and Sciences, a member of the National
Institute of Arts and Letters, and a Chancellor of the Academy of
American Poets. He served the PSA as President in 1949-50 and
again in 1952-4. For nineteen years he was Boylston Professor of
Rhetoric and Oratory at Harvard. He is now Professor of English at
the University of Delaware. He was born in East Orange, N. J. on
June 3, 1895.

HIMMELL, SOPHIE is a Russian by birth, long resident in New
York. She is the winner of several PSA monthly awards, and the
author of *Within the Crucible* (Wings Press 1938), *Spontaneous
Now* (The Fine Editions Press 1948) and *Checkerboard of Talk*
(Bookman Associates 1955).

HOBSON, KATHERINE THAYER was born in Denver, Colo. and
educated in private schools, here and abroad, where she majored in
law and sculpture. Her poems have appeared in newspapers and
magazines. She makes her home in New York.

HOFFMAN, PHOEBE W. was born and educated in Philadelphia,
Pa. Many of her one-act plays as well as poems have appeared in
magazines and anthologies. In 1917 she was awarded the Browning
Society (Philadelphia) medal for poetry. She is a resident of Alpine,
Calif.

HORNER, JOYCE was born in England in 1903. She received her
B.A. from Oxford and her M.A. from Smith. She teaches English at
Mt. Holyoke College. Miss Horner has published two novels *The
Wind and the Rain* (1943) and *The Greyhound in the Leash* (1949)
both brought out by Doubleday here, and by Faber & Faber in Lon-
don. She has contributed poetry to Harper's, The New Yorker, Amer-
ican Scholar, and other journals. In 1957 she won the PSA Annual
Award.

HOWARD, FRANCES MINTURN was educated in private schools.
She hails from New York but makes her home in Boston. In 1950 her
book ms. *All Keys Are Glass* won the $1000 Borestone Mt. Poetry
Award, which Dutton published the same year. Dutton also brought
out her second book *Sleep Without Armor* (1953). Mrs. Howard is
a winner of the PSA Annual Award and co-winner of the Reynolds
Lyric Award, as well as of the Ficke Sonnet Award. She has served
many years on the Governing Board of the Poetry Society.

HOWES, GRACE CLEMENTINE, a resident of Boston, was born
in Somerville, Mass. 1874. Her work has appeared in Voices, The
Lyric West, and elsewhere. A national prize poem given her by
Delineator is included in four anthologies. With others she founded,
in the 20's, the Boise (Idaho) Writers Club and is the first honorary
member of that organization.

HUGHES, DOROTHY has published in The New Yorker, American
Scholar, Poetry, and other magazines. Her book, *The Green Loving,*

was brought out by Scribner in 1953. Born in St. Louis, Mo. in 1910, she received her B.A. from Barnard and her B.S. in library science from Columbia. She has served as library assistant at the Horace Mann School and at the New York Public Library.

HUGHES, TED, a native of Yorkshire, England, holds the B.A. and M.A. degrees from Cambridge University. A prize-winning volume of his poems *The Hawk in the Rain* (1957) was published simultaneously by Harper in this country and by Faber & Faber in England. He is also the winner of the Guinness Poetry Award (1958) and is a John Simon Guggenheim Fellow. He is married to Sylvia Plath. Mr. Hughes was born in 1930 and makes his home in Wellesley, Mass.

INGALLS, JEREMY was Fulbright Professor in American Literature, Japan, 1957-58; a Rockefeller Foundation lecturer in American Poetry, Japan, 1958; and is the recipient of a Guggenheim Fellowship, a Ford Foundation Fellowship, and other grants, including one from the American Academy of Arts and Letters (1944). Born in Gloucester, Mass. in 1911, Miss Ingalls received her B.A. and M.A. from Rockford College and is Professor of English and Asian Studies there. She won the Yale Series of Younger Poets Award in 1941 and in 1950 the PSA Shelley Memorial Award. She is the author of four books of poetry and two of prose.

ISH-KISHOR, SULAMITH was born in London, where her first poem was published at the age of ten. She attended Hunter College in New York. Among her books are *Magnificent Hadrian* (Minton, Balch, N. Y. and Victor Gollancz, London) and *American Promise* (Behrman House). Her writing has appeared in many periodicals. The Reader's Digest printed her "Appointment with Love." Miss Ish-Kishor is currently working on a historical novel and a play.

JACOBS, CATHERINE HAYDON is a native and resident of New York. She attended Vassar College and is a teacher at Julia Richmond High School in New York. She has contributed to Good Housekeeping, Ladies Home Journal, and other magazines and newspapers.

JACOBSEN, JOSEPHINE is the author of *Let Each Man Remember* (1940) and *For the Unlost* (1946), the latter a volume in the Contemporary Poetry Distinguished Poets Series. She makes her home in New Hampshire in the summer and Baltimore in the winter.

JACOBY, GROVER has been editor and publisher of Variegation: A Magazine of Free Verse since 1946, and of Recurrence; A Magazine of Rhyme since 1950. A volume of his own verse, *The Human Patina*, was published in 1937. He was born in Los Angeles, Calif. in 1911.

JEFFERS, ROBINSON was born in Pittsburgh, Pa. in 1887. He studied at private schools in this country, Switzerland, and Germany. He received his A.B. from Occidental College in 1905. Graduate study took him to the University of Southern California Medical

School, the University of Zurich, and the University of Washington, School of Forestry. *Flagons and Apples,* his first volume of verse, appeared in 1912. Jeffers' desire to pursue a literary career was realized when a cousin died and left him a legacy. In 1914 he moved to Carmel, Calif. and there, on a bluff overlooking Carmel Bay, built himself the stone house and tower in which he has lived and worked for upward of forty years. He is the recipient of many major awards and is a member of the National Institute of Arts and Letters. His published works include *Tamar* (1924), *Roan Stallion* (1925), *Candor* (1928), *Give Your Heart to the Hawks* (1933), *Selected Poetry* (1938), *Medea* (1946), *Double Axe* (1948) and *Hungerfield* (1954).

JEFFRIES, CHRISTIE is the author of *Until This Moment,* a book of poems published in 1942 by Banner Press. She has published poetry, literary criticism and articles in various magazines. A native of Odessa, Mo., she received her M.A. from the University of Missouri and did graduate work at Columbia. She is chairman of the Department of Communication Arts at Paterson (N. J.) State College.

JENKINS, OLIVER has been a political columnist for the Boston Herald, and consultant to the Governor of New Hampshire. He is a native Bostonian. Among his published books are *The Sky Is Falling* (Page 1931) and *Captain's Walk,* a collection of poems (Caxton, Ltd. 1940).

JENNINGS, LESLIE NELSON was born in Ware, Mass. in 1890. His early years were spent in California where he was a protege of George Sterling. On his return to the East he became associate editor of Current Opinion. His verse has appeared in The New Yorker, Saturday Review, Poetry, The Nation, The New Republic, etc. He is the author of *Mill Talk & Other Poems* (The Fine Editions Press 1942). He is currently active as literary consultant, critic, and editor.

JONES, CULLEN has been an Army officer, beginning with service on the Mexican Border and extending through World War II when he was Control Officer and Commander of the North Service Command. He has served as headmaster and superintendent of preparatory schools and taught creative writing in college. His collected poems *Finger Prints,* was published by Marshall Jones in 1952. He won the American Weave publication award in 1950. He is a native Nevadan (born 1890) and lives in San Rafael, Calif.

JONES, MARY HOXIE is a Pennsylvanian by birth and residence. An alumna of Mt. Holyoke College, she published two volumes of prose and a collection of poems, the latter, *Arrows of Desire,* brought out by Macmillan in 1931. She is at work on a history of Quakers in New England.

JORDAN, BARBARA LESLIE (Mrs. John Ingle Yellott) was born in New York in 1915. She studied technique of poetry at Columbia. Falmouth Press published her *Web of Days* in 1949 and Arkwright Press her *Comfort the Dreamer* in 1955.

KAHN, HANNAH is a New Yorker by birth. She now resides in Miami, Fla., where she serves as poetry review editor for the Miami Herald. Her work has appeared in anthologies and magazines. She is the winner of a number of national awards.

KANE, DOUGLAS V., formerly in the Portuguese Consulate General's office in San Francisco, is now with the travel department of the American Express Company in New York. Born in 1903 in New York, he received his B.S. from City College and did graduate work at Columbia and at the University of California. He has published two books. At one time he was New York representative of the poetry magazine Wings.

KAPLAN, MILTON, chairman of the English Department of George Washington High School, was born in New York in 1910 and educated at City College and Columbia University, where he earned his M.A. and Ph.D. He has contributed to Poetry, Harper's, and other magazines. His *Radio and Poetry* was published by the Columbia University Press in 1949.

KEATING, NORMA has been represented with work in Scribner's, Poetry, New York Times, etc. She is the author of *Giants and Dwarfs, Songs of a Salamander,* and *Dark Doves & Other Poems.* She has also written children's stories and done newspaper reporting. In private life she is Mrs. Matt Mattlin. She is a resident of Spring Lake, N. J.

KEITH, JOSEPH JOEL is the author of several collections of verse, among them *The Proud People, The Long Nights, The Hearth Lit,* and *Two Laughters,* the last named published in 1958 as a Book Club for Poetry selection. Mr. Keith's individual poems have appeared in the Saturday Review, Argosy (London), Kenyon Review, Harper's, Prairie Schooner, Spirit, etc. He has lectured widely and has served as Secretary-Treasurer of the Los Angeles Center of P.E.N.

KELLER, MARTHA (Mrs. Edmund Rowland) is a resident and native of Pennsylvania. She received her A.B. at Vassar and did graduate work at Stanford University. She worked in publishing houses from 1926 until 1932. Among her books are *Mirror to Mortality* (Dutton 1937) and *The War Whoop of the Wily Iroquois* (Coward-McCann 1954).

KENNEDY, MARY is the author of *Mrs. Partridge Presents* and other plays. In 1933 Doubleday brought out her *Surprise to the Children,* for which Deems Taylor provided the music. She has also written a Dodd, Mead publication, *Star on Her Forehead,* in collaboration with Helen Hayes. Miss Kennedy is a native of Claxton, Ga. In 1954 she won the William Rose Benét Memorial Award.

KEYSNER, BLANCHE WHITING was born in 1881 in Glenville, W. Va., was educated at Glenville Teachers College, and has taught in her home county as well as in Brooklyn public schools. Wings

Press published her *Far Hills Are Blue* in 1947. She is a past President of the Pennsylvania Poetry Society.

KILMER, KENTON was for seven years poetry editor of the Washington Post and is now editorial specialist in legislative reference for the Library of Congress. He has edited five anthologies of poetry and published poems of his own in America, Catholic World, and other magazines. He was born in Morristown, N. J. in 1909 and holds degrees from St. Mary's College (A.B.) and Georgetown University (M.A.). He is the son of the late Joyce Kilmer.

KING, ETHEL is a native New Yorker, educated at the Convent of the Sacred Heart, Columbia University, and other schools. She has contributed to the Lyric, Spirit, etc. and is the author of two published works.

KOCH, JAMES H., currently engaged in completing a novel, was born in Milwaukee in 1926 and is a graduate of Carleton College. He also studied at the University of Wisconsin under Karl Shapiro, at Middlebury, and at Princeton, the first year as Woodrow Wilson Fellow. Since 1952 he has been employed by Dun & Bradstreet, where he is Art and Copy Chief. His poems have appeared in Western Review, Furioso, Manuscript, etc.

KRUGER, FANIA of Wichita Falls, Tex. is a native of Sevastopol. She attended Russian gymnasia and Harvard, Columbia, and Brandeis Universities. She is the author of *Cossack Laughter* (1937) and *The Tenth Jew* (1949), both Kaleidograph Press publications. Her short story "Sabbath Magic" was cited in Martha Foley's 1952 *Best American Short Stories.* She was born in 1893.

KUMIN, MAXINE W. is the author of *Sebastian and the Dragon,* a children's story in verse recently published by Putnam. Her work in poetry has appeared in The New Yorker, Harper's and other magazines. An alumna of Radcliffe (A.B., M.A.) and a native of Philadelphia, Mrs. Kumin is an instructor in English at Tufts College. She won the PSA Annual Award, second prize, in 1959.

LaBOMBARD, JOAN was born in San Francisco, Cal. in 1920 and was graduated from the University of California at Los Angeles. Her work has appeared in The Atlantic, Poetry, and elsewhere.

LANKFORD, FRANCES STOAKLEY is a past president of the Norfolk Poets' Club and has been published in a number of magazines and newspapers. She has taught creative writing at the University of Virginia (Norfolk Extension) and has been a junior high school teacher. She was born in New Orleans, La. in 1909. She received her B.A. from Hollins College and her M.A. from Columbia University.

LAUBE, CLIFFORD JAMES began a fifty-year career in journalism on a Rico (Colo.) newspaper in 1903, retiring as national news editor of The New York Times in 1953. For two terms he was president of the Catholic Poetry Society, and is an editor and co-founder of the magazine, Spirit. Monastine Press published his book of verse, *Crags*, in 1938. Born in Telluride, Colo. in 1891, he holds honorary degrees from St. Bonaventure University, Manhattan College, and Boston College.

LAY, NORMA, an alumna of Elmira College, did graduate work at Wellesley. Decker Press brought out her book of poems *Interval to Sun* in 1949. She was born in Ithaca, N. Y. in 1904.

LeGEAR, LAURA LOURENE hails from Waco, Tex. She is the winner of many poetry awards, including the PSA Annal Award in 1949. An animal fancier, she raises show cats for TV and the movies.

LEIGHTON, LOUISE is founder, past president, and life member of the Wisconsin Fellowship of Poets, and is a board member of the Wisconsin Regional Writers' Association. She is the author of two books *The Great Carrying Place* and *Journey to Light*. She was born in Wauwatosa, Wisc. in 1890.

LENGYEL, CORNEL has been editor, music critic and columnist for The Argonaut, and a Warrant Officer during World War II in the Merchant Marine. He has published poetry in the Saturday Review and other journals, and is the author of *American Testament* (Grace Books 1956) and *Four Days in July: The Story Behind the Declaration of Independence* (Doubleday 1958). He is the recipient of the Maxwell Anderson Poetic Drama Award (first prize), a Huntington Hartford Fellowship, and other grants and awards. He was born in 1915 in Fairfield, Conn.

LEVI, ADELE FRANCES is a native of San Francisco and received her A.B. at University of California. Since 1934 she has been a social service worker with the San Francisco Public Welfare Department. While a college undergraduate she won the Emily Chamberlain Cook prize in poetry for her *Dwellers in the Hills*, published by the University of California Press. In 1956 she received the Laramore-Rader Poetry Award.

LIEBERMAN, ELIAS is a retired Associate Superintendent of Schools in New York City. As permanent chairman of judges for the Inter-High School poetry contests, he has done much to encourage creative expression among talented students. At one time he served as member of the editorial staff of Puck. His published works include *Paved Streets, The Hand Organ Man, Man in the Shadows, To My Brothers Everywhere*, and *Poems for Enjoyment* (the latter an anthology and guide to poetry appreciation). The Spoken Word Inc. recently issued an album record of a number of his poems. Some years ago the Alumni Association of City College awarded him the Townsend Harris Medal for distinguished service as educator and author. He was created a PSA Fellow at the Society's 50th Anniversary Dinner in January, 1960.

LINK, CAROLYN WILSON is a native of Newark, N. J. and an alumna of Vassar. She is the author of *Fir Trees and Fireflies* (Putnam 1920) and *There is Still Time,* the 1945 prize volume of The League to Support Poetry.

LINK, GORDDEN S. has been director of the Link Psychotherapy Clinic and Guidance Center since 1948, and of the Armed Forces Guidance Center, R.O.A. since 1955. He is also executive secretary of the American Association for Social Psychiatry and Lecturer in Psychology at George Washington University. He has published four books, including *Three Poems for Now* (University Press 1953). He was born in Chicago in 1907.

LITTLE, KATHARINE DAY was born in 1889 in Brookline, Mass. and attended the Boston School of the Museum of Fine Arts, and the Universities of Maine and Michigan. Harper brought out her *Fenelon, Study of a Personality* in 1952. Her work has appeared in the Saturday Review, Prairie Schooner, and elsewhere. She is on the board of the Poetry Club of New England.

LITTLEFIELD, HAZEL (Mrs. Dennis V. Smith) was born in Farwell, Mich. in 1889. She received her B.A. in 1913 from the University of Michigan. She is the author of two books of verse: *Mortal Harvest* and *A Flame of Faith.* In 1959 her biography of Lord Dunsany was brought out by Exposition Press.

LIVINGSTON, EDNA was born in 1897 and is a resident and native of New York. She studied education, music and English at Columbia and New York University, has done editorial and research work and is currently teaching in the New York City school system. Her verse has appeared in the North American Review and other periodicals.

LODGE, EDITH, resident of Salem, Va., is a native of New York (1908). She received her B.A. from Oberlin College. She contributes to Kaleidograph, the Saturday Review, and other magazines and newspapers.

LORD, MAY CARLETON is president (third term) of the Akron branch of the Ohio Poetry Society. She was born in Kansas City, Mo. in 1883 and studied piano and creative writing and painting, as well as history and psychology. Her verse has appeared in Kaleidograph and elsewhere.

LOUIS, LOUISE is the author of two books of verse: *This is for You* (1947) and *Dervish Dance* (1958), and of two books for use in secondary schools. She has lectured, has had her own radio program, and is a professional reader. She was born in New York in 1906 and took her B.A. degree at Hunter College. She is the winner of the 1960 Leonora Speyer Award.

LUTZ, GERTRUDE MAY was born in Oakland, Cal. in 1899. She began the serious study of poetry in 1942. She has since published a book of poems, *Point the Sun Tomorrow* (Golden Quill Press 1956) and has been the winner of several poetry prizes, including the PSA Leonora Speyer Award in 1959. She lectures on the technique and appreciation of poetry.

MacARTHUR, GLORIA was born in 1924 in Washington, D. C. She attended Vassar and holds a B.A. cum laude from the University of Minnesota. She studied under Joseph Warren Beach and Robert Penn Warren. Her poetry has appeared in many anthologies and magazines.

MADELEVA, SISTER MARY THERESE is the author of four books of verse: *Give Joan a Sword, Now There Is Beauty, Selected Poems,* and *Moment in Ostia,* the last published in 1959 by Doubleday. Born in Wisconsin, she joined the Sisters of the Divine Savior and spent many years teaching English at their training school in Milwaukee. She is president of St. Mary's College, Notre Dame, Ind. and holds M.A., Ph.D., and Litt. D. degrees conferred on her by many institutions of learning.

MALESKA, EUGENE T. began his career in education as a teacher of English and Latin in New Jersey, has been a school principal, and now is N. Y. C. Director of Teacher Recruitment. He was born in New Jersey in 1916, and took his bachelor's and master's degrees at Montclair State College, and his Ed.D. at Harvard. His first book of poems is to be published in the Spring of 1960.

MANSFIELD, MARGERY was born in 1895 in Chicago and studied at Smith College (B.A.), the New School, and elsewhere. She was business manager of Poetry under Harriet Monroe and corresponding secretary of the PSA. Her work has appeared in about forty periodicals. She is the author of *Workers In Fire: A Book about Poetry* (Longmans Green 1937) and co-author of *New England's Monterey* (Monterey Congregational Church 1950).

MARGOLIS, SILVIA was born in Poland, emigrating to America early in life. She was educated at the University of Dayton and at Ohio State University. Wings Press published her two books of poetry: *The Argent Flame* (1958) and *The Singing Elm* (1959).

MARS, ANN (Annalita Marsigli) has contributed verse, in English and Italian, to Il giornale dei poeti, Il Progresso D'Italia, and other publications. She is a native of Bologna and received her early education in Switzerland, England, and Chile. In this country she trained at Vassar and Barnard. Her first book of poems is in preparation.

MARSHALL, LENORE G. took her B.A. at Barnard College and worked as a literary editor from 1929 to 1932. She has published three novels and two books of verse: *No Boundary* (Holt 1943) and *Other Knowledge* (Noonday Press 1957). She has contributed to Partisan Review and other magazines, and has done a recorded reading of her work issued by Spoken Arts. Her most recent work in prose, *The Hill is Level* (a novel), was issued by Random House in 1959.

MARX, ANNE was born in Germany in 1913. After receiving her B.S. degree, she studied medicine at the University of Heidelberg. A volume of her poetry in German was published by Kaufmann Verlag. She has lived in the United States since 1936 and now writes poetry in English. Her work has appeared in various magazines and has won several prizes.

MASEFIELD, JOHN, O. M., has been Poet Laureate of England since 1930. He was born in 1878, son of a solicitor of Ledbury, Herefordshire. After a brief schooling, he took to sea (on training ships and windjammers), but after two and a half years decided to become a writer. His first book of poems, *Salt-Water Ballads*, appeared in 1902. In 1911, with the publication of *The Everlasting Mercy*, his fame as one of the leading poets of his day was firmly established. Oxford, Cambridge, Harvard, Yale have honored him with degrees. Among his works other than those already mentioned are: *The Widow in the Bye-Street, Dauber, Reynard the Fox*, and *Right Royal*.

MASON, MADELINE is the author of four books and a translation into French of Gibran's *The Prophet*. She is the winner of the 1957 Diamond Jubilee Award of Distinction in Poetry (Nat. League of American Penwomen) and the Lyric magazine Reynolds Award in 1955. Born in New York in 1913, she has been political columnist, lecturer, reader, and writer of radio scripts. Her work is in permanent collections at the Lamont Library, Lockwood Memorial, and Yale. Her latest book *At the Ninth Hour*, a sonnet-sequence in a new form, was published by The University Press of Washington, D. C.

MASTERS, MARCIA, daughter of the late Edgar Lee Masters, was born in Chicago in 1910. She attended the University of Chicago and returned there in 1943 on a President's Remission for special studies. She has done reporting and feature writing for the Chicago Sun-Times and other papers, and was editor of the Los Angeles Times Home Magazine. Her poetry has appeared in the Saturday Review, Voices, and elsewhere. She is the mother of three children and lives in Kenilworth, Ill.

MASTIN, FLORENCE RIPLEY was graduated from Barnard College (B.A.) and taught English in a Brooklyn High school. In 1918 she published *Green Leaves*, and in 1935 *Cables of Cobweb*. She is a native of Wayne, Pa. and a resident of Piermont-on-the-Hudson, N. Y.

MATTHEWS, ALICE CLEAR, born in Albany, N. Y., is an alumna of New York State College for Teachers and holds a Master of Arts degree from the Bread Loaf School of English, Middlebury College, Vt. Before her marriage, she taught English at Albany High School.

McGARVEY, MARGARET has been a journalist, secretary, and stenotype reporter, and has done publicity for a concert association and a Little Theatre. Born in 1899 in Brunswick, Ga., where she still lives, she studied at the University of Georgia. She contributes to mnay magazines and newspapers and has won a number of poetry prizes.

McGINLEY, PHYLLIS (Mrs. Charles Hayden) was born in Oregon in 1905 and studied at country schools and at the universities of Utah and California. For a time she did free lance writing and served as assistant editor of Town and Country. She early gained a reputation as a writer of light verse. Her most popular recent volume in that field was *The Love Letters of Phyllis McGinley.* She has also published a prose book, *The Province of the Heart* (Viking Press 1959). Individual poems of hers have appeared in The New Yorker, Atlantic, Saturday Review, etc.

McKEE, GLADYS (Mrs. Eugene E. Iker) was born and educated in Irontown, O., and has lived in Cincinnati since she was sixteen. Her work has been appearing in poetry magazines and newspapers for the past twenty years. She acquired her early writing training as Continuity and Program Director of a local radio station. She is married and has one son.

MEACHAM, HARRY M. is a native Virginian, born in Petersburg in 1901 and now residing in Richmond. He took special courses in Greek Literature and Philosophy at St. Johns College. He is a past president of the Poetry Society of Virginia and serves on a number of boards, including that of the Richmond Professional Institute, The Lyric, and the Valentine Museum. His work has appeared in various anthologies and periodicals.

MEYER, GERARD PREVIN was born in New York in 1909. He holds B.A. (cum honoribus) and M.A. degrees from Columbia. His second collection of poems, *Louder Than the Drum,* was the 1943 prize volume of The League to Support Poetry. He teaches at Queens College and writes for WNYE, the Board of Education broadcasting station.

MILLETT, WILLIAM, now a resident of California, is a native of New York. He studied journalism at San Diego Junior College and painting at the School of Fine Arts in Lima, Peru. His work has appeared in The Olivant Quarterly, Epos, Harlequin. etc. He was born on December 21, 1925.

MOORE, MARIANNE had her first volume of poems published by friends in England without her knowledge. At that time (1921) and for four years thereafter she served as an assistant at the New York Public Library. Her first American book *Observations* (1924) won the Dial Award. The following year she joined the Dial magazine as editor and remained with it until 1929, when it ceased publication. During and after that time Miss Moore continued writing and

winning awards, several from Poetry magazine of Chicago, the
PSA Shelley Award, a Guggenheim fellowship, and a grant from the
National Institute of Arts and Letters. Additional honors came to
her with the Bollingen Award and Pulitzer Prize. Her works include
Selected Poems, with introduction by T. S. Eliot (1935); *What Are
Years* (1941); *Nevertheless* (1944); *Collected Poems* (1951); *Like
a Bulwark* (1956). Her most recent collection of poems, *O To Be a
Dragon,* was published by Viking Press in 1959. She was awarded
the PSA Gold Medal at the Society's 50th Anniversary Dinner in
January, 1960. Miss Moore was born in 1887 in St. Louis, Mo.

MORRIS, HARRY has contributed poetry to Kenyon Review, New
Republic, and other magazines. Born in New York in 1924, he took
his B.A. and M.A. at the University of Miami and his Ph.D. at the
University of Minnesota. He is now a Professor of English at Tulane
University in New Orleans.

MOUSLEY, JAMES P. is a native of Wilmington, Del., where he
was born in 1937. He was awarded two scholarships, one for
Huckleberry Mt. Writers Camp in 1954 and the other for Washington College (Md.), 1956-57. His work has appeared in *Six
First State Poets* and elsewhere.

MOWRER, PAUL SCOTT served as foreign correspondent, war
correspondent, diplomatic correspondent, and editor of the Chicago
Daily News. In 1928 he won the Pulitzer Prize as best foreign cor-
respondent for that year. Born in 1887 in Bloomington, Ill. he was
a special student at the University of Michigan, receiving his L.L.D.
(Hon.) in 1941. He is the author of ten books, seven in poetry.
Dutton brought out his first book of poems *Hours of France* in 1918.
His most recent book *Twenty-One and Sixty-Five* is a 1958 Wings
Press publication.

MUNDORF, FRANK has been a contributor to Poetry, Saturday
Review and other periodicals, and has published one book of
poems, *Saturday Night in the Accident Ward* (American Press
1955). He won the 1952 first prize, Poetry Awards (Occidental
College, Calif.). Born in 1916 in Philadelphia, he attended the University of Pennsylvania. In 1945 he served as warrant officer in the
War Crimes Office at General MacArthur's Headquarters in Manila.

NEILSON, FRANCIS, resident of Long Island, is a native of Birken-
head, England, where he was born in 1867. He has been a stage
director (The Royal Opera in London) and a Member of Parliament
(from 1910 to 1916). He has published three score books, including
plays, novels, poetry—*Manabozo* (Macqueen 1899), *Blue and Purple*
(Huebsch 1920), *Poems* (Nelson 1956)—and three Shakespearean
studies. He is founder of the Neilson Expedition to the Near East,
a member of the Governing Body of the Shakespeare Memorial
Theatre (England), and Honorary Governor of the John Rylands
Library (England).

NELSON, PAULA is the author of three volumes of poetry: *Full Heart Remembering, Race in the Sun,* and *Always the Search.* She was born in 1897 and studied at Cornell University and the University of Arizona, where she received her B.A.

NELSON, STARR was born on Long Island and studied violin at the Ithaca Conservatory of Music. She lives in New Britain, Conn. and is the wife of an artist. Her first book of poems, *Heavenly Body,* was a prize volume of the League to Support Poetry (1942). Her work has appeared in The Saturday Review, Fantasy & Science Fiction, Contemporary Poetry, Voices, etc. A novel and a new collection of poems are in the offing.

NICHOLL, LOUISE TOWNSEND is the author of seven books of poetry, the latest of which, *The World's One Clock,* appeared in 1959 (St. Martin's Press). Her previous books were *Water and Light, Dawn in Snow, Life Is the Flesh, The Explicit Flower, Collected Poems,* and *The Curious Quotient.* In 1954 she was awarded the $5000 Fellowship of the Academy of American Poets. Miss Nicholl is an Editor and Literary Advisor in New York. She was created a PSA Fellow at the Society's 50th Anniversary Dinner in January 1960.

NUTTER, MEDORA ADDISON for four years was associate editor of House Beautiful magazine. She is a native of Fitchburg, Mass. Her *Dreams and a Sword* was published in the Yale Series of Younger Poets in 1922. In 1950 William Morrow brought out her *Mountain Creed and Other Poems.*

O'BRIEN, KATHARINE was born in Amesbury, Mass. in 1901 and now lives in Portland, Me. She was educated at Bates College, Cornell University, and Brown University (A.B., A.M., Ph.D.) and is a member of Phi Beta Kappa and Sigma Xi. She is head of the Mathematics Department at Deering High School in Portland, Me. Her poetry has appeared in the Saturday Review, Christian Science Monitor, etc. She has also published a three-part chorus for women's voices.

ORENTE, ROSE J. was born in 1919 in New York and received her B.A. at Hunter College. She is publicity director for John Wiley & Sons, publishers. She is the author of *Carlotta's Serape,* first-prize winner in the 1957 verse-play contest sponsored by The Academy of American Poets.

PALEN, JENNIE M. is a graduate of New York University and a native of New York State. Accountant, editor, teacher and writer, she has published two books of verse: *Moon Over Manhattan* (Wings Press 1949) and *Good Morning, Sweet Prince* (American Weave 1957), as well as a book on accounting. She has won numerous prizes for her poetry.

PALMER, WINTHROP is the author of books in the field of dance criticism, poetry, ballet, and fiction. In 1945 two books of hers ap-

peared simultaneously: *Theatrical Dance in America* (Bernard Acker-
man) and *The Invisible Wife and Other Poems* (The Fine Editions
Press). She published two novels in 1946. In 1951, Farrar, Straus
brought out her *The New Barbarian*. She is on the faculty of Post
College, and has an Hon. Litt.D. from Long Island University. In
1959 her *Fables and Ceremonies,* a collection of poems, translated
into French, appeared in Paris over the Jean Grassin imprint.

PELOUBET, MAURICE E., member of the certified public ac-
countants firm of Pogson, Peloubet & Co. of New York, is Treasurer
of the PSA. He has contributed poetry to various magazines and
newspapers, has written books and articles of a technical nature, and
is the author of *Ballads, Songs and Snatches* (1937). He is a collector
of Blake and creator of the Emily S. Hamblen Memorial Award,
given annually for an outstanding work on the English poet and
painter. Mr. Peloubet was created a PSA Fellow at the Society's
50th Anniversary Dinner in January 1960.

PENNANT, EDMUND is a native New Yorker. He was born in
1917 of Hungarian and Russian Jewish parents. Scribner's brought
out his *I, Too, Jehovah* (poems) in 1952. He has done original stories
and narratives for documentary TV films. One of his films won honorable mention at the 1955 Venice Film Festival.

PHILLIPS, MARIE TELLO is the author of seventeen published
books, including three novels, seven volumes of poetry, and a book
of critical essays. Among her many awards are: a decoration from
Institute Litteraire et Artistique de France "for distinguished writing"; the English professional Fraternity, Sigma Tau Delta, Diamond
Torch in 1927, and doctor's degrees for literary achievement. She is
a founder-member of the American Academy of Poets. She was born
in Louisville, Ky. in 1874.

PINKNEY, DOROTHY COWLES was born in New Rochelle, N. Y.
in 1904. Her verse has appeared in more than fifty magazines and
newspapers. In 1956 The Fine Editions Press brought out her first
collection of poems *The Town Not Yet Awake.* She has a second
book in preparation.

PLATH, SYLVIA (Mrs. Ted Hughes) has been the recipient of a
Fulbright grant to England (1955-57), The Academy of American
Poets Prize at Smith College (1955), The Lyric Young Poets' Prize
(1955) and Poetry's Bess Hokin Prize (1957). Her verse has ap-
peared in Harper's, The Nation, London Magazine, The New
Yorker, etc. She has degrees from Smith College and from Cambridge
University. She was born in Boston in 1932.

PORTER, JENNY LIND (M.A., Ph.D.) is a native Texan (1927).
Educated at Texas Christian University and the University of Texas,
she is currently teaching at West Texas State College. She has published extensively in magazines and has to her credit four books,
among them *The Lantern of Diogenes* (1954), *Peter Bell the Fourth*
(1955), and *The Siege of the Alamo* (1958).

POWERS, STAR hails from Wisconsin. A delegate to UNESCO in 1954, she is a professional lecturer on poetry and was editor of American Poetry Magazine from 1950 to 1957. In 1939 she published *My Poems,* verse for children (Hyde Park Press) and *Selections* (Kenyon Press 1949).

PRAY, BENJAMIN STURGIS was born in Cambridge, Mass. and took his A.B. and M.L.A. degrees at Harvard. His poems have appeared in The Christian Science Monitor, the New York Times, and elsewhere.

RAINSFORD, CHRISTINA is a native New Yorker. She attended the Spence School. For several semesters she studied under Leonora Speyer. Her poetry has appeared in the New York Times, American Weave, and other periodicals.

RANDALL-MILLS, ELIZABETH is a Vassar alumna, a native of St. Louis, Mo. (1906). She has contributed to such publications as Poetry, Spirit, Virginia Quarterly, American Mercury, etc. She is a Phi Beta Kappa.

ROBINSON, HENRY MORTON, a native of Brooklyn, was educated at Columbia University (B.A., M.A.) where he later became instructor in English literature. In 1925-27 he edited Contemporary Verse. Since 1935 has been an editor of Reader's Digest. He is the author of more than a dozen books, among them *Stout Cortez, Buck Fever, Second Wisdom, The Perfect Round,* and *The Cardinal.* He saw active service as gunner's mate in the U. S. Navy in World War I. He makes his home in Tenafly, N. J.

ROCHE, PAUL has lived most of his life in London, but spent his early years in India. He began his education at Ushaw College, Durham (a pre-Elizabethan stronghold of the humanities), and completed it at the Gregorian University in Rome, taking a Ph.B. and Ph.L. in scholastic philosophy. He is the author of a novel *Vessel of Dishonour;* English versions of *The Oedipus Plays of Sophocles* and *The Murder of Agamemnon* (from the Oresteian cycle of Aeschylus); a book of legends, *The Rat and the Convent;* and an allegorical work, *O Pale Galilean.* Mr. Roche's poems and short stories have appeared in Encounter, The Listener, Saturday Review, Town & Country, New World Writing, etc. Recordings of his work exist at the Lamont Library, Harvard, and the library of the University of Chicago.

ROMANO, LIBORIA has a B.A. cum laude and an M.A. from Hunter College. While still an undergraduate she won the Dante Medal. Since 1958 she has conducted a monthly column for The Writer's Voice. Her first book of poems, *Venus for a Crown,* appeared in 1959. Mrs. Romano was born in New York on July 17, 1899.

ROSENBAUM, NATHAN is a Russian by birth. He emigrated to the U.S.A. in 1903 and was educated in Philadelphia where he attended Temple University. He is director of a firm of commercial bankers. He has, to date, published five books, among them *Songs and Symphonies, Each in His Time, My Hand and Seal* and *A Man from Parnassus.*

ROSS, ALLISON (Mrs. Robert E. Anderson, Jr.) has contributed to the American Scholar, Antioch Review, etc. A native of Baltimore, she attended and graduated from Goucher College. She now makes her home in Albuquerque, N. M.

ROSS, DAVID is a native and resident of New York and a pioneer in poetry reading on the radio. In 1933 the American Academy of Arts and Letters awarded him radio's gold medal for diction. His *Poet's Gold* anthology, first published in 1933, has been reissued in 1945 and again in 1958. Mr. Ross was created a PSA Fellow at the Society's 50th Anniversary Dinner in January 1960.

RUBIN, LARRY holds the B.A., M.A. and Ph.D. degrees from Emory University. Although he has had no book published, his poems have appeared in a great variety of periodicals: Saturday Review, Beloit Poetry Journal, New Mexico Quarterly, Fiddlehead, etc. He has had critical articles in Modern Language Notes and Twentieth Century Literature. His doctoral dissertation consisted of a study of thematic imagery in the novels of Thomas Wolfe. He is assistant professor of English at Georgia Institute of Technology. A native of Bayonne, N. J., he was born on February 14, 1930.

RUSS, VIRGINIA did the choreography for the University of California-sponsored Greek Theatre performance of *The Birds* and has performed in her own ballet at the New School, the Guild Theatre, and elsewhere. Her poetry has appeared in anthologies and magazines and is included in a published volume of verse. Mrs. Russ was born in San Francisco in 1916.

RUSSELL, ETHEL GREEN was born, near Fort Scott, Kans. of Quaker ancestry and spent her childhood in the Valley of the Gila, Arizona. She has been a teacher, is married, and has raised three sons, all of whom served as Air Force officers in World War II and in Korea. Mrs. Russell's work has appeared in many publications in this country and in England.

RUSSELL, SYDNEY KING is the author of eleven books, among them *Proud Universe* (Putnam 1940), *Songs for America* (The Fine Editions Press 1943), *The Listening Year* (Peter Pauper Press 1953), and *Clock and Bottle* (Falmouth 1959). He is the composer of many concert songs, one of which, "Harbor Night," won the Kimball award in 1945. He has been an editor of The Poetry Chap-Book and a member of the Executive Board of the PSA.

SALOMON, I. L. was born in Hartford, Conn. in 1899 and claims Vermont as his second home. Much of his poetry deals with the way of life in the Green Mountain State. He is the winner of a first and second PSA Annual Award. He was the first to introduce the poetry of Carlo Betocchi in English translation, and is the author of *Unit and Universe* (1959).

SALZ, HELEN is an artist by profession and has had many one-man shows at the San Francisco Museum and elsewhere. She was educated in San Francisco, where she was born in 1883, and studied art under Gottardo Piazzoni and Robert Henri. Her verse has appeared in various periodicals.

SAMPLEY, ARTHUR M. is a professor of English and a vice-president of North Texas State College. Born in Texas in 1903 and educated at the University of Texas and Columbia, he has published three books of poetry with Kaleidograph Press. He is a regional Vice-President of the PSA.

SANDBURG, CARL was born in 1878 in Galesburg, Ill. He left school at thirteen and worked at harvesting, bricklaying, and other odd jobs. During the Spanish-American War he served in Puerto Rico with the Sixth Illinois Infantry. After four years at Lombard College, he left without taking a degree. In Milwaukee, from 1910 to 1912 he was secretary to the mayor of that city. His first literary recognition came to him with his winning the Helen Haire Levinson Prize (1914). He won the Pulitzer Prize for his six-volume life of Lincoln in 1940. He won the Pulitzer Prize again in 1951, this time for poetry. The Gold Medal for History from the American Academy of Arts and Letters and the PSA Gold Medal for Distinguished Service were also awarded him. His principal works include *Chicago Poems* (1916), *Cornhuskers* (1918), *Smoke and Steel* (1920), *Slabs of the Sunburnt West* (1922), *Selected Poems* (1926), *Abraham Lincoln: The Prairie Years* (1929); *The People, Yes* (1936), *Complete Poems* (1950), and an autobiography, *Always the Young Strangers* (1953).

SARTON, MAY, a native of Belgium, was born in 1912. She has served as instructor of English at Harvard in 1950-53, Phi Beta Kappa Visiting Scholar 1958-9, and is now a lecturer at Wellesley. She is the author of six novels, two books of non-fiction and five books of poetry, among them *Inner Landscape* (1939), *The Land of Silence* (1953) and *In Time Like Air* (1958). Among her awards are a Guggenheim Fellowship in 1953, an American Academy of Arts and Sciences Fellowship (1958) and an Hon. Litt. D. from Russell Sage (1959).

SAUL, GEORGE BRANDON is the author of sixteen books and chapbooks. He has been professor of English at the University of Connecticut since 1924. A native of Shoemakersville, Pa., he received his A.B., A.M. and Ph.D. from the University of Pennsylvania.

SAVAGE, FRANCES HIGGINSON is a great grandniece of Thomas Wentworth Higginson. She is a Bryn Mawr alumna and a native of New York and the author of two published volumes.

SCARBROUGH, GEORGE is a native and resident of Tennessee and received his M.A. from the University of Tennessee. He was awarded a Literary Fellowship to the University of the South in 1941 and has published three books with Dutton, the most recent *Summer So-Called* (1956).

SCHEUER, MARJORIE SOMERS was born in New Haven, Conn. in 1890 and graduated from what is now Curry College. She studied voice at the New England Conservatory of Music. Her poetry has appeared in the Lyric, Catholic World, and elsewhere.

SCHIERLOH, SAMUEL has published two books, *Grains That the Huskers Lost* and *Down the Bright Stream*. He is a retired Post Office Superintendent. A resident of Cincinnati, he was born in Reading, O. in 1889.

SCHMID, CONSTANCE M. is a native of New York, a former teacher, now living on a Maine farm. Her poems have been published in American Weave, Epos, and elsewhere.

SCHMULLER, AARON was born in 1910, attended City College and, after holding a variety of jobs, now owns and manages his own business in Brooklyn. His poems and translations from the Yiddish have appeared in many magazines. He is the author of four volumes of verse, with a fifth to appear early in 1960.

SCHOECK, R. J. attended McGill University and received his A.M. and Ph.D. from Princeton. He is an associate professor at Notre Dame. He has received fellowships from the Ford Association for the Advancement of Education, and from Yale for research on St. Thomas More. His writings have appeared in Commonweal, Virginia Quarterly Review, and elsewhere.

SCHOLTEN, MARTIN is associate professor of English at the University of Toledo, O. He was born at Muscatine, Ia. in 1911, and was educated at the University of Iowa (B.A.) and the University of Michigan (M.A. and Ed.D.). His *A Later Shore* (poems) was published in 1951.

SCHULTZ, LULU MINERVA is a resident of Washington, D. C. She is the author of two books of verse: *Wide Country Dusk* (1941) and *But the Stars Come Out* (1958).

SEXTON, ANNE is a native and resident of Massachusetts. Her first book of poems, *To Bedlam and Partway Back*, was recently brought out by Houghton, Mifflin. She has appeared in Partisan Review and other magazines, and was awarded the Robert Frost Fellowship at Bread Loaf Writers Conference in 1959.

SHAW, CHARLES was born in New York in 1892 and attended Yale (Ph.D.) and Columbia School of Architecture. Among his seven published books are *Heart in a Hurricane* (Brentano's 1927), *It Looked Like Spilt Milk* (Harper 1949), and *Into the Light* (The

Fine Editions Press 1959). Mr. Shaw is a well known artist whose
work is represented in more than twenty of the country's leading
art museums.

SHEPARD, ELIZABETH ALSOP is the author of a book of poems,
White Fox, published by Dodd, Mead in 1956. Born in Brooklyn
in 1888, she received her A.B. from Smith College and has done
executive work in the fields of education and welfare.

SHERRY, RUTH FORBES is a native of Chicago. She was educated
at Vassar, Stanford, and the Sorbonne. She has published several
volumes of verse. Her writings have appeared in more than two
hundred periodicals.

SHERWOOD, GRACE BUCHANAN was born in New York in
1883 and was graduated from the Spence School. She has published
five books, including *Water Meadows* (1937) and *No Final Breath*
(1940), both brought out by Wings Press.

SHUFORD, GENE has taught at several colleges and universities
and is now director of the North Texas State College, Department
of Journalism. He was born in Fayetteville, Ark. in 1907. His poetry
has appeared in Scribner's, New Republic, and other magazines.

SIELLER, WILLIAM VINCENT is a native (1917) and resident
of Norfolk, Conn. He took his B.A. at the University of Buffalo and
his A.M. at Canisius College. He is a teacher of English at Pearson
School, in Connecticut. He has published two books with Falmouth
House, and has won a number of poetry prizes.

SLOAN, JOCELYN MACY was born in Avon, N. Y. in 1901. She
attended Miss Porter's School in Farmington, Conn., as well as
schools in New York and in Canada. Her work has appeared in
American Weave, Voices, Four Quarters, and elsewhere. She served
as guest editor of a recent number of Voices.

SMYTH, FLORIDA WATTS was born in San Antonio, Tex. in
1873 and was educated at Washington, St. Louis, and Columbia
Universities. She has won, among other awards, one from Poetry and
one from the PSA. She succeeded Sara Teasdale as State Poet of
Missouri. A book of her verse *Only on the West Wind* (Middlebury
College Press) has a foreword by Louis Untermeyer.

SMYTHE, DANIEL teaches English at Bradley University and is
the author of four books of poetry. Born in Brockton, Mass. in 1908,
he was educated at Union College (B.A.) and the University of
Pennsylvania (M.A., Ph.D.). He received a $500 prize for creative
work at Union College in 1948.

SOLOMOS, GEORGE (who formerly wrote under the pen name of
Themistocles Hoetis) is of Greek descent but American born. During
World War II he served in the US Air Force and was awarded four
citations for combat duty. After his military discharge he studied at

Wayne State University in Detroit, at the U.C.L.A. in California, and at the Julian Academy and the Sorbonne in Paris. He founded and edited the literary magazine Zero and established The Zero Press. He is the author of a prose work *The Man Who Went Away* (1952). During the years 1948 and 1956 he lived in Europe and North Africa.

SORELL, WALTER has been play producer, lecturer, editor, columnist and translator. He was born in Vienna in 1905 and received his B.A. and M.F.A. at Columbia, where he has served as lecturer. He translated a Goethe Anthology for New Directions and Remarque's *Arch of Triumph.* Of his own two books, one is a modern version in free verse of the medieval play: *Everyman Today* (Dramatists Play Service).

SPEARS, WOODRIDGE is a native Kentuckian. He was educated at Transylvania College, Morehead State College, and the University of Kentucky. At present he is Associate Professor of English at Georgetown College. He has published two books: *The Feudalist* (1946) and *Elizabeth Madox Roberts: A Biographical and Critical Study* (1955).

SPINGARN, LAWRENCE P. is author of two books of verse, *Rococo Summer and Other Poems* (Dutton 1947) and *The Lost River* (Heinemann 1951), and of a novel. He is Professor of English at Valley College, Los Angeles. A native of Jersey City, N. J., he was born in 1917.

STARBUCK, GEORGE has contributed to The New Yorker, Harper's and other magazines, and is represented with a book in the Yale Younger Poets Series. He was born in 1931 in Columbus,O. and attended California Tech., University of Chicago, and Harvard Graduate School. He is an editor at Houghton Mifflin Company.

STARKWEATHER, PAULINE studied music in Brussels and has taught professionally. She has won a score of poetry prizes. Her work appears in Saturday Review, Christian Century, etc. She was born in Springfield, O. in 1885.

STEESE, EDWARD is a resident and native (1902) of Scarsdale, N. Y. He received his A.B. (Latin Salutatorian) and MFA in Architecture at Princeton and is a partner in the architectural firm of Noyes & Steese. Among his published books are *Storm in Harvest* (1923) and *First Snow* (1954). He has served as editor of a Princeton Anthology.

STEINMAN, D.B. is a native New Yorker and attended City College (B.S., Sc.D. Hon.) and Columbia (A.M., C.E., Ph.D., Sc.D. Hon.). He has published scores of books on engineering. A master bridge builder, he has received many awards for the excellence and beauty of his designs. He is author of two books of verse: *I Built a Bridge* (1956) and *Songs of a Bridgebuilder* (1959).

STEVENSON, CANDACE has published one book, *First the Blade* (Dutton). She was born in Brooklyn and studied at Smith College, Columbia, and the Sorbonne. Her verse has appeared in Century, Saturday Review, and a number of other magazines.

STICKNEY, HELEN FRITH is a former vice-president of the PSA. She is the author of three books of poetry, has published widely in magazines and newspapers, and won numerous awards. She is a member of the Cosmopolitan Club and Pen and Brush.

STOPPLE, LIBBY is a native Texan, born in Dallas in 1910, and is a graduate of a Nurses Training School. Her *Never Touch a Lilac* won the brochure award of the Southwest Writers' Conference in 1959. She has published two books and has contributed to anthologies and magazines.

STORK, CHARLES WHARTON is poet, novelist, playwright, translator and former college professor. He was born in Philadelphia in 1881 and received his A.B. and A.M. from Haverford and Harvard. He has published four books of verse and a novel and has done many translations, both in poetry and prose, from German, Danish, Norwegian and Swedish. In 1922 he was decorated by King Gustav V of Sweden. He was editor of Contemporary Verse from 1917 to 1925; in 1927-28 he served as president of the PSA.

STRONG, GEORGE was born in New York on January 11, 1917. His work has appeared in Flame, Quicksilver, and The Compass Review.

STRONG, JULIA HURD is a fifth generation Texan, resident in Houston. She was born in 1908 and received her B.A. from the Rice Institute (1930). She has won a dozen first prizes in the Texas Poetry Society's annual contests and has contributed poetry to various national magazines.

STUART, JESSE was born August 8, 1907 in a one-room shack near a coal mine on a hill overlooking W-Hollow in Greenup, Ky., where he still lives. In 1926 he was graduated from the local high school, then went on to do college and university work equivalent to requirements for a Ph.D. degree but did not wait to get it, although he has, today, six degrees, five of them honorary. He has published over a score of books, the best known among them *Man with a Bull-Tongue Plow* (poems), *Taps for Private Tussie* (novel), *The Year of My Rebirth* (autobiography). Poems, stories, and articles of his have appeared in the Atlantic, Harper's, Saturday Review, Esquire, and a host of other publications.

SULLIVAN, A. M., president of the PSA (1940-43; 1950-52) was born in Harrison, N. J. and educated at St. Benedict's Preparatory College, Newark. He is editor of Dun' Review and Modern Industry. He conducted the Radio Forum of Poetry over the Mutual network from 1932 to 1940. His published work includes *The Three Dimen-*

sional Man, Elbows of the Wind, and *Psalms of the Prodigal.* In 1952 he was awarded the Alexander Droutzkoy Memorial Gold Medal. He is active in many enterprises, literary and business, as organizer, counselor and lecturer.

SUMMERS, HOLLIS is a professor of English at Ohio University. Thus far he has published four books, including *The Weather of February* (1957) and *The Walks Near Athens* (1959), both brought out by Harper's. He was born ni 1916 in Eminence, Ky.

SWANN, THOMAS BURNETT is a native Floridian who is currently completing his doctoral work at the University of Florida. From 1950 to 1954 he was Personnel Man II in the U. S. Navy. He has published three books: *Driftwood* (1952), *Wombats and Moondust* (1956), and *I Like Bears* (1959).

TALL, GRACE CORNELL was born in Neponsit, L.I., and is now a resident of Montrose, N. Y. She was educated at New York University and Chestnut Hill College in Philadelphia, where she received her B.A. in 1941. The mother of two children, she contributes verse regularly to a Westchester County newspaper.

TAYLOR, SARAH WINGATE teaches Shakespearre and Creative Writing at Dominican College in California. Summers she spends on Clark's Island, Mass., a property with which her family has been associated since 1690. Over fifty of her poems have appeared in national magazines and in anthologies. Born in Newton, Mass. in 1906, she studied at Smith College (A.B.), Boston University (M.A.), London University, and the Sorbonne.

TERRELL, MYRA BURNHAM has been a piano teacher for the past twenty-five years. Born in Newport, Ky. in 1897, she is an alumna of Southwest Texas Teachers' Normal. Her work is widely published. She is also active in groups working with poetry.

THOMPSON, DOROTHY BROWN was born in 1896 in Springfield, Ill. She received her A.B. from the University of Kansas. Her work has appeared in more than one hundred periodicals and in numerous textbooks and anthologies. A number of her poems have been transcribed in Braille.

TIEMER-WILLE, GERTRUDE, a native of Orange, N. J., divides her time between New York City and Cundy's Harbor, Me. She studied at the Art Students League and in Rome. A pioneer in fourth dimensional photography, she has had many one-man shows. Her poetry has appeared in various magazines and newspapers.

TRIEM, EVE was born in New York but grew up and was educated in San Francisco. She attended the University of California at Berkeley. Her book *Parade of Doves* (Dutton 1946) won the award of The League to Support Poetry the year it was published.

TROUBETZKOY, ULRICH is an alumna of Vassar and the University of Chicago (B.A.), a research officer for the City of Richmond, Va. and a feature writer, columnist, and art critic for the Richmond Times-Dispatch. She is author of *Out of the Wilderness* and *Richmond, City of Churches*. Her poetry awards include four Ficke Memorial Awards; PSA monthly and annual prizes; Jamestown Award; AAU W prize, etc. She was born in Hartford, Conn. in 1914.

TUSIANI, JOSEPH is a native of San Marco (Lamis), Italy. At 25, after earning a summa cum laude doctorate of letters at the University of Naples, he taught Latin and Greek at the Classical Lyceum of San Severo. At present he is a Professor of Romance Languages at New York University and Hunter College. Author of *Emily Dickinson, Melos Cordis,* and other books of poems and criticism, he is the recipient of the Grenwood Prize of England (1956). A verse translation of his of all the extant poems of Michelangelo is to be brought out this year by The Noonday Press.

TUTTLE, STELLA WESTON was born March 6, 1907, in Minneapolis, Minn. Her first book of poetry *Daguerreotypes* was published during her senior year at Robbins College, of which she is a graduate. Other books include *Of Hopeful Greenstuff Woven* (1936) and *Nor Bitter Nor Profane,* which won the Kaleidograph Book Publication Award in 1953. Mrs. Tuttle edited the national Poetry Contest Chart from 1951 to 1959.

VAN DOREN, MARK was born in 1894 in Hope, Ill. He received his B.A. and M.A. from the University of Illinois (1914-1915). After serving in the Infantry during World War I, he spent a year abroad on a traveling fellowship. In 1920 he earned his Ph.D. at Columbia, and has been on the faculty of that university ever since. He won the Pulitzer Prize in 1940 for his *Collected Poems.* In addition to poetry, Mr. Van Doren has written numerous critical studies, and has edited a long list of anthologies. Among his published works are: *Shakespeare* (1939), *The Mayfield Deer* (1941), *The Seven Sleepers* (1944), *Spring Birth and Other Poems* (1953), and an autobiography (1959). He is president of the American Academy of Arts and Letters. He won the PSA Gold Medal (the Droutzkoy Memorial Award) in 1957.

VAN SLYKE, BEREN was born in Fort Wayne, Ind. in 1891 and is now a resident of Valley Cottage, N. Y. She received her B.A. from Wellesley. She has published two novels, *Power of the Sun* (Dodd Mead 1931) and *This Was Sandra* (Funk & Wagnalls 1938) and a translation from the French. She is the most recent winner of the PSA Annual Award.

VAN VOORHIS, LINDA LYON, a native of Rochester, N. Y., attended The Masters' School, Dobbs Ferry, N. Y. and the Art Students League. She has appeared in numerous magazines and is the author of two books of poems.

VERRY, ISABEL WILLIAMS earned her B.S. from Bucknell University. By profession she is a teacher of English. Her work has appeared in the University of Kansas City Review, Antioch Review, Common Ground, etc. She was born in Pittston (Pa.) in 1909.

VIERECK, GEORGE SYLVESTER is a charter member of the PSA and was, in fact, its first secretary. He is the author of many books in verse and prose, for a number of which he used various pen names. His *My Flesh and Blood*, subtitled "A Lyric Autobiography," was brought out in 1931 by Liveright. In collaboration with Paul Eldridge he wrote the best-selling novel *My First Two Thousand Years*. A stormy political figure of the two World Wars, he is now living in peaceful retirement in New York. His most recent work is a memoir on prison life called *Men Into Beasts*.

VINAL, HAROLD, founder and editor of Voices, divides his time betwen New York City and Vinalhaven, Me., the island of his birth. He spent his early years in Boston, where he studied the piano. His interest in poetry stems from the 1920's when his first book *White April* was published (1922), followed by *Voyage* (1923), *Nor Youth Nor Age* (1924), *A Stranger in Heaven* (1927), *Hymn to Chaos* (1931), and *Hurricane* (1936), the latter a blank verse book-length chronicle of the Maine coast. He served the PSA as secretary for many years.

WABNITZ, WILLIAM S. has published in the Saturday Review, the New Yorker, etc. and is President of the Alliance Francaise of Cincinnati. Born in Wyoming, O., in 1890, he attended Ohio State University (A.B.), the University of Grenoble in France, and Harvard University. He is Professor of English and Historic Literature at the University of Cincinnati.

WAGNER, CHARLES A. was born in New York, graduated from Columbia College, and was named Nieman Fellow at Harvard in 1945. Formerly book and art critic for the New York Mirror, he is now editor of the N. Y. Sunday Mirror Magazine. He is the author of *Poems of the Soil and Sea* (Knopf), *Nearer the Bone* (Coward-McCann), and *Harvard*, a biography (Dutton). Some years ago he edited *Prize Poems* for Boni.

WAGNER, MARY BOYD hails from Yreka, Cal. but has spent most of her life in New York. Her book, *Roots,* was published by Wings Press in 1954. A winner of numerous awards, she has had poems in The New York Times, Better Homes and Gardens, Wings, etc.

WALKER, DEE was born in Corsicana, Tex. in 1902, received his B.S. from Stephen F. Austin State College, and his M.A. from the University of Houston. At 31 he resigned as a public school superintendent to enter business, and after heading three corporations, retired at the age of fifty to devote his time to lecturing, writing and world travel. His two books of poetry *Salt Spray and Honey* (Wilson Publishing Co. 1951) and *Sky Trails* (Story Book Press 1952) are now in their third printing.

WARD, MAY WILLIAMS is a native of Holden, Mo. and received her education at the University of Kansas. She was editor of The Harp from 1926 to 1931. Her *Poems for Choral Speaking* appeared in 1945. She is consulting editor of Kansas Magazine.

WARREN, HAMILTON M. was born in New Rochelle, N. Y. in 1898 and now lives in Maplewood, N. J. He earned his Litt. B. at Princeton in 1919. His work has appeared in the Saturday Evening Post, Freedom and Union, and elsewhere.

WARREN, JAMES E. JR. is the author of *This Side of Babylon* (1938) and *Against the Furious Men* (1946), as well as of a book on the teaching of English. In 1937 he won the PSA Annual Award. Born in Atlanta, Ga. in 1908, he was educated at Emory University (A.B., M.A.).

WASSALL, IRMA has published more than six hundred poems in magazines in this country and Canada. She is the author of a book of poems, *Loonshadow*, brought out by Sage Books in 1949 and re-issued in 1958 by Experiment Press.

WEBB, TESSA SWEAZY has been a teacher at Ohio State University (1918-1954) and an editor of poetry journals for many years. The latest of her three publishd books is *Window by the Sea* (1942).

WEIL, JAMES L. is a native New Yorker, born in 1929 and educated at the University of Chicago (B.A.) and Oxford. In 1958 he received the American Weave Chapbook Award for the most recent of his three published books of poetry, *Quarrel with the Rose,* which has a foreword by Robert Hillyer.

WESLEY, CECIL COBB is a native and resident of Georgia, where he attended Cox College. His work appears in Good Housekeeping, Reader's Digest, Lyric, etc., and in anthologies.

WHEELOCK, JOHN HALL was born in 1886 at Far Rockaway, L. I., is a graduate of Harvard, and has done post-graduate work at the universities of Gottingen and Berlin. His first book, *Verses by Two Undergraduates* (in collaboration with Van Wyck Brooks) appeared in 1905. He has since published eight volumes of poetry, including *Poems Old and New* (1956), which was awarded the Ridgely Torrence Memorial Award and the Borestone Mountain Poetry Award. He served as an officer of Charles Scribner & Sons for many years, and as a vice-president of the PSA. He is a Chancellor of the Academy of American Poets. Though in retirement, he edits and writes critical forewords for Scribner's *Poets of Today,* an annual publication featuring the work of younger poets.

WIDDEMER, MARGARET, a native of Doylestown, Pa., is a long-time resident of New York. While still a child, she won several prizes in poetry. In 1919 she shared a PSA-Pulitzer award with Carl Sandburg and, in 1923, won the Saturday Review of Literature award for her "Tree with a Bird in It." She is also a popular novelist. Her volumes of poetry include *Factories* (Henry Holt 1917), *Ballads and Lyrics* (Harcourt Brace 1923), *Hill Garden* (Farrar & Rinehart 1936) and *The Dark Cavalier,* collected poems (Doubleday 1958).

WILSON, DEDIE HUFFMAN has been a delegate to UNESCO. She founded The Poets' Workshop of San Jose, Cal., of which she is still director. Born in Texas in 1897, she won an essay award at the age of ten, and at fifteen sold a short story to Holland's. She has also won a number of poetry awards.

WINTER, MARY A. is a graduate of the Art Institute in Chicago, her native city. She is interested in sculpture, and has published one book, *The Archaic Smile.* Her work has appeared in Archaeology, Voices, the New Yorker, and elsewhere. In 1958 she won the Leonora Speyer Award.

WINWAR, FRANCES is the Italian-born American biographer and novelist. She won the Atlantic Monthly prize for her first "group" biography, *Poor Splendid Wings* (1933). Since then she has published many other notable studies of such 19th Century literary figures as Coleridge, the Wordsworths, Byron, Shelley, Keats, the Brownings, etc. Her most recent work, *The Haunted Palace,* a life of Poe (Harper 1959), has gone into six printings.

WOODBOURNE, HARRY was born in Kiev, Russia in 1896, the son of the Chief Forester to the Czar, and grew up in the vast forests of the Ukraine. He began to write poetry at an early age. He emigrated to the United States in his late teens and entered the field of horticulture. His book *The Green Kingdom,* a garden text in wide use by garden clubs, contains fifty of his nature poems.

WRIGHT, CATHARINE MORRIS, a painter as well as a poet, founded the Fox Hill School of Art at Jamestown, R. I. in 1950. She has published three books, the most recent of which, *The Color of Life,* was brought out by Houghton Mifflin in 1957. Born in Philadelphia in 1899, she was educated in private schools and at the School of Design for Women. In 1959 she received an honorary degree of Doctor of Fine Arts from Moore Institute, Philadelphia.

YEATMAN, JENNETTE conducts discussion groups in Modern Poetry at the Pasadena Area Liberal Arts Center (Cal.). She received her M.A. from Occidental College, her thesis being a series of verse translations from the French of Sully Prudhomme, first winner of the Nobel Prize for Literature. Born in Wilkinsburg, Pa. in 1905, Mrs. Yeatman has published one book of poems, *Four Men West* (Dierkes Press 1952).

YOUNG, VIRGINIA BRADY was for many years secretary to the Pre-Medical Adviser at Columbia College. At present she is assistant to the Director of the Colgate Foreign Policy Conference. Born in New York in 1911, Mrs. Young was educated in the local public schools and at Columbia University Extension.

Acknowledgments

For permission to include copyrighted material reprinted in this Anthology, grateful acknowledgment is made to the following authors, authors' agents, editors, and publishers:

ALICAT PRESS for "We Shall Say" from *Outcast Poets* by Miriam Allen deFord.

THE AMERICAN PRESS for "Remembering Lincoln" from *Saturday Night in the Accident Ward* by Frank Mundorf.

CECIL ANDERSON for "Not for its Own Sake" from *A Flame of Faith* by Hazel Littlefield.

AUGUSTANA BOOK CONCERN for "Sifting" from *The Winnowing Years* by Victor E. Beck.

BALLANTINE BOOKS for "After a Game of Squash" by Samuel L. Albert from the anthology *New Poems by American Poets*.

BANNER PRESS for "On Going Home" from *And the Moon Be Still As Bright* by Marjorie L. Agnew; and "The Grapevine" from *Heart on my Sleeve* by Zoe Kincaid Brockman.

JOHN F. BLAIR for "Rescue" from *The Spotted Hawk* by Olive Tilford Dargan.

CLARKE & WAY for "Song for the Greenwood Fawn" from *Unit and Universe* by I. L. Salomon.

DEVIN-ADAIR COMPANY for "D-Dawn" by Margaret McGarvey from the anthology *One Word*.

DIERKES PRESS for "Exile" from *Four Men West* by Jennette Yeatman.

DIETZ PRESS for "Earth's Bondman" from *The Ancient Bond* by Betty Page Dabney; and "To a Young Poet" by Harry M. Meacham from the anthology *Lyric Virginia Today*.

DODD, MEAD & COMPANY for 'White Fox" from *White Fox* by Elizabeth Alsop Shepard.

DORMER HOUSE for "Late Comer" from *One Stone Unturned* by Fanny de Groot Hastings.

DORRANCE COMPANY for "Hester Macdonagh" from *Inward from the Sea* by Jeannette Slocomb Edwards.

E. P. DUTTON & COMPANY for "Keepsake from Quinault" from *Beach Fire* by Dorothy Alyea; "Grant at Appomattox" from *Sunday in Virginia & Other Poems* by Gertrude Claytor; "Narcissus in a Cocktail Glass" from *Sleep without Armor* by Frances Minturn Howard; and "Classroom in October" from *To My Brothers Everywhere* by Elias Lieberman.

FALMOUTH HOUSE for "The Quest" from *Selected Poems* by Harold Vinal.

FARRAR, STRAUS & CUDAHY for "Playmates" from *Journey to the Future* by Lillian Everts.

THE FINE EDITIONS PRESS for "Pinkletinks" from *The Mother Beach* by Grace Elisabeth Allen; "Candle Song" from *Cantabile* by Anna Elizabeth Bennett; "Coin in the Fist" from *Pendulum* by Florence Kerr Brownell; "Praise of New England" from *Cornucopia: 1919-1953* by Thomas Caldecot Chubb; "Planetary Arc-Light" from *Rendezvous in a Landscape* by August Derleth; "Bird at Night" from *Bird at Night* by Marion Ethel Hamilton; and "On Laying Up Treasure" from *"My House and My Country* by Lois Smith Hiers.

THE GOLDEN QUILL PRESS for "Precarious Ground" from *This Tilting Dust* by Leah Bodine Drake; "Gardener" from *The Small Hour* by Evelyn Eaton; "Duel in the Park" from *No Light Evaded* by Lisa Grenelle; and "Old Fence Post" from *Wide the Gate* by Leigh Hanes.

GRANITE STATE PRESS for "Flood" from *Across a Covered Bridge* by Mary Grant Charles.

GREENBERG INC. for "Desert River" from *Signature in Sand* by Patricia Benton.

HARCOURT, BRACE & COMPANY for "Each to Each" and "Presence of Snow" from *And Pastures New* by Melville Cane; and "Little Candle," "Little Girl, Be Careful What You Say," and "On a Flimmering Floom You Shall Ride" from *The People, Yes* by Carl Sandburg.

HARPER & BROTHERS for "Valentine" and "Family Reunion" from *The Walks Near Athens* by Hollis Summers.

HENRY HOLT & COMPANY for "A Tuft of Flowers," "A Drumlin Woodchuck," and "Departmental" by Robert Frost from *The Complete Poems of Robert Frost;* and "This Amber Sunstream" from *Selected Poems* and "When the World Ends" from *Spring Birth & Other Poems* by Mark Van Doren.

KALEIDOGRAPH PRESS for "The Contentment of Willoughby" from *Time at the Window* by Frances Alexander; "Passover Eve" from *The Tenth Jew* by Fania Kruger; and "The Defender" from *Furrow with Blackbirds* by Arthur M. Sampley.

KENYON PRESS for "Harvest Time" from *Selections* by Star Powers.

ALFRED A. KNOPF, INC. for "The Relic" and "The Bats" from *The Relic & Other Poems* by Robert Hillyer.

HORACE LIVERIGHT for "After the Battle" from *My Flesh and Blood* by George Sylvester Viereck.

THE MACMILLAN COMPANY for "Sonnet XI" from *Love's Argument* by Adele Greeff; "Ballade on Eschatology" from *The Four Last Things* (collected poems) by Sister M. Madeleva, C.S.C.; "June Twilight," "Lollingdon Downs XVIII," and "Sonnet" from *The Story of a Round-House, Lollingdon Downs,* and *Good Friday* by John Masefield.

MARSHALL JONES COMPANY for "Now That the Flowers" from *Finger Prints* by Cullen Jones.

THE MAVERICK PRESS for "Second Wisdom" and "November Fugitive" from *Second Wisdom* by Henry Morton Robinson.

MONASTINE PRESS for "Dimidium Animae Meae" from *Wings over Patmos* by Charles A. Brady; and "At the Battery Sea-Wall" from *Crags* by Clifford James Laube.

WILLIAM MORROW & COMPANY for "Mountain Creed" from *Mountain Creed & Other Poems* by Medora Addison Nutter.

THE MOSHER PRESS for "Death Was a Woman" from *Lost Warrior* by Sydney King Russell.

NEW ORLANDO PUBLICATIONS for "Challengers" from *Flamenco Dancer & Other Poems* by Alfred Dorn.

NOONDAY PRESS for "Invented a Person" from *Other Knowledge* by Lenore G. Marshall.

PAGEANT PRESS for "Homestead—Winter Morning" from *This Instant Joy* by Mary Ballard Duryee.

RANDOM HOUSE for "Signpost," "Return," and "The Answer" by Robinson Jeffers from *The Selected Poetry of Robinson Jeffers*.

ROYAL PUBLISHING COMPANY for "Breaking Point" from *The Grace of the Bough* by Sylvia Auxier.

RYERSON PRESS (Canada) for "Prayer" from *Words on a Page* by Doris Hedges.

CHARLES SCRIBNER'S SONS for "Bottle Should Be Plainly Labeled 'Poison'" from *The Delicate Balance* by Sara Henderson Hay; and "Lost Explorer" from *I, Too, Jehovah* by Edmund Pennant.

WILLIAM SLOANE ASSOCIATES for "Close Clan" from *New Poems* by Mark Van Doren.

SOUTHWEST PRESS for "Beauty's Hands Are Cool" from *Dreamers on Horseback* by Karle Wilson Baker.

STORY BOOK PRESS for "Calvary" from *Red Metal* by Libby Stopple.

ALAN SWALLOW for "Fugue" and "Transformation Scene" from *The Middle Voice* by Constance Carrier; and "Shore Birds" from *Several Houses* by Vi Gale.

UNIVERSITY OF MINNESOTA PRESS for "Portrait in Winter" from *The Other Journey* by Katherine Garrison Chapin.

UNIVERSITY OF PITTSBURGH PRESS for "The Daily Manna" from *The Stone and the Shell* by Sara Henderson Hay.

THE VIKING PRESS for "O To Be a Dragon" and "To a Chameleon" from *O To Be a Dragon* by Marianne Moore.

WAKE-BROOK HOUSE for "Mountain Convent" from *In Love with Time* by Laura Benét; and "Mozart's Grave" from *And Let the Glory Go* by Paul Scott Mowrer.

THE BOND WHEELWRIGHT COMPANY for "Janus" from *The Cage of Years* by Madeline Mason.

WHITTIER BOOKS for "Pictures at an Exhibition" from *Create the World* by Nathan Rosenbaum.

WINGS PRESS for "Westering" from *Westering* by Douglas V. Kane; "Old River Road" from *Far Hills Are Blue* by Blanche Whiting Keysner; and "The House" from *Always the Search* by Paula Nelson.

YALE UNIVERSITY PRESS for "My Head on my Shoulders" from *The Metaphysical Sword* by Jeremy Ingalls.

THE AMERICAN BARD for "Legend of his Lyre" by Aaron Schmuller.

AMERICAN MERCURY for "Two Solitudes" by Evelyn Ames; "Old Men's Ward" by Elma Dean; and 'Belden Hollow" by Leslie Nelson Jennings.

AMERICAN SCHOLAR for "Spring Mountain Climb" by Richard Eberhart; "Echo" by Elizabeth Stanton Hardy; "Eppur Si Muove" by Robert Hillyer; and 'My Six Toothbrushes" by Phyllis McGinley.

AMERICAN WEAVE for "Renaissance" by Robert Avrett; "Flood" by Mary Grant Charles; "Villa Sciarra: Rome" by Christine Turner Curtis; "Suspended Moment" by Mariana B. Davenport; "In the Month of Green Fire" by Sophie Himmell; "Earthly Illusion" by Louise Leighton; "Old Man with a Mowing Machine" by May Carleton Lord; "Public Library" by Candace T. Stevenson.

ARIZONA HIGHWAYS for "On the Edge of the Copper Pit" by Pauline Henson.

ATLANTIC MONTHLY for "Horizon Thong" by George Abbe; "An Autumn Walk" by Witter Bynner; "A Thought of Marigolds" by Janice Farrar; "Morning in Spring" by Louis Ginsberg; "Silence Spoke with your Voice" by Ryah Tumarkin Goodman; "Notation in Haste" by Elias Lieberman; "Dame Liberty Reports from Travel" by Dorothy Cowles Pinkney; "Green Mountain Boy" by Florida Watts Smyth; and "The Shepherds" by Beren Van Slyke.

AUDIENCE for "Anticipation" by Joseph Tusiani.

BELOIT POETRY JOURNAL for "Heron in Swamp" by Frances Minturn Howard; and "Eliza Telefair" by Jocelyn Macy Sloan.

CANADIAN POETRY MAGAZINE for "No Escape" by Harriet L. Delafield.

CARMEL PINE CONE for "The Lairdless Place" by Kate Rennie Archer; "Song of the Hill" by Edith Lodge; and "Late" by Helen Salz.

CHICAGO JEWISH FORUM for "The Pigeon-Feeders in Battery Park" by Julia Cooley Altrocchi.

CHICAGO REVIEW for "Birth by Anesthesia" by George Scarbrough.

CHRISTIAN SCIENCE MONITOR for "Brief History" by Olga Hampel Briggs; "Father of the Man" by Elizabeth Mabel Bryan; "Cat on the Porch at Dusk" by Dorothy Harriman; "Late Comer" by Fanny de Groot Hastings; "Wind of the Prairie" by Grace Clementine Howes; "Motorcycle" by Benjamin Sturgis Pray; and "Out of the Wilderness" by Ulrich Troubetzkoy.

CHRISTIAN CENTURY for "Apology of the Young Scientists" by Celia Dimmette.

CINCINNATI POST AND TIMES-STAR for "Sailor's Woman" by Annette Patton Cornell.

CITY LIGHTS for "I Am Ham Melanite" by William Millett.

COLORADO QUARTERLY for "Game out of Hand" by Allison Ross.

COMMONWEAL for "The Animals" by Josephine Jacobsen; and "The Exile" by Larry Rubin.

CONTEMPORARY POETRY for "We Shall Say" by Miriam Allen deFord.

COUNTRY POET for "Neighbors" by Marilyn Francis.

DELTA for "Letter from the Vieux Carre" by Ethel Green Russell.

EDUCATIONAL FORUM for "Codicil" by Mabel MacDonald Carver; and "Newton to Einstein" by Jeannette Chappell.

ENCOUNTER (England) for "Thrushes" by Ted Hughes.

EPOS for "Tree Tag" by Mary E. Caragher; and "Prisoner" by Marguerite George.

ESSENCE for "Raccoon on the Road" by Joseph Payne Brennan; and "Momist" by Amy Groesbeck.

EVE for "The Dusting of the Books" by Dorothy Hughes.

EXPERIMENT for "Oh, You Wholly Rectangular" by E. R. Cole.

FIDDLEHEAD for "Ear Is Not Deaf" by Irene Dayton; and "Blueprint" by D. B. Steinman.

FLAME for "The Epiphany" by George Strong.

FLORIDA MAGAZINE OF VERSE for "Soliloquy by the Shore" by Martin Scholten.

GEORGIA REVIEW for "As Night Comes On" by Cecil Cobb Wesley; and "Blessing the Hounds" by Mary Winter.

GOOD HOUSEKEEPING for "September Afternoon" by Margaret Haley Carpenter; and "Garland for a Storyteller" by Jessie Farnham.

HARPER'S MAGAZINE for "Because I Live" by Evelyn Ames; "The Train Butcher" by Thomas Hornsby Ferril; "To Be Black, To Be Lost" by Hannah Kahn; "Halfway" by Maxine W. Kumin; "Kind Sir: These Woods" by Anne Sexton.

HARTFORD (Conn.) TIMES for "With Lilacs in my Eye" by Lucile Coleman.

HIGH HORIZONS for "Creative Force" by Maude Miner Hadden.

HUDSON REVIEW for "American Vineyard" by Mildred Cousens; and "Arlington Cemetery—Looking Toward the Capitol" by Winthrop Palmer.

THE HUMANIST for "When Silence Divests Me" by Henry Birnbaum.

IRISH TIMES for "Garland Sunday" by Padraic Colum.

JOURNAL of the AMERICAN ASSOCIATION OF UNIVERSITY WO-MEN for "Mask" by Elizabeth Cox.

KALEIDOGRAPH for "The Soul Remembers" by Richard Burdick Eld-ridge; and "Old River Road" by Blanche Whiting Keysner.

THE KANSAS MAGAZINE for "The Teacher" by Virginia Brady Young.

THE KAPUSTKAN for "Stone from the Gods" by Irma Wassall.

KENYON REVIEW for "Where Unimaginably Bright" by Oliver Hale; and "In the First House" by Joseph Joel Keith.

THE LANTERN for "Remainder" by Frederika Blankner.

LADIES HOME JOURNAL for "Heart-Summoned" by Jesse Stuart.

THE LITERARY REVIEW for "After the Storm" by Elizabeth Bartlett; "A Room I Once Knew" by Henry Birnbaum; and "Alcestis" by Isabel Williams Verry.

THE LONDON MAGAZINE for "The Addict" by Larry Rubin.

THE LONDON POETRY REVIEW for "Old Essex Door" by Agnes Mac-Carthy Hickey.

THE LYRIC for "Funeral" by Murray Bennett; "Deserts" and "Old Fence Post" (the latter published under the title "Surprised") by Leigh Hanes; "A Gentle Park" by Moss Herbert; "Never Ask Me Why" by Silvia Mar-golis; "Early Dutch" by Jennie M. Palen; and "Crossing the County Line" by Elizabeth Randall-Mills.

McCALL'S MAGAZINE for "Pawnshop Window" by R. H. Grenville.

MORNING STAR for "Prisoner of War" by Gertrude May Lutz.

THE NATION for "The Circus" by Milton Kaplan; "Two Views of a Cadaver Room" by Sylvia Plath; and "Conversation in Black and White" by May Sarton.

NEW ATHENAEUM for "Bucko-Mate" by Samuel Schierloh.

NEW HAMPSHIRE PROFILES for "New Hampshire Farm Woman" by Rachel Graham.

NEW MEXICO QUARTERLY for "The Death of Friends" by Adele Levi.

NEW YORK HERALD TRIBUNE for "New York City" by George Abbe; "Like a Whisper" by Ethan Ayer; "Child of the World" by Edna L. S. Barker; "When You Reach the Hilltop the Sky Is on Top of You" by Etta Blum; "Snow Anthology" by Arthur S. Bourinot; "Nevertheless" by Gustav

Davidson; "Evensong" by Carleton Drewry; "Etruscan Warrior's Head" by Helen Rowe Henze; "The Lacemaker (Vermeer)" by Anne Marx; "Shadbush" by Christina Rainsford; "Lyric Barber" by Liboria Romano; "Duck in Central Park" by Frances Higginson Savage; "Habitue" by Helen Frith Stickney; "A Japanese Birthday Wish" by Thomas Burnett Swann.

NEW YORK TIMES for "A Little Girl" by Charles Angoff; "The Rowers" by Laura Benét; "Old Voyager" by Walter Blackstock; "Fame" by Eleanor Hollister Cantus; "Earth's Bondman" by Betty Page Dabney; "John Butler Yeats" by Jeanne Robert Foster; 'Wisdom" by Phyllis Hanson; "Of the Mathematician" by Alice Clear Matthews; "Fox" by Marjorie Somers Scheuer; "Windmill on the Cape" by William Vincent Sieller; "From my Thought" (original title "All-Being") by Daniel Smythe; "Three City Cantos" (published separately) by Charles A. Wagner; and "The Lethal Thought" by Mary Boyd Wagner.

NEW YORKER for "Exodus from a Renaissance Gallery" by Ellen Acton; "The Zoo in the City" by Sara Van Alstyne Allen; "Now in Bloom" by Florence Kiper Frank; "Merry-Go-Round" and "Time Out" by Oliver Jenkins; "Deadfall" by Martha Keller; "Journey toward Evening" by Phyllis McGinley; "Hardcastle Crags" (original title "Night Walk") by Sylvia Plath; "Bone Thoughts on a Dry Day" by George Starbuck; "The Divine Insect" by John Hall Wheelock; and "Lower Forms of Life" by Mary Winter.

OPPORTUNITY for "Assembly: Harlem School" by Eugene T. Maleska.

OREGONIAN for "Pedro" by Phoebe W. Hoffman.

OUTPOSTS for "Promises" by Ruth Forbes Sherry.

PARTISAN REVIEW for "Invented a Person" by Lenore G. Marshall; and "News Reel" by David Ross.

PENNSYLVANIA LITERARY REVIEW for "One No. 7" by John Frederick Frank.

POETRY (Chicago) for "After Speaking of One Dead a Long Time" by Padraic Colum; "Blind, I Speak to the Cigarette" by Joanne de Longchamps; "The Sibyl" by Joan LaBombard; "Blessing Mrs. Larkin" by Margery Mansfield; "Impressions of my Father" by Marcia Masters; and "Wet Summer" by May Williams Ward.

POETRY CHAP-BOOK for "Elements" by Carolyn Wilson Link.

POETRY REVIEW (London) for "Sorrow" by Marie Tello Phillips.

POETRY SOCIETY OF TEXAS YEARBOOK for "Harvest" by Gene Shuford; and "The Huckster's Horse" by Julia Hurd Strong.

PRAIRIE SCHOONER for "A Peony for Apollo" by Charles Edward Eaton; "Tomorrow Is a Birthday" by Gwendolen Haste; "Hazlitt Sups" by Katharine Day Little; and "In the Beginning" by Jenny Lind Porter.

QUEENS QUARTERLY for "Spring Song" by George Brandon Saul.

RECURRENCE for "Desert Shipwreck" by Barbara Leslie Jordan; and "As I Lay Quiet" by Margaret Widdemer.

SAN FRANCISCO REVIEW for "Dissembler" by Charles Shaw.

SATURDAY EVENING POST for "Crow's Nest" by Richard F. Armknecht; "Diary of a Raccoon" by Gertrude Ryder Bennett; "Late October" by Sara King Carleton; "Secret" by Catherine Haydon Jacobs; "Lone Huntsman" by Christie Jeffries; and "Spring Cellar" by Gladys McKee.

SATURDAY REVIEW for "Image in a Mirror" by Mae Winkler Goodman; "The Unfortunate Mole" by Mary Kennedy; "Sea Sonnet" by Norma Lay; "Return to Spring" by Florence Ripley Mastin; "The White Rainbow" by Starr Nelson; "Spring Song" by Katharine O'Brien; "The Lesson" by Larry Rubin; "Eternal Contour" by Florida Watts Smyth; "A Bronze Statuette of Kwan-Yin" by Charles Wharton Stork; "Monument" by A. M. Sullivan; and "Schoolroom: 158–" by James E. Warren, Jr.

SEWANEE REVIEW for "Witches" by Ted Hughes.

THE SONNET for "Wood Music" by Ethel King.

SPARROW for "At a Loss" by James L. Weil.

SPIRIT for "Snowflakes" by Alice Behrend; "Duality" by Katherine Thayer Hobson; "Homage (Diptych 2)" by R. J. Schoeck; "With Metaphor" by Sarah Wingate Taylor; and "Rest O Sun I Cannot" by Joseph Tusiani.

THE TABLET for "Eugenio Pacelli" by Francis Neilson.

TACOMA NEWS TRIBUNE for "Two Mountains Men Have Climbed" by Pauline Starkweather.

TRAILS for "Long-Billed Gannets" by Frances D. Emery.

TWELFTH STREET QUARTERLY for "The Wounded" by Louise Louis.

UNIVERSITY OF KANSAS CITY REVIEW for "Museum Piece" by Lawrence P. Spingarn.

VARIEGATION for "Juxta" by Grover Jacoby; and "The Shape of Autumn" by Virginia Russ.

VERSECRAFT for "What Price" by Lulu Minerva Schultz.

VESPERS for "Piazza di Spagna" by Willard M. Grimes.

THE VILLAGER for "Deer in Aspens" by Kay deBard Hall.

VIRGINIA QUARTERLY for "Public Holiday: Paris" by Joyce Horner and "Autosonic Door" by Dorothy Brown Thompson.

VOICES for "Changeless Shore" by Sarah Leeds Ash; "Exercise in a Meadow" by Jean Elliot; "Lines Written in a Mausoleum" by Lillian Grant; "Conversation with Rain" by Louise D. Gunn; "The Great Farewells" by Amanda Benjamin Hall; "Restoration" by Woodridge Spears; "Gardens Are All my Heart" by Eve Triem; and "The Quickening" by Stella Weston Tuttle.

WESTERN HUMANITIES REVIEW for "A Walk in Kyoto" by Earle Birney.

WISCONSIN POETRY MAGAZINE for "The Flute of May" by Harry Woodbourne.

YANKEE for "Madaket" by Isabel Harriss Barr.

ZERO for "Wisdom of the Gazelle" by George P. Solomos.

Index of Poems